FINDING
COURAGE

FINDING COURAGE
writings by women

EDITED BY IRENE ZAHAVA

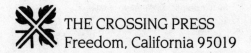
THE CROSSING PRESS
Freedom, California 95019

Dedicated to my grandmother, Yetta Kaplan,
for her courage, dignity and indomitable sense of humor

Grateful acknowledgment is made for permission to use the following previously published material:

"As We Are Now" (an excerpt), from *As We Are Now*, by May Sarton. Copyright © 1973 by May Sarton. Reprinted by permission of W.W. Norton & Company, Inc.

"The Chipko," by Sally Miller Gearhart from *Love, Struggle and Change*, by Irene Zahava. Copyright © 1988 by Sally Miller Gearhart. Reprinted by permission of the author.

"The Field is Full of Daisies and I'm Afraid to Pass," from *The Question She Put To Herself*, by Maureen Brady. Copyright © 1987 by Maureen Brady. Reprinted by permission of the author and The Crossing Press.

"Grey Is The Color of Hope" (an excerpt), from *Grey Is the Color of Hope*, by Irina Ratushinskaya, translated by Alyona Kojevnikov. Translation Copyright © 1988 by Alyona Kojevnikov. Reprinted by permission of Alfred A. Knopf, Inc.

"I Used to Like the Dallas Cowboys," from *Sans Souci and Other Stories*, by Dionne Brand. Copyright © 1988 by Dionne Brand. Reprinted by permission of Williams-Wallace Publishers, Inc. (Canada) and Firebrand Books.

"The Long Night," from *The Sea Birds Are Still Alive*, by Toni Cade Bambara. Copyright © 1974, 1976, 1977 by Toni Cade Bambara. Reprinted by permission of Random House, Inc.

"Mrs. Morris Changes Lanes," from *More Tales I Tell My Mother*, by Zoë Fairbairns, Sara Maitland, Valerie Miner, Michele Roberts, Michelene Wandor. Copyright © 1987. Reprinted by permission of the author.

"Nore and Zelda," from *Two Willow Chairs*, by Jess Wells, Copyright © 1987 by Jess Wells. Reprinted by permission of the author.

"Nothing Safe in Crabtree Meadow," from *The Notebooks of Leni Clare and Other Short Stories*, by Sandy Boucher. Copyright © 1982 by Sandy Boucher. Reprinted by permission of the author.

"Ruthy and Edie," from *Later The Same Day*, by Grace Paley. Copyright © 1985 by Grace Paley. Reprinted by permission of Farrar, Straus and Giroux, Inc.

"Seeing San Antonio," from *The Odyssey of Katinou Kalokovich*, by Natalie L.M. Petesch. Copyright © 1974 by Natalie L.M. Petesch. Reprinted by permission of the author.

"Snowwalker," by Joyce Renwick originally appeared in *The Southern Review*, January 1989. Reprinted by permission of the author.

"Things To Do," by Binnie Kirshenbaum originally appeared in *The Beloit Fiction Journal*, Fall 1987. Reprinted by permission of the author.

"West With The Night," from *West With The Night*, by Beryl Markham. Copyright © 1942, 1983 by Beryl Markham. Reprinted by permission of North Point Press.

"When It Happens," from *Dancing Girls and Other Stories*, by Margaret Atwood. Copyright © 1977, 1982 by O.W. Toad, Ltd. Reprinted by permission of Simon and Schuster, Inc.

"A Window On Soweto" (an excerpt), from *A Window On Soweto*, by Joyce Sikakane. Copyright © 1977, 1980. Reprinted by permission of the International Defense and Aid Fund for Southern Africa.

Cover art by David Eason
Cover design by Betsy Bayley
Book design and production by Martha J. Waters
   text in Baskerville ultra (11/12.5), titles in Novarese italic

Printed in the U.S.A.

Library of Congress Cataloging-in-Publication Data

Finding courage: writings by women/edited by Irene Zahava.
   p.   cm.
ISBN 0-89594-379-4
ISBN 0-89594-378-6 (pbk)
1. American prose literature -- Women authors. 2. English prose literature -- Women authors. 3. Women -- fiction.
I. Zahava, Irene.
PS647.W6F48   1989
808.8'99287 – dc 20   89-15914
                                                                          CIP

Contents

vii **Preface**
Irene Zahava

1 **Misty, Tiled Chambers**
Valerie Miner

9 **When It Happens**
Margaret Atwood

18 **Emei Shan**
Canyon Sam

29 **Seeing San Antonio**
Natalie L.M. Petesch

40 **As We Are Now** (an excerpt)
May Sarton

45 **In a House of Wooden Monkeys**
Shay Youngblood

50 **West With the Night**
Beryl Markham

61 **The Long Night**
Toni Cade Bambara

69 **Things to Do**
Binnie Kirshenbaum

85 **Walking Steel**
Merril Mushroom

92 **A Window on Soweto** (an excerpt)
Joyce Sikakane

99 **The Chipko**
Sally Miller Gearhart

111 **Mrs. Morris Changes Lanes**
Zoë Fairbairns

122 **Her Wild Barbarian Heart**
Martha Shelley

130 **The Great Shakedown**
Judy Freespirit

135 The Steps Involved in Falling
     Teresa Noelle Roberts

141 A Saturday in August
     Terri de la Peña

151 Ruthy and Edie
     Grace Paley

159 The Field is Full of Daisies and I'm Afraid to Pass
     Maureen Brady

167 I Used to Like the Dallas Cowboys
     Dionne Brand

179 Mz. Kitty Leaves the Longbranch to Win the Battle
     at the O.K. Corral
     Anne Cameron

192 Grey is the Color of Hope
     Irina Ratushinskaya

204 The Year I Was Ten
     Bonnie Morris

213 How Grandmother Spider Brought the Light
     Paula Gunn Allen

217 Solitary Pleasure
     Kitty Tsui

230 Nothing Safe in Crabtree Meadow
     Sandy Boucher

238 Snowwalker
     Joyce Renwick

256 Nore and Zelda
     Jess Wells

294 Contributors' Notes

Preface

I am a fearful person. This is something I have always known about myself. For the most part I am able to present a calm exterior and many people fail to recognize the fear that lurks just beneath the surface. But others have pegged me from the start. My first grade teacher wrote on my report card, "Irene is afraid to try new things, but once she does she seems to like them."

When the suggestion to edit this anthology was first made, I jumped at the opportunity. After all, I have always learned so much from books. I assumed that by reading stories about women who were courageous, brave and heroic I would learn their secrets.

What I learned is that there are no secret formulas, no magical incantations. The women whose lives are described in this book weren't born without fear genes. They didn't burst into this world in protective armor, eager to march into battle. They didn't grow up in some idyllic childhood, free of all pain. They weren't granted immunity from cruelty or indifference, nor were they granted the gift of prophecy so they could anticipate all obstacles and successfully avoid them.

Most of the women described in this collection would not call themselves courageous. They'd say that they have simply found ways to survive in this world with their dignity and self-respect intact. They'd say that what they do is common-place; that they don't want to be singled out as heroines or role models; that they are ordinary women who have fears, uncertainties, self-doubts, divided loyalties and set-backs. These are women who don't act because they are fearless, they act *in spite of* their fears.

I've learned that it is a lot easier for me to say "I am a fearful person" than it is to say "I am a courageous person." I now know that both statements are true.

IRENE ZAHAVA

Misty, Tiled Chambers

VALERIE MINER

"Nine is old enough to learn to swim," Mom said, letting me have the window seat on the bus.

"But *you* don't know how to swim," I protested.

"Exactly!" she pronounced with the infallible logic she always used when refuting arguments with my own words.

Mom made me wear my heavy jacket and her own long, wool scarf. She wore the old red coat and her neck looked too long that morning. When I was mad at my mother I found fault with her appearance — especially with her skinny face and bowed legs. I was furious with her today because it was 20° outside and she was dragging me all the way to Hackensack for swimming lessons.

"But, Mom, it's too *cold* for a bathing suit. Why don't we wait for summer?"

"It's crowded in the summer. This way you'll be able to swim at the pond when hot weather starts; won't that be nice?"

"I'd rather learn piano."

She looked past me at snowmen guarding white lawns along Monroe Avenue.

"Why can't I take piano? Jackie has lessons."

"Music lessons are expensive, dear. Besides, you'd have to practice. We could hardly afford a *piano*."

1

I stared at an icicle forming on a telephone wire. "I could practice on Jackie's." I looked back with expectation.

She was picking absent-mindedly at a callous on her palm. It was about to bleed and I tapped her. "No, don't do that; it's bad for you."

She smiled, then peered out the window again. We were silent for the rest of the trip.

As we pulled into Hackensack, she took my hand. "You'll like swimming. Give it a chance."

The YMCA was an imposing building, but lacking the ornate drama of St. Mary's Catholic School. Here I noticed one crucifix, no statues, a lot of plain windows and a big desk. A woman with kinky, blond hair gave Mom a form and took some money. She nodded at me insincerely. Soon Mom was marching me down a dark corridor and I remembered a movie where ancient peoples sacrificed their children to the gods.

The locker room had a green smell. It was hot and humid, like July. I caught a glimpse of a fat woman without any clothes, before Mom hauled me over to a stall and handed me the regulation suit. The dark blue knit material was scratchy and stank of disinfectant. I thought about Mom taking me to the doctor, telling me to get undressed and lie on the table while she stood by, tall and invulnerable in that horrid red coat. How could she wear a heavy coat in this muggy room? This wasn't the first time I had doubted her sanity. Maybe I could run away to Jackie's and sleep under the piano.

"Hurry along, dear, we only have five minutes before we meet your teacher."

Mitch was waiting for us outside the Ladies' dressing room. He was a tall man with red hairs on his chest and head. At first glance, he reminded me of Buster Crabbe. Shyly, I stared at the locker room door. The italicized "Ladies" was so much more adult than the block lettered "Girls" marking the bathroom at school. "Ladies," I tilted my head at the same angle as the white letters. I would tell Jackie about this.

"How do you do?" Mitch had a broad smile, but I didn't register the rest of his face because he reached down to shake my hand. And I noticed that he had several fingers missing. I watched the goosebumps rise along my arm.

Mom nudged me. Maybe she saw, too, and we could go home now. Instead, she said, "Say 'How-do-you-do?' Gerry."

I knew it was rude to stare at people's handicaps. I knew I should be too adult to mention it. And yet I imagined his hand sticking in my throat, right above the "How-do-you-do?"

"Well, a lot of people are shy at first."

I noticed he was talking to me rather than to my mother.

"You'll be fine once we get in the water. Shall we test the temperature?"

He took my hand and I tried not to *feel,* just as I would try not to smell when I went to the bathroom at the movies. Instead, I concentrated on the high, winding echoes of the Hackensack pool. For the first time I noticed that there was a whole class of swimmers in the far end — the deep end — of the water. Mitch nodded toward the wading section.

He turned gently to Mom. "You'll want to sit up there," he said, pointing to the bleachers. "That way you won't get wet."

Coward, I thought, as she found a seat and let the strange man lead me down the cold metal ladder. I soon forgot her when he showed me how to dunk my head in and out of the water. Then I experienced the miracle of floating. I hardly thought about his hand until he lead me back to my mother beneath the italicized "Ladies" sign.

"A natural," he patted my shoulder. "Regular mermaid. See you next week, Gerry?"

"Oh, yes, next week," I answered, surprised by my enthusiasm.

It was a very cold winter, but each week we took the bus to Hackensack. Once I had learned to dogpaddle, Mitch graduated me from the wading section. Every so often I would look up and see Mom watching closely and pretending to be brave. After the lesson she always took me to Woolworth's for an egg salad sandwich and a gingerale. I had completely forgotten about the piano. I hardly saw Jackie any more because she spent so much time indoors, practicing.

One night I dreamt I was sitting on the edge of the pool, dangling my feet. The water had turned black and I was singing, trying to entice the missing fingers to surface from the

3

bottom of the water.

During the day, I tried not to think about Mitch's hand. I never mentioned it to Mom. At first I thought it would be impolite to talk about his handicap—for surely she must have noticed it too. Then I worried that she hadn't noticed and that if I told her about the missing fingers, she would cancel the lessons. None of the reasons made sense, but it seemed important to remain silent. I succeeded in forgetting about Mitch's hand until the week we began diving lessons.

He took me to the deep end, dove in himself, cutting the water sharply, swimming underneath, graceful as a dolphin. He surfaced with a big smile. "See how easy it is?"

"Sure," I stood shivering, suddenly remembering this was late January and it was sleeting outside.

"Just try jumping first," he called. "I'll catch you."

I stood there, bolstered by his smile. Then I glanced over at Mom's encouraging face. The air was an endless expanse; the water, I knew, would be worse, for it went down fourteen feet. Suddenly I jumped. Down. Down. I couldn't decide between terror and exhilaration, and then I was safe. Mitch was holding my hands; we were looking at each other, sputtering and laughing.

"Brave girl," he said.

I laughed, pumped my feet up and down and held onto his hands. Suddenly I was conscious of the missing fingers and panicked about drowning.

"Don't worry," he caught my frown. "Just hold on and I'll swim us to shore."

Those four feet were interminable as I struggled to keep afloat, to hide my revulsion, to keep from throwing up.

"There," he said as we reached the safe metal ladder. "It's a little early to knock off, but you've done a lot for one day."

I nodded, not daring to meet his eyes, for he must have known the cause of my distress. "Thank you, Mitch. See you . . . next Saturday."

I couldn't eat the egg salad sandwich. When Mom asked what was wrong, I broke down and sobbed, finally managing to confess.

She regarded me carefully. She listened as all my fears

4

spilled out. Did he have a kind of leprosy? Was it catching? Or polio? Sometimes the Salk vaccine didn't work and I knew kids got polio from swimming. Were the missing fingers dangerous? Would he lose his grip and let me slip to the bottom of the pool? Mom patted my perfectly formed hand and reassured me that I was safe. She speculated on how he might have lost his fingers — in an industrial accident, in the war.

The war, I decided. That night, watching a World War II movie on TV, I imagined Mitch on the frontline, perhaps the scout who went ahead of other soldiers to clear the way for his buddies and in the process. . . .

Sergeant Mitch taught me the crawl, the sidestroke, the breast stroke, the elementary back stroke. I still had trouble diving. But he was impressed with my progress and told Mom I was his best student.

I liked the sidestroke because I could see all around me. I would look up at the ceiling and consider the funny, yellow light pouring through the high windows. I liked to peer down the length of the pool and watch the fat lady doing her laps and the toddlers splashing each other. Searching the bleachers, I would wave to Mom, who smiled as I swam past her fears. When I looked up at her nowadays she seemed more relaxed. Sometimes she even sat back in her seat with her feet out on the bench in front of her.

The sidestroke made me feel like a graceful machine or one of those scissor bugs at the pond. It always put me in a quiet mood. I found the back stroke too slow, just as I considered the crawl too fast. With the breast stroke, I could fly, clearing a path through the cool water with my strong arms. Sometimes Mitch and I played tag and he would dare me to chase after his sleek shadow on the chlorine floor.

The locker room felt more comfortable now. I watched steam weaving around the dented grey lockers and I imagined this mist as angelhair breathing from the naked female forms. Mom made me get dressed in the cubicle, but many swimmers, particularly the older women, weren't at all shy. The different shapes were fascinating: tall, lean women with tiny breasts; others with chubby legs and big tummies. Everyone with that

5

triangle of fur above the legs. I had a big curiosity because my
mother was always very modest about her own body. Despite
Mom's efficient method of whisking me in and out of the dressing room, I learned a lot. One woman always creamed her
legs, slowly, as if she were putting on delicate silk stockings,
her hands rising higher and higher until she almost touched the
triangle. Everyone had a different system for attaching the
bra — some would snap it in front and then ponderously turn
the bra around before putting their arms through the straps.
Others were astonishingly quick at hooking from behind. The
bras came in all sorts — flimsy cheesecloth models like the one
my friend Karen wore; lacy, black styles and large, white contraptions with metal supports which made me think of the hair-
shirts Sister Martin talked about. Maybe women saints wore
metal under their breasts. I loved the mingling scents of talcum
powder and deodorant and perfume. I eavesdropped on the
ladies' quick conversations about gaining and losing weight,
raising kids and shopping. By late February I was a regular;
several women began to greet me by name.

Sister told us we could write about anything we liked, so I
was surprised when she asked me to stay after school to discuss
my essay on Mitch's swimming lessons.

"Sit here," she said in that voice she reserved for serious
talks.

"Is it true, what you've written in your paper?" she asked
slowly.

I looked into her long face, relieved that I could reassure
her it wasn't a lie, that I had, indeed, mastered four strokes
although my diving was still giving me trouble.

"Very nice dear. But is it true that you're taking lessons at
the YMCA?"

"Yes, Sister," I answered proudly. "All the way in Hackensack. Every Saturday."

She breathed deeply and looked at me with kindness. "But
what can your mother be thinking about? The YMCA is a *Protestant* organization."

"Oh, I know that, Sister. There are no statues, anywhere.
It's a very plain building. But the pool is pretty, with lots of

blues and greens. . . ." I stopped at her impassive face.

"Dear, remember what we learned in catechism class about the First Commandment. You shouldn't be participating in a Protestant organization."

"Oh, I see," I said, in that voice Mom used when she didn't want to make a decision right away and planned to talk with my father first.

She changed her tack. "And swimming in the middle of winter? Hackensack is a long way to travel. Have you considered piano? Mrs. Sullivan teaches piano in her home."

"No," I shrugged. "Swimming is more useful." The anger rose suddenly in my throat. "Music requires too many fingers."

Sister decided not to pursue this last point. She tapped my knee and said conclusively, "Gerry, I'm afraid that you'll just have to stop going there."

"I see." I wasn't sure how convincing my neutrality was because I was concentrating on holding back the tears.

The next week Mom and I were back on the bus to Hackensack. Mom explained that Sister was mistaken. She couldn't have understood that I was just learning how to swim, that it involved no religious instruction.

I stared out at the grey slush and the lawns peeking through the snow. This was a moral crisis for me because I didn't want to displease God. I didn't want my attendance at the YMCA to damn me to hell—what good would swimming do me there? On the other hand, I loved that old building and my new friends in the locker room. And Mitch.

"Don't worry," Mom repeated. "Trust me. Sister Martin means well, but sometimes the nuns are a little . . . innocent about the world. They could get lost in their rules and regulations."

I shrugged, but I felt very grown up. Although Mom complained about the nuns to Dad, this was the first time she had ever said anything to me. I tried to conceal my satisfaction.

"Trust me. Wasn't I right about swimming being fun?"

That was the day I did it. I wasn't sure what had got into me. I walked out to the fourteen foot sign, put my head down and dove straight into the green water.

"Perfect," Mitch called, treading gracefully, holding out his hands to congratulate me.

"Perfect," Mom called from the bleachers.

"Perfect," I surfaced, reaching eagerly for his hands.

All winter during my ninth year I took the long bus ride from Dumont to Hackensack. Through the snow I travelled to those misty, tiled chambers where I learned how not to drown.

When It Happens

MARGARET ATWOOD

Mrs. Burridge is putting up green tomato pickles. There are twelve quarts in each lot with a bit left over, and that is the end of the jars. At the store they tell her there's a strike on at the factory where they get made. She doesn't know anything about that but you can't buy them anywhere, and even before this they were double what they were last year; she considers herself lucky she had those in the cellar. She has a lot of green tomatoes because she heard on the weather last night there was going to be a killer frost, so she put on her parka and her work gloves and took the lantern out to the garden in the pitch-dark and picked off all the ones she could see, over three bushels. She can lift the full baskets herself but she asked Frank to carry them in for her; he grumbles, but he likes it when she asks. In the morning the news said the growers had been hit and that would shoot the price up, not that the growers would get any of it themselves, everyone knows it's the stores that make the money.

She feels richer than she did yesterday, but on the other hand there isn't that much you can do with green tomatoes. The pickles hardly made a dint in them, and Frank has said, as he does every year, that they will never eat twenty-four quarts of green tomato pickle with just the two of them and the chil-

9

dren gone. Except when they come to visit and eat me out of house and home, Mrs. Burridge adds silently. The truth is she has always made two batches and the children never liked it anyway, it was Frank ate them all and she knows perfectly well he'll do it again, without even noticing. He likes it on bread and cheese when he's watching the hockey games, during every commercial he goes out to the kitchen and makes himself another slice, even if he's just had a big meal, leaving a trail of crumbs and bits of pickle from the counter across the floor and over the front-room rug to his big chair. It used to annoy Mrs. Burridge, especially the crumbs, but now she watches him with a kind of sadness; she once thought their life together would go on forever but she has come to realize this is not the case.

She doesn't even feel like teasing him about his spare tire any more, though she does it all the same because he would miss it if she stopped. "There you go," she says, in the angular, prodding, metallic voice she cannot change because everyone expects it from her, if she spoke any other way they would think she was ill, "you keep on munching away like that and it'll be easy for me to get you out of bed in the mornings, I'll just give you a push and you'll roll all the way down the stairs like a barrel." And he answers in his methodical voice, pretending to be lazy even though he isn't, "You need a little fun in life," as though his pickles and cheese are slightly disreputable, almost like an orgy. Every year he tells her she's made too much but there would be a fuss all right if he went down to the cellar one day and there wasn't any left.

Mrs. Burridge has made her own pickles since 1952, which was the first year she had the garden. She remembers it especially because her daughter Sarah was on the way and she had trouble bending down to do the weeding. When she herself was growing up everyone did their own pickles, and their own canning and preserving too. But after the war most women gave it up, there was more money then and it was easier to buy things at the store. Mrs. Burridge never gave it up, though most of her friends thought she was wasting her time, and now she is glad she didn't, it kept her in practice while the others were having to learn all over again. Though with the sugar going up the way it is, she can't understand how long anyone is going to

10

be able to afford even the homemade things.

On paper Frank is making more money than he ever has; yet they seem to have less to spend. They could always sell the farm, she supposes, to people from the city who would use it as a weekend place; they could get what seems like a very high price, several of the farms south of them have gone that way. But Mrs. Burridge does not have much faith in money; also it is a waste of the land, and this is her home, she has it arranged the way she wants it.

When the second batch is on and simmering she goes to the back door, opens it and stands with her arms folded across her stomach, looking out. She catches herself doing this four or five times a day now and she doesn't quite know why. There isn't much to see, just the barn and the back field with the row of dead elms Frank keeps saying he's going to cut down, and the top of Clarke's place sticking over the hill. She isn't sure what she is looking for but she has the odd idea she may see something burning, smoke coming up from the horizon, a column of it or perhaps more than one column, off to the south. This is such a peculiar thought for her to have that she hasn't told it to anyone else. Yesterday Frank saw her standing at the back door and asked her about it at dinner; anything he wants to talk to her about he saves up till dinner, even if he thinks about it in the morning. He wondered why she was at the back door, doing nothing at all for over ten minutes, and Mrs. Burridge told him a lie, which made her very uneasy. She said she heard a strange dog barking, which wasn't a good story because their own dogs were right there and they didn't notice a thing. But Frank let it pass; perhaps he thinks she is getting funny in her old age and doesn't want to call attention to it, which would be like him. He'll track mud all over her nice shiny kitchen floor but he'd hate to hurt anyone's feelings. Mrs. Burridge decides, a little wistfully, that despite his pigheadedness he is a kind and likeable man, and for her this is like renouncing a cherished and unquestionable belief, such as concentrating on the paper — she writes on the backs of used-up days of the page-a-day calendar Frank gives her every New Year's — she is gazing around the kitchen, looking at all the things she will have to leave behind when she goes. That will be the hardest part. Her mother's china, her silver, even though it is an old-fashioned pattern and the silver is wearing off, the egg timer in the shape of a chicken Sarah gave her when she was twelve, the ceramic salt and pepper shakers, green horses with perforated heads, that one of the other children brought back from the Ex. She thinks of walking up the stairs, the sheets folded in the chest, the towels stacked neatly on the shelves, the beds made, the quilt that was her grandmother's, it makes her want to cry. On her bureau, the wedding picture, herself in a shiny satin gown (the satin was a mistake, it emphasized her hips), Frank in the suit he has not worn since except to funerals, his hair cut too short on the sides and a surprising tuft at the top, like a woodpecker's. The children when they were babies. She thinks of her girls now and hopes they will not have babies; it is no longer the right time for it.

Mrs. Burridge wishes someone would be more precise, so she could make better plans. Everyone knows something is going to happen, you can tell by reading the newspapers and watching the television, but nobody is sure what it will be, nobody can be exact. She has her own ideas about it though. At first it will simply become quieter. She will have an odd feeling that something is wrong but it will be a few days before she is able to pin it down. Then she will notice that the planes are no longer flying over on their way to the Malton Airport, and that the noise from the highway two miles away, which is quite distinct when the leaves are off the trees, has almost disappeared. The television will be non-committal about it; in fact, the television, which right now is filled with bad news, of strikes, shortages, famines, layoffs and price increases, will become sweet-tempered and placating, and long intervals of classical music will appear on the radio. About this time Mrs. Burridge will realize that the news is being censored as it was during the war.

Mrs. Burridge is not positive about what will happen next; that is, she knows what will happen but she is not positive about the order. She expects it will be the gas and oil: the oil delivery man will simply not turn up at his usual time, and one morning the corner filling station will be closed. Just that, no explanations, because of course they — she does not know who "they" are, but she has always believed in their existence — they do not want people to panic. They are trying to keep things looking normal, possibly they have already started on this program and that is in fact why things still do look normal. Luckily she and Frank have the diesel fuel tank in the shed, it is three-quarters full, and they don't use the filling station anyway, they have their own gas pump. She has Frank bring in the old wood stove, the one they stored under the barn when they had the furnace and the electricity put in, and for once she blesses Frank's habit of putting things off. She was after him for years to take that stove to the dump. He cuts down the dead elms, finally, and they burn them in the stove.

The telephone wires are blown down in a storm and no one comes to fix them; or this is what Mrs. Burridge deduces. At any rate, the phone goes dead. Mrs. Burridge doesn't particularly mind, she never liked using the phone much anyway, but it does make her feel cut off.

About now men begin to appear on the back road, the gravel road that goes past the gate, walking usually by themselves, sometimes in pairs. They seem to be heading north. Most of them are young, in their twenties, Mrs. Burridge would guess. They are not dressed like the men around here. It's been so long since she has seen anyone *walking* along this road that she becomes alarmed. She begins leaving the dogs off their chains, she has kept them chained at night ever since one of them bit a Jehovah's Witness early one Sunday morning. Mrs. Burridge doesn't hold with the Witnesses — she is United — but she respects their perseverance, at least they have the courage of their convictions which is more than you can say for some members of her own church, and she always buys a *Watchtower*. Maybe they have been right all along.

It is about this time too that she takes one of the guns, she thinks it will be the shotgun as she will have a better chance of hitting something, and hides it, along with the shells, under a piece of roofing behind the barn. She does not tell Frank; he will have the twenty-two. She has already picked out the spot.

They do not want to waste the little gasoline they still have left in the pump so they do not make unnecessary trips. They begin to eat the chickens, which Mrs. Burridge does not look

13

forward to. She hates cleaning and plucking them, and the angriest she ever got at Frank was the time he and Henry Clarke decided to go into turkey farming. They did it too, despite all she had to say against it, and she had to cope with the turkeys escaping and scratching in the garden and impossible to catch, in her opinion they were the stupidest birds in God's creation, and she had to clean and pluck a turkey a week until luckily the blackhead wiped out a third of the flock, which was enough to discourage them, they sold off the rest at a loss. It was the only time she was actually glad to see Frank lose money on one of his ventures.

Mrs. Burridge will feel things are getting serious on the day the electricity goes off and does not come back on. She knows, with a kind of fatalism, that this will happen in November, when the freezer is full of the vegetables but before it is cold enough to keep the packages frozen outside. She stands and looks at the Pliofilm bags of beans and corn and spinach and carrots, melting and sodden, and thinks, Why couldn't they have waited till spring? It is the waste, of food and also of her hard work, that aggravates her the most. She salvages what she can. During the Depression, she remembers, they used to say those on farms were better off than those in the city, because at least they had food; if you could keep the farm, that is; but she is no longer sure this is true. She feels beleaguered, isolated, like someone shut up inside a fortress, though no one has bothered them, in fact no one has passed their way for days, not even the solitary walking men.

With the electricity off they can no longer get the television. The radio stations, when they broadcast at all, give out nothing but soothing music, which Mrs. Burridge does not find soothing in the least.

One morning she goes to the back door and looks out and there are the columns of smoke, right where she's been expecting to see them, off to the south. She calls Frank and they stand watching. The smoke is thick and black, oily, as though something has exploded. She does not know what Frank is thinking; she herself is wondering about the children. She has had no news of them in weeks, but how could she? They stopped delivering mail some time now.

14

Fifteen minutes later, Henry Clarke drives into the yard in his half-ton truck. This is very unusual as no one has been driving anywhere lately. There is another man with him, and Mrs. Burridge identifies him as the man three farms up who moved in four or five years ago. Frank goes out and talks with them, and they drive over to the gas pump and start pumping the rest of the precious gas into the truck. Frank comes back to the house. He tells her there's a little trouble down the road, they are going along to see about it and she isn't to worry. He goes into the back room, comes out with the twenty-two, asks her where the shotgun is. She says she doesn't know. He searches for it, fruitlessly—she can hear him swearing, he does not swear in her presence—until he gives up. He comes out, kisses her goodbye, which is unusual too, and says he'll be back in a couple of hours. She watches the three of them drive off in Henry Clarke's truck, towards the smoke, she knows he will not come back. She supposes she ought to feel more emotional about it, but she is well prepared, she has been saying goodbye to him silently for years.

She re-enters the house and closes the door. She is fifty-one, her feet hurt, and she does not know where she can go, but she realizes she cannot stay here. There will now be a lot of hungry people, those that can make it this far out of the cities will be young and tough, her house is a beacon, signalling warmth and food. It will be fought over, but not by her.

She goes upstairs, searches in the cupboard, and puts on her heavy slacks and her two thickest sweaters. Downstairs she gathers up all the food that will be light enough for her to carry: raisins, cooking chocolate, dried prunes and apricots, half a loaf of bread, some milk powder which she puts into a quart freezer bag, a piece of cheese. Then she unearths the shotgun from behind the barn. She thinks briefly of killing the livestock, the chickens, the heifers and the pig, so no one will do it who does not know the right way; but she herself does not know the right way, she has never killed anything in her life, Frank always did it, so she contents herself with opening the henhouse door and the gate into the back field. She hopes the animals will run away but she knows they probably will not.

She takes one last look around the house. As an after-

15

thought, she adds her toothbrush to the bundle: she does not like the feel of unbrushed teeth. She does not go down into the cellar but she has an image of her carefully sealed bottles and jars, red and yellow and purple, shattered on the floor, in a sticky puddle that looks like blood. Those who come will be wasteful, what they cannot eat themselves they will destroy. She thinks about setting fire to the house herself, before anyone else can do it.

Mrs. Burridge sits at her kitchen table. On the back of her calendar page, it's for a Monday, she has written *Oatmeal,* in her evenly spaced public-school handwriting that always got a star and has not changed very much since then. The dogs are a problem. After some thought she unchains them, but she does not let them past the gate: at a crucial moment they might give her away. She walks north in her heavy boots, carrying her parka because it is not yet cold enough to put it on, and her package of food and the shotgun which she has taken care to load. She passes the cemetery where her father and mother and her grandmother and grandfather are buried; the church used to be there but it burned down sixteen years ago and was rebuilt closer to the highway. Frank's people are in the other cemetery, his go back to the great-grandfather but they are Anglican, not that he kept it up. There is no one else on the road; she feels a little foolish. What if she is wrong and Frank comes back after all, what if nothing, really, is the matter? *Shortening,* she writes. She intends to make a lemon meringue pie for Sunday, when two of the children are coming up from the city for dinner.

It is almost evening and Mrs. Burridge is tired. She is in a part of the country she cannot remember, though she has stayed on the same road and it is a road she knows well; she has driven along it many times with Frank. But walking is not the same as driving. On one side there is a field, no buildings, on the other a woodlot; a stream flows through a culvert under the road. Mrs. Burridge kneels down to drink: the water is icecold and tastes of iron. Later there will be a frost, she can feel it. She puts on her parka and her gloves, and turns into the forest where she will not be seen. There she will eat some raisins and cheese and try to rest, waiting for the moon to rise so she can continue walking. It is now quite dark. She smells earth, wood, rotting leaves.

Suddenly her eye is caught by a flicker of red, and before she can turn back — how can this happen so quickly? — it takes shape, it is a small fire, off to the right, and two men are crouching near it. They have seen her, too: one of them rises and comes towards her. His teeth bare, he is smiling; he thinks she will be easy, an old woman. He says something but she cannot imagine what it is, she does not know how people dressed like that would talk.

They have spotted her gun, their eyes have fastened on it, they want it. Mrs. Burridge knows what she must do. She must wait until they are close enough and then she must raise the gun and shoot them, using one barrel for each, aiming at the faces. Otherwise they will kill her, she has no doubt about that. She will have to be fast, which is too bad because her hands feel thick and wooden; she is afraid, she does not want the loud noise or the burst of red that will follow, she has never killed anything in her life. She has no pictures beyond this point. You never know how you will act in a thing like that until it actually happens.

Mrs. Burridge looks at the kitchen clock. On her list she writes *Cheese,* they are eating more cheese now than they used to because of the price of meat. She gets up and goes to the kitchen door.

Emei Shan

CANYON SAM

Finally I am away from the brown, choking haze of the cities, from the clouds of cigarette smoke in restaurants, buses, and trains throughout China. The air here is moist, clean, unaffected.

Steep, twisting mountain paths. Cobbled mosaics of rough-hewn boulders form a trail. Drifting houses of fog obscure views of lush fir and cedar landscapes. The light rain makes the already testy path even more treacherous. It is late April on Emei Shan in Szechuan Province, one of the five sacred Buddhist mountains in China.

Young Chinese in groups hoot through the hushed green canyons, toss empty cigarette packages into the ferns, out-talk each other in front of girlfriends. The Emei Shan porters have muscled calves like Olympians, taut, honey-glazed skin, and stout, sturdy bodies. They wear wood-frame packs to haul their loads to the monasteries above: stacks of red brick, jerry cans of cooking oil, heaps of quilted comforters, crates of soda bottles, bluging sacks of charcoal. When an item is especially unwieldy, like a thirty-foot wooden roof beam, a team of four porters carry it together, chanting a low rhythmic ditty as they step in unison, the weight of the load swinging to and fro.

When the porters rest, they place their walking stick under

the bottom of their pack behind them and let the pressure of the load — often equal or greater in weight to their own body — fall into the earth through the pole's length. Chests heaving, sweat pouring from their foreheads, they mop themselves with cotton kerchiefs tied around their necks. Five minutes and they're off, trudging steadily, backs held upright in the frames. Their upper body strapped high and wide with goods as if a moving van was upended and emptied onto their back; their legs churning beneath like a human locomotive. Because of their load the porters cannot turn their heads to see behind or very far to either side as people scurry behind or beside them. They wear cotton culotte pants, tank tops with drooping arm holes and thin rubber shoes.

In heavy prolonged downpour they eventually cover their load with a plastic tarp and don flimsy raincoats that are thin as tissue, the kind you buy from souvenir hawkers at the base of the mountain, their soaked dripping heads left bare. Some porters are babyfaced, as young as 15, but even they have the full-muscled proportions of men twice their age. Black black stunning irrefutable thick black hair. In China, a bobbing sea of black hair, medium-framed bodies, curious brown eyes. Like my grandparents, like my family, like me. It is normal.

After the porters deliver a load along the trail, they look for other ferries up and down the mountain. They take passengers up the steep climb: grandmothers, cranky children, high-heeled city ladies straddle the porter's wooden packframe looking alternately terrified or bored with each step. The porters zero in on me immediately. I wear Patagonia hiking shorts that bare my legs, Hong Kong eyeglasses, a Western hairstyle. Lady tired. Lady wants a ride. I'll take you, I'll take you. Come on, come on, I'll take you.

They see: tourist, American money, business opportunity. C'mon, c'mon, they hound, following me for long stretches up and down and around the meandering trails. A low, reassuring entreaty. Constant, repetitious. That tone of voice that hums into one's bones, echoes into the quiet layers of one's mind like a subliminal recording.

Sometimes they touch me lightly, tapping the inside of my elbow with the calloused fingers of their hand; when I turn and meet their eyes boldly, they don earnest looks as thin as their raincoats. Forty yuan, it's a good price, they drum. Thirteen dollars. Their eyes baleful on the surface, steely as I look more deeply. Okay thirty yuan! thirty yuan! they jog alongside me, their wooden contraptions bobbing like some medieval back brace.

No, no. No thanks. I like to walk. I *want* to walk, I tell them. They tail me endlessly, and soon I stop bothering to answer. Lady take a ride, you don't want to walk. It's so far. You can't make it. It's tiring. It's steep and dangerous. Let me carry you, let me carry you. It is as if they can't believe people from developed countries would ever want to engage in physical labor, let alone seek it out, enjoy it. Especially a woman.

At the end of the first long day the mountain falls into a shadowed hush as the rain comes down in cold, sobbing slivers and light is squeezed from the tree-veiled track. Most hikers stopped off earlier for the night; the once-crowded trail is virtually deserted. When I finally see another trekker I pounce upon him, asking how much farther to Elephant Temple Monastery? How much longer to walk? Twenty minutes, he answers.

Twenty minutes in the wet chill, in my weary state. I have walked all day up thousands of stone steps, chipped crudely from huge granite boulders and dug into a winding staircase. Because of the irregularity of the steps my ankle twists differently, my leg raises to a new height, my muscles arch at unpredictable angles with each step toward Elephant Temple, my place of rest for the night. A porter rounds the bend heading downhill as I head up. In the fading light I see rain dripping from his brow, falling from his chin. Carry? Carry? he ventures in a low tenor. How much? I ask, suddenly curious in my weariness. Thirty yuan, comes the answer. Thirty yuan! I gasp. For twenty minutes ride! And I drudge on under my own power.

It takes two days to reach the top. People head for Wanfo, the summit, to see the sunrise at daybreak. When the clouds clear, a full-circled rainbow of light, a haloed aura off the northern ledge, can be seen in the sky — and seen at this time only.

I've seen postcards of this natural wonder called Buddha's Aureole.

We get up in the freezing pre-dawn—three or four hundred people in long green Mao overcoats 10,000 feet high, packed together on a narrow outcropping like penguins in Anarctica. Huddled together in shivering clusters, we stomp our feet to resurrect numb toes, lower our heads into the wind, and bury our hands in the pillow-sized pockets. Hundreds of pairs of eyes fix on the northern sky waiting for the clouds to part as if awaiting heaven's benediction. Freezing minutes pass. The sun rises. We wait. We stamp our feet and watch our frosty out-breaths. The clouds do not clear. After an hour and a half the thick cover still has not moved away, a floating ethereal mass between us and the view of Buddha's halo. People eventually stray, scatter to scenic outlooks to pose for photos. The top of Emei Shan: Emei Mountain, Szechuan Province, late spring; we were there.

The weather going down is more comfortable. I fold my blue collapsing umbrella, a birthday present from my friend Nan years ago, into my day pack. Shifting constantly, fog occupies the verdant gorges like a phantom army, framing different vistas throughout the day—eclipsing scenes once visible, unveiling views never shown: ridges of rockface, pockets of jungle, windows of blue horizon. Foggy fringes border every vantage point and then melt seamlessly into the overcast sky. Wild monkeys swing from vine to vine, crashing with reckless grace through the dewy forest. The descent is even harder on my body than the climb up. The spongy part at my knee joint is jarred sharply with each downhill step. After several hours my leg muscles feel light and tingly beneath me.

At six o'clock the light is fading fast. Luckily I have just come to my destination for the night: Xianfeng, Magic Peak Monastery, a large monastery backed into rugged cliffs. It is such a gigantic complex that it takes half an hour before I find the right place to register for a room. I am in luck: a single room is available and their prices are reasonable. At the summit we were hostage to whatever exorbitant fee the inn proprietors charged. The clerks here are pleasant, composed young women with long black hair. They sit in a single-lightbulb-lit cubicle, a vision of warm bright order that creates a feast of anticipation in me for when I will shortly be bathed and resting in my own room. Dry, sheltered, and most importantly, off my feet.

"Please give me the English form," I ask, for I cannot read the Chinese one they've handed me.

"What?" they ask puzzled, staring into my Cantonese features.

"The English form."

Ahh, much better. I fill it out, answer the routine questions. "Date" it reads before a blank space. But I've lost track of time out here. "What is the date?" I ask.

"30th day, fourth moon," the clerks reply.

April 30, I write. I've planned this trek at a leisurely pace: two days to go up and two days to go down.

A strange, queasy feeling starts to come over me. Slowly at first like spilled ink touching the edge of rice paper.

"Are you sure it's 30th day, fourth moon?" I ask.

They point at a calendar posted on the wall. Now the uneasy feeling spreads quickly. A quiet panic rises, as if I watch helplessly the ink-spill race toward beautiful calligraphy on the paper.

I force myself to think rationally. "Thirty days has September . . . April, June, and November . . ." I recite silently. I tap the grooves on my knuckles counting the long and short months as I was taught in grade school.

I carry a ticket in my wallet for a bus leaving May 1 for Chengdu, the capital of this province, connecting to a flight to Lhasa, Tibet, the next day. Reservations are hard to come by and normally take at least a week of waiting. I suddenly realize that I have made the mistake of counting one extra day in April. I must be at the bottom of this mountain *tomorrow* morning at 7, not the next day, to catch my bus. I am at over 5,000 feet atop a mountain in China, weary from a full day of hiking, and night is falling.

The trail is the same pattern of huge stone steps for another half hour till the next temple. Gradually they narrow to a dirt

22

footpath, which begets more footpaths, which beget more footpaths. They cross and entwine—meandering in all directions like a bevy of snakes. Crossroads, crossroads, always a choice to be made, leading to another set of choices to be made, leading to another set of choices to be made. After awhile I find myself standing in the center of a dozen hectares of farmland, the sky looming charcoal grey above with little moonlight. The trail has vanished mysteriously and entirely. Disappeared. I stand looking over terraced farmland with thatched cottages in the far distance, cradled by a ridge on the uphill side. I pick my way back to the last set of crossroads. Farmland surrounds me—dark mounds of earth furrowed in neat rows. From here on the way is never clear. Two times I must go great distances out of my way upon sight of a moving shadow, intimations of a late-working farmer, to ask the way. It is eight o'clock, and I pray to reach the monastery at the foot of the mountain by midnight.

The farmers are wary at first. Their grizzled faces lines and closed as if peering at me from behind the drawn shades of a window. Their heads nod slowly upwards at me. What am I doing here so late in the middle of their land? A stranger—a Westerner at that—wandering across their farm at such an improper hour. But sensing my urgency to find my way down they become larger, animated in their thin wiry frames. They gesture empathically as they speak, become helpful and verbose.

It is of little use. The language problem is always present, always hard. On a cold dark mountainside lost in the bowels of China, it is even harder. I see the pointed finger, follow their head jerking in the direction I must follow. I see the earthy fire in their eyes, hear it crackle through their speech: the fire of someone as borne from this earth as any stalk they cultivate from it by labor of their cracked, brown hands. I accept the help, pretend to understand.

What they're saying, I imagine, is: Follow this footpath till you reach the wheat crop, take the path towards the mountain short of a kilometer till you come to the irrigation stream. Head east into the forest. Walk towards the moon until the stand of old fir trees. Take the west path and in an hour it will open to a hilly meadow; look for a spur and head towards it over the low ridge, not the high ridge. You'll see a small temple. Enter through the main gate but leave by the south gate and there'll be a flight of stairs. . . .

What I understand . . . is the fire and the pointed finger.

At the edge of one hilly village I walk past an open food stall. The wooden benches are stacked in a corner. The hearth is cool, the fire extinguished. Soot-bottomed cauldrons have been pulled alongside cardboard and burlap screens behind which an oil lamp shines and a family of voices is heard. The food vendors along the crowded tourist path work long, long hours from before daybreak till hours past nightfall. A lone porter appears down the trail heading towards me. He is a shadowy figure in the low-lit sky.

"Siuje, where are you going?"

"To Fuhusi."

"You need a ride? I'll take you there."

"No, no. I'll walk."

"Siuje, let me porter you. You'll get tired; the trail is very difficult. It is late and dark, and Fuhusi is a far way."

"I know the way," I bluff, "I can walk. No thanks."

"It is very late. Why not go tomorrow? It is easy to get lost."

I explain my situation: the bus . . . the plane . . . I must reach Fuhusi by tonight. Is it far? I inquire. My estimate is about four hours.

"It is a long way, maybe three hours if you know the way. You have a torch?" I pull out my Mini Mag Light from Whole Earth Access; I show him how it focuses wide like a floodlight or narrow to a pinpoint. He's not impressed. Neither am I right then.

"Siuje, come on," he says gently, soothingly, ". . . let me carry you. Good price, cheaper for you. . . . You'll get lost otherwise. Come along now . . . come with me, come with me."

For half an hour he walks with me pursuing a fare. At one point he asks, "Why are you alone?" "No mother or father . . . no husband?"

I nod in answer. No mother, no father, no husband. He is

startled. I shrug.

"No companion? Why don't you have a friend?"

It's unheard of in China for a woman to travel alone.

"Because I am alone," I reply.

"It's not proper for a woman, it's not right," he scolds. He asks questions I don't understand. I give murmurs of acknowledgement but am unable to hold up my part of the conversation, even if I was in the state of mind to do so. As the night grows long, his entreaties taper off. Sometimes he walks near me and sometimes paces behind. On dangerous twists of trail he coaxes, "Mandiar, mandiar, siuje." Slowly, slowly, miss. For I am still at full speed, clamoring over slippery ridges intent to make it down this mountain; and now after what I've just told him, intent to show him I can do it without his help. Over rough rocky passes he is touching the back of my elbow lightly. Lightly like an infant's breath. Touching, hovering beneath. Touching, hovering. Touching, backing away . . . as I trek on determinately.

We walk in silence for he finally understands that I will walk, I will not hire him to carry me. There is no wind, only the sound of pebbles crushed underfoot as we step. Deeper and deeper the dark becomes. The glimmering bodies of a few stars are covered by haze. The mountainside is dead asleep, and the trail completely obscure in some places and then streaming in all directions in other places like a tangle of wild vines.

He says he is going to a friend's house near the bottom of the mountain to spend the night, that he has another load to take up in the morning. Hatless, he is lean, sinewy, slightly taller than me. He is one of the older porters I've seen, perhaps in his 30's but it is impossible to judge age in rural China. I act as if I know the way, just happen to be on the trail at the same time he is. Coincidence. I could take off on my own at any time. In fact I already know the trail winds under the ruffled shadows of trees, chisels across tracks of graveled mountain path, absolutely untraceable lest one knew the way or had benefit of daylight to find it. Having never been on this mountain before, let alone at night, I don't really know the way but it can't be that hard: just head downhill.

He has pulled on long pants against the chill of evening. I

wear my cowl-neck wool sweater and a vest to keep out the cold. My walking stick pokes gently ahead of me in step with my left foot.

The night stands around me, such a dark encompassing void it is as if it could take people into it and swallow them alive. It is still of any human activity except for me and this late-trodding porter. My feet are swollen from 13 hours of trekking, most of it earlier today on the jarring trek downhill. Pound! on the ball of my foot. Bounce! at the knee. The stone steps had no give against my thin crepe-soled shoes. Pound! and bounce. Pound! and bounce. Over and over on unpolished steep surfaces. The guidebook says there are over 3,000 stairs from top to bottom. My lower legs feel enlarged now as if they've reacted to a bee sting. My feet rush with blood as they expand against the soft leather sides of my shoes.

I come to a juncture. I look around. One way the path leads over a ridge, one way it crosses an open field, one path dips further along the edge of the forest. They all point downhill but in widely divergent directions. So much for my theory of just heading downhill. Without even really trying to decipher this, I find myself waiting for him, taking advantage of the lapse of moments between us to rest my legs. A few paces later he approaches, and without breaking stride marches down the left path — his footsteps as grounded and certain as the earth lying beneath us.

Fear walks with me silently. Fear of this unfamiliar land. Fear to be lost and in danger. Fear to miss my connection tomorrow. It is like a whisper without a voice, this fear — too threatening to be fully acknowledged. I tell myself I can spend one night in the open, without food. Wake up at first light. Better to miss a flight than to walk foolishly towards misfortune. I was raised in cities of straight-grid sidewalks and street signs at every corner. I am loosely attached to this human being, but who is he? And where is he leading me? What lies behind a low caressing voice and gentle solicitous mannerisms? Is he not a man? And are men not men all over the world? I am never absolutely sure where we are going. To a place out from which voices will not penetrate?

The narrow dirt trail on which I walk suddenly ends and I

face open land. I reach for my flashlight. The trail divides in opposite directions. To the right and to the left. I flash the light in each direction. Which way might lead to Fuhusi, the sixteenth century monastery sunk in the forest near the bottom of the mountain? There is no indication at all — not footprints, not the grade. The land is completely level so it is impossible to tell which way is downhill. Fuhusi is southwest of Emei Shan, but which was is that? I give up, and just try and get a *sense* of the right way. Nothing comes through. I try again. Nothing . . . nothing clear.

He comes up from behind, his wooden pack frame arched slightly, laden with only a few personal items. He gets out his torch and ricochets a beam of light down one dark trail then crossing the field in front of us, shoots the beam down the opposite trail.

"Which way, Suije?" he queries.

I pause a moment. Check both ways. Still no answer. He is silent. His dark outline shifts over his feet. His eyes watch me in the dark. I know him more by his voice, by the sense of his physical energy in motion than by what he looks like. He is shadow and voice and movement. He does not offer help. I think left more than right, so I take a stab. Left. The town is this way, I say.

I expect him to respond brightly, "Hou la, Good, right" and truck down the left trail. He says nothing and does not move, but I can feel his eyes rapt upon me. He stands looking at me a long time in the dark. No, he says. It's this way. To the right.

I fear that he can see all the way through me . . . to my fear . . . to my lostness that I have tried so hard to hide. With sure soundless steps he sets off down the right-hand trail. I look quickly down into the darkness of both directions again as his figure retreats. Can it be that the opposite way from town *leads* to town?! Can that be true?

"Coming?" he turns back looking at me.

Is this really the way? Am I being foolish or worse yet, naive, to follow him? *Are* men not men all over the world? Shall I keep surrendering my will to this nameless mountain porter? Who exactly am I following? When did he change from hustler to guide? *Has* he in fact changed? Can I trust him? . . . Do I

27

have a choice?

I don't stop to rest. I don't know how long this journey might take, and were I to get lost, I could lose hours backtracking. I never stop to look at him directly, not wanting to feel his eyes on my face, his soothing, lulling voice lick the air between us as we stand on a deserted trail. I follow him down the right-hand path. I pray to arrive by midnight.

In an hour we begin to see clusters of dark buildings — temples and houses — sunk back in the trees. The trail becomes a wide dirt road. We stride together at a brisk, relaxed pace under tall pines. I feel tremendously relieved as I start to recognize the way. Fuhusi is not far now. The hard part is over, from here Fuhusi is half an hour of easy walking.

I hear him speak; I turn around. He is five feet above on the road embankment, one leg bent against the upslope like a mountain goat.

"I go this way to sleep," he nods his chin towards some buildings across the clearing. He stands on a short ribbon of trail that slants sharply to the other side — a deer path I never would have seen in the dark.

"Jijian!" he says in a low voice.

"Jijian," I answer back promptly. Surprised to lose him so abruptly I cast a last look at his dim silouhette but the moonlight is so deeply shadowed under the pines that I cannot make out his features.

"Thank you!" I say, backing up and watching him go. "Goodbye!"

And then he is out of sight. Vanished like a trail that disappears after a bend.

After a long moment I walk on. The porter, the hustler, the guide . . . is gone. Veering away from its tree-lined edges, I move to the center of the road, and march down the moonlit aisle — even more joyful and triumphant to reach the bottom of Emei mountain, than I was to reach the top.

Seeing San Antonio

NATALIE L.M. PETESCH

Kate discovered that the abortion laws were inflexible: no less than a clear threat to the mother's life would satisfy the medical authorities that Kate should not bear this child. Her own wishes had nothing to do with it; she should have thought of that before she began fucking, the doctors implied, turning away with a severe look. The fact that she was a married woman ironically militated against her; she had a cover behind which she could conceal her crime; unlike thousands of others she need not have her child at a home for unwed mothers. Her child would have a name: what else did she, in her condition, feel she had a right to—a reward? a stipend? Other doctors, they inferred, (unlike themselves) were getting altogether too lax about such things.

The fact that she did not want to exploit Shaddy's name, that she would have to bring up the child alone (unless she married Caleb); that at this time in her life she wanted to study art—all these were considered callow, selfish and even irrelevant grievances. You can always study later, they said. Or in a more surly, even envious tone which she had grown to recognize, as if she were preempting a freedom they themselves coveted, one man and wife team of physicians observed drily: "Why are you so different from everybody else? We all want to

29

do things we can't. We have to assume responsibility for our actions."

She tried to argue logically that she had assumed "responsibility" when she had undertaken to prevent this birth. The physician himself had incorrectly fitted the diaphragm: why wasn't *he* responsible? To this she received only angry, suspicious looks: what was Kate trying to suggest about the medical profession? Doctors were not perfect. Did she think this was a Margaret Sanger Clinic or something? This was a busy hospital. They had no time for women who wanted to sleep with every tomdickandharry and then expected doctors to get them out of their predicament. *They* hadn't had the fun of it, they didn't see why they should risk disgrace and imprisonment just because she. . . .

She would not be able to get a professional abortion, that was clear; so Kate began inquiring of the girls at the art school. At the school she discovered, there was a cordon of silence protecting every girl; the subject was taboo. Some pretended to be scandalized; some offered sympathy; one or two "knew a woman who. . . ." Only one knew a practicing abortionist who charged a thousand dollars and Kate would have to arrange to meet him across the border in Mexico. The thought was intimidating: suppose there were complications? Why should the Mexican government care what happened to a sick American girl whose own country would have permitted her to ship herself across the border like cattle. In desperation Kate wrote down the (pseudonymous) names of a couple of women who were actually classified as *curanderas* by the Mexican-American population. She rationalized that they were women: after all they would have personal knowledge of their own bodies. One girl offered the amazing statistic of a woman (name unknown) who had performed eleven such "simple" abortions on herself, so it could not be difficult.

As the difficulties of obtaining a legal abortion mounted, Kate's anger and stubbornness intensified. She was barely eighteen years old; she had neither money nor education nor strength to undertake the rearing of a child by herself. She had tried to protect herself (*and* the unborn) by taking pains to be measured for a diaphragm. Clearly they were trying to punish her, to rub her nose into guilt and shame: where would *they* be if their mothers had decided it was inconvenient to have babies?

"She's all right," whispered the art student Magenta, handing Kate the name and address of a *curandera*.

Magenta's real name was Margaret, but the other students flattered her by calling her—like "Mauve"—by her favorite color. Actually the poor girl was only a moderately talented watercolorist, but her obsession with Texas sunsets was something everyone could understand; the Impressionists had done such things to perfection, their teacher told them, and it was natural to imitate until one achieved a style of one's own. Kate's own conviction was that the girl ought to be whipped for painting sunsets like the Impressionists: it might be good for her technique but very bad for her soul. The girl ought, Kate felt, to be set adrift to sink or swim in some passionate medium of her own. But Kate never criticized her art teachers: her sense of economic determinism spared her that particular sin of pride. She never for a moment believed that they were teachers of painting because they could not paint, but only that they were obliged to teach, for the sake of bread and (perhaps) a little wine. . . .

"Is it far?" asked Kate. "I'd rather stay right in town."

The girl looked at her incredulously. "You can't be too choosy. You've got to get it done as soon as you can. You'd be surprised . . ."

But Kate did not want to hear horror stories. It was going to be hard enough on her nerves so she interrupted: "Can I get there and back the same day?"

"Well: San Antonio's not far if you're just driving to see your folks . . . But if you're on the bus and you don't feel so good. . . ." The girl shrugged.

"Do you bleed much?" Kate felt she couldn't very well sit on the bus for several hours, saturating the seat; that would be asking for trouble. She tried to remain lucid, but panic was rising in her. Even the simplest problems could become overwhelmingly complicated when one was alone. "I mean, do I have to stay in bed? Will I need to take stuff along? Food? There won't be anybody visiting me." The thought of Caleb's moral

31

indignation at what she felt it was necessary to do made her quail with guilt. It was hard enough to sustain one's will about such an action without hearing moral proclamations: *what are you fixin' to do with MY child?*

"Well, no. Not till it starts coming, at least. It's not like a D&C, you know. It causes contractions, more like a miscarriage, you know."

"Oh." She felt fortunate at that moment that such words did not evoke associative responses from her. She preferred her ignorance: ignorance kept the anxiety from watering down her courage. She decided to ask no more questions, but simply wrote down the name and address of the woman in San Antonio.

"Perdita?" she observed with heavy irony. "That's one hell of a bad symbol."

She packed her bag for a weekend in San Antonio. Instead of a confrontation with Caleb she decided to send him a note which would, in fact, arrive Monday morning, by which time she hoped to have been through the worst. She thought she could face his recriminations afterwards, but not his moral arguments before: he made her feel like a murderer.

But by the time the bus rolled into San Antonio on Saturday morning she felt more like a victim. Her body ached from what felt like an oncoming case of flu. The lunging and growling of the bus had given her a headache. She had risen at six in order to catch the express; then the bus had turned out not to be an express after all, had seemed to stop at a Stuckey's every twenty miles. She had bought a San Antonio newspaper and map at the bus station and she now mulled over the classifieds, carefully scanning the columns for a cheap room in the event she should have to stay over. A hotel would be out of the question; it would cost her as much for the night as a room would cost for the week: she carefully outlined her itinerary on the map, calculating the distance between a well-known Mexican-American neighborhood where the rents would be cheapest and the distance to the house of Señora Perdita. As she descended from the bus the first sight that struck her was a billboard for a tourist company: SEE OLD SAN ANTONIO;

blazoned across the name of the company, like flying pennants were pictures of Spanish missions, of antique bridges and mossy riverbanks lined with Spanish-style restaurants: and of the Alamo.

It took about two hours after her arrival to find a room, wash up in the bathroom (which was on the second floor), and make her way to Señora Perdita's address. It was, as she might have predicted, a slat-strewn shack with outdoor plumbing. Chickens roosted on the twisted metal fence which separated the Perdita territory from the unpaved streets gullied by gas pipes which the city was in the process of laying down. Two long-haired brown and white dogs, very dirty and of uncertain breed, barked hoarsely at Kate as she climbed the splintered wooden porch. Corn feed had been strewn on the porch, apparently for the chickens. A sign on the bell in Spanish said the bell was out of order, and an arrow pointed to the rear. Kate wearily shifted the bag of clean towels she had been instructed by Magenta to bring along. ("Take along extras, in case," Magenta had added warningly. *In case what?* Kate had wanted to know, but had not dared ask.)

Her heart sank as she plodded through the back yard. The outhouse was open; flies buzzed like bees over the atmosphere, scenting out the decomposition of the race: *human beings, human beings,* they seemed to be repeating, their buzz rising to a crescendo as Kate passed and they moved away in a triangular swarm.

She did not need to knock. The old woman, who was apparently Señora Perdita, had heard the dogs barking and seen the chickens scuttle away, clucking at Kate's approach. She now stood at the screen door, nodding at Kate in that friendly mute way of people who expect not to understand the language they will hear. At her side was a dirty barefooted boy of about eight who stood nervously clutching at his crotch as if he had already been punished into believing that these parts were the cause of mankind's Sin and Suffering.

The old woman continued to nod to everything Kate said. She spoke from time to time to the child at her side and Kate realized with horror that the boy was her grandchild, (he said *si madre* to everything she instructed him to do), and that he was

33

also her assistant. The thought that the boy could be in the house at all during this delicate procedure made Kate miserable: there was no end to the psychological damage one inflicted on people, she thought in despair. How many women had this child witnessed his aging, impoverished grandmother performing abortions on? "He's not going to *be* here? . . ." she demanded at last, plucking up the will to ask this decisive question at least. If he were to be present, Kate would leave at once.

"No, no. He helpin' me," said Señora Perdita. "He gonna play. You gonna play later, Fernando. First, you put the teakettle."

Kate closed her eyes briefly; she felt faint. She saw the boy unhook a huge white enamel teakettle from the wall and place it on the black stove. Kate's habitual eye managed to take in the stove: it was obviously used for heat in the winter; there were three black burners on each side while the oven was overhead — its door a soft Delft-like blue enamel finish, strangely out of place in that house. If the old woman had been a witch about to roast Kate alive, the sight of her standing over the teakettle could not have been more terrifying. At the same time Kate could not overcome a feeling of sadness, of compassion, for the slovenly grandmother who managed to keep herself and the boy too from going hungry by practicing these ancient arts.

The old woman said with pride: "He my grandson. He go to school." She patted the boy on the head as he carefully dropped into the teakettle what looked to Kate like a small rubber hose, a pair of thick rubber gloves and some sort of arrow-shaped object which Kate could not see clearly. It was in fact difficult to see anything at all: every shade in the house was drawn against the blinding sunlight outdoors: Kate wondered how the señora would see to do her work if there were no electrification in the house. But as if sensing her thought, Señora Perdita now cautiously hauled a long outdoor extension cord in from the porch. This she placed on a hook in the ceiling of the kitchen and screwed into the open socket a blinding bulb of about two hundred watts. *An experienced surgeon,* thought Kate bitterly, and waited to see if the woman would wash her hands.

The señora did not in fact remember to wash her hands until she asked Kate for the towels. Then, with a confidential grimace, she gestured to Kate to wait *uno minuto* and hobbled over to a sink in the corner of the kitchen where she self-consciously washed her hands with what smelled to Kate like naptha soap. From where Kate stood, nervously waiting and watching, she could clearly see long brown and white hairs on the soap. Then with a surprisingly gracious smile the woman summoned Kate to a cracked leather chair which boasted an adjustable headrest, like a dentist's chair. Evidently Señora Perdita was proud of this reclining chair. She patted the headrest for Kate to be comfortable on: but first she dramatically (and admiringly) took out the towels Kate had brought and covered every inch of the shredding leather couch to her satisfaction. She then ordered her grandson out to play. Kate was so relieved at the boy's departure that she forgot for a moment to be frightened.

Señora Perdita then plucked out her sterilized instruments from the teakettle, lifting them with ice tongs. Kate watched from her semi-reclining position on the couch as the woman put on the black rubber gloves. Then, evidently remembering something, and still wearing her gloves, the señora walked over to a closet commode evidently used for storage, took out a white sheet with which she wrapped herself from bosom to toe. So much for sterile conditions, thought Kate grimly, and thought that in a moment she, Kate, would start praying to be released from this grotesque but dangerous nightmare. She could still get up and leave—but what then? She tried consciously to whip up her courage with admonitions, but had to admit she was scared. Her terror increased when, suddenly, during the insertion of the catheter, the two brown and white dogs began scraping and whining at the door. Tenderly cursing them, the señora abruptly left Kate's side: while holding her hands self-consciously in the air, she slewed her body sidewise at the screen door to push it open for the dogs. . . . The dogs promptly ran over to Kate and began sniffing at her with curiosity and excitement. Señora Perdita shoved them into the bedroom and latched the door. "Lotta trouble," she observed affectionately of the animals, and returned to Kate.

What followed took only a few minutes; the insertion of the catheter seemed ludicrously simple when Kate considered the terror which had preceded it all. Kate stood up gingerly, and handed the woman two twenty dollar bills. It was with mild surprise that she realized that in spite of her poverty, the woman had trusted Kate to hand over the money after her work was done and had not insisted on receiving cash before hand—a kind of *cortesia* which had not died with the indignities of poverty and old age.

"That's all?" asked Kate incredulously.

"Ahhh. . . ." Señora Perdita shrugged ambiguously. "Later, later. You'll see. All gotta come out." She indicated by clenching and unclenching her fists the labor contractions Kate might expect to feel. Kate sighed with discouragement, already exhausted from the psychological fear and trembling and dreading the ordeal. Enough, she wanted to cry. I've been through enough already.

The señora took the bills Kate had given her and pushed them into an empty milk bottle on the kitchen sink; the bills moved languidly, unfolding and spreading themselves in the bottle like green leaves floating upwards from their watery depths. The two women stood a moment watching the money float in the glass bottle, fascinated by its movement as though it were a living thing, a snake or water plant. But the dogs had begun whining again impatiently behind the bedroom door. With a groan of feigned impatience (it was obvious the woman adored her dogs) the señora allowed the dogs out of the room. Then she rolled Kate's towels into a paper shopping bag and returned them to Kate. At the sight of the shopping bags, the dogs began sniffing around the bag, nuzzling Kate's crotch as though the smell of her body had put them in heat. Kate quelled a rising nausea long enough to say feebly: *À díos,* smiling—what felt to her like a smile of complicity between two women who had been forced to use each other to disadvantage: what we ought to do is beg each other's pardon, thought Kate, and stepped out into the air. She did not feel giddy, but she was too emotionally upset to eat. The strain of the past two weeks had exhausted her, especially the gruelling and humiliating interviews with doctors in an attempt to get a legal abortion. Now, at least, she was free. She bought some milk and a few cans of food and returned to her room. She fell onto the unmade bed as if she had somehow survived a disaster.

When she awoke the room was dark. Several mosquitoes were tasting her blood, but she was too tired to beat them away. One of the things she had neglected to buy was insecticide, she would either have to get up to fight the mosquitoes or allow them to feast on her blood. With an effort she struggled to her feet; she at once began trembling with cold and realized she had been lying under a heavy blanket: yet the sunlight streaming through the paper window shade as though through heated glass testified to the relentless summer heat. Flies buzzed inside the shade, trying to get out; their bodies, elongated against the parchment-colored paper, made flying shadows big as bats.

She tried to open a can of sardines, reminding herself that food was necessary to recover strength, but the smell of fish oil as powerful as iodine sucked into her lungs and nostrils as though she were drowning in oil. There was no wash basin in the room; if she wanted to vomit she'd either have to use an empty can in the clothes closet or walk down the hall, then upstairs to the bathroom. She chose to stay motionless, fighting nausea. It was as if there were no air left in the universe, the face of the earth had been taken over by tropical fauna, these buzzing flies and snarling mosquitoes. Kate put her head down on the table and resisted an overwhelming impulse to cry.

Her head on her arm was hot, and the realization struck her (what seemed her first rational thought since she had arrived in this *barrio*): fever. The concept was as clear as her first vision of sunflowers years ago, followed by that illness which had struck the sound from one ear and left her with those star-shaped scars which were only beginning to fade. Fever, she knew by heart and experience, was not something sardines could do anything about. With relief she pushed the food aside. Stick to water. *Feed a cold and starve a fever,* as the ancient almanacs said. She finally forced herself to stagger out to the hallway and climb the twelve steps to the bathroom (the fact that she counted them seemed to her a miracle of pure clearheadedness). Here she filled two empty milk cartons with water.

All night long she carefully remembered to wake herself and to *sip water, sip water, it prevents dehydration.* But by morning her mouth was parched, her skin like coarse blotting paper spotted over with small bites from the bloodthirsty misquitoes. The flies which had quieted down resounded like helicopters in her brain. She must do what was necessary, she must manage to climb those twelve stairs *(again!)* to where she had seen a phone not far from the bathroom and telephone for a taxi. Otherwise she was certain to be found in this room a week later when the rent was due, stretched out on the bed, her body blossoming with flies, her tongue hanging out with thirst. . . . With an effort she pushed all her things into the sack Señora Perdita had given her and made her way toward the pool of light which lay upon the stairwell.

In the street she waited anxiously for the taxi. She stood leaning against a fire hydrant for support until she saw a black driver moving his cab cautiously up the unpaved street, avoiding the ditches ploughed by the gas company. He looked at her suspiciously as he approached, afraid, perhaps, that she had been knifed, or would bleed to death in his car.

For some reason, perhaps the fever itself, perhaps because she was in a Mexican-American neighborhood and the driver was black — she was inspired to tell the truth. Luckily her instinct did not betray her. The driver understood at once and, clucking his teeth sympathetically, scolded her like a child all the way to the County Hospital. "Look like you ought to of knowed better," he said, and helped her out of the cab. She smiled at him tenderly — she was all her life to remember the scar on his forehead as though someone had meant to cleave him in two and the axe had slipped; by then her fever was so high, her brain so giddy that she never noted his company nor his name nor anything about him but his voice. He vanished, having unwillingly stuffed the five-dollar bill she insisted on giving him into his pocket.

By the time they had laid her on the table to prepare her for a dilatation and curretage, her temperature was 104°. She could hear the doctors in the clinic cursing her and all those ignorant *curanderas* who kill off more people a year, they said, than diphtheria; they were like a plague upon 'the people.' Until these ignorant people learned to go to real doctors, she heard someone say, they would continue to die off like flies. Someone then quoted the San Antonio annual death rate, but by this time Kate was staring, half-blinded, at the blazing light which hung over the surgery table. She could feel them quickly and expertly shaving her pubic hair: an anesthetist hovered efficiently over her with fumes from a cone-shaped cup: *why couldn't I have had all this before? NOW they want to save me, when only a day or so ago they were willing to see me murdered?*

She had not time to separate the "they" from the "me" however; for with the first whiff of ether (*if that's what it is,* thought Kate doubtfully — adding to herself with what she imagined was enormous lucidity: *je doute, donc je suis*), she seemed to hover over and fall into the bright light which was pouring into her eyes; and she shut her eyes until she waked to a clean bed with a spotlessly white nurse pushing penicillin into her hip with a sharpness which felt to Kate like the distilled savagery of the world and who was saying: "There, that wasn't so bad, was it?"

As We Are Now

(an excerpt)

MAY SARTON

I am not mad, only old. I make this statement to give me courage. To give you an idea what I mean by courage, suffice it to say that it has taken two weeks for me to obtain this notebook and a pen. I am in a concentration camp for the old, a place where people dump their parents or relatives exactly as though it were an ash can.

My brother, John, brought me here two weeks ago. Of course I knew from the beginning that living with him would never work. I had to close my own house after the heart attack (the stairs were too much for me). John is four years older than I am and married a much younger woman after Elizabeth, his first wife, died. Ginny never liked me. I make her feel inferior and I cannot help it. John is a reader and always has been. So am I. John is interested in politics. So am I. Ginny's only interest appear to be malicious gossip, bridge, and trying out new recipes. Unfortunately she is not a born cook. I find the above paragraph extremely boring and it has been a very great effort to set it down. No one wants to look hard at disagreeable things. I am not alone in that.

I am forcing myself to get everything clear in my mind by writing it down so I know where I am at. There is no reality now except what I can sustain inside me. My memory is failing. I have to hang on to every scrap of information I have to keep my sanity, and it is for that purpose that I am keeping a journal. Then if I forget things later, I can always go back and read them here.

I call it *The Book of the Dead.* By the time I finish it I shall be dead. I want to be ready, to have gathered everything together and sorted it out, as if I were preparing for a great final journey. I intend to make myself whole here in this Hell. It is the thing that is set before me to do. So, in a way, this path inward and back into the past is like a map, the map of my world. If I can draw it accurately, I shall know where I am.

I do not blame John. That is the first thing. In his way he is fighting to keep whole, as I am, and Ginny was making life intolerable for both of us. Far better to dump me here than lose me in a quicksand of jealousy and hatred. He had to make a choice. The only thing I do not know is why he has not come to see me. Perhaps he is ill. Perhaps they have gone away. It does seem queer.

Also, although it is clear in my mind that I had to go somewhere, it is not clear why the place chosen should seem a place of punishment. But I must not dwell on this if possible. Sometimes old people imagine that everyone is against them. They have delusions of persecution. I must not fall into that trap.

It is better to smile at the image of that big white Cadillac turning off macadam onto a rough dirt road, the rain—of course it had to be raining, and not just a quiet rain, but a real downpour that would make almost anyone consider building an ark! I wondered whether Ginny had taken a wrong turning. When we stopped at a small red farmhouse that looked as though it had been gradually sinking into the mud for years, I thought it must be to ask directions. There was no sign, only two elms—the nursing home is called "Twin Elms." Five enormous geese stretched out their necks and hissed at us when we got out of the car. I noticed there was a barn over to the right. In the rain, the whole place seemed enclosed in darkness.

"Well," John said, "here we are, Caro." His voice had become unnaturally cheerful in the way voices do when addressing children or the feeble-minded.

There were two doors, but the front door opened into a sea

of mud and was evidently not used. Ginny had parked close to the side door. We pushed our way in without ringing because of the downpour. Even in those few minutes I got soaking wet. There was no hall. We found ourselves in a large room with four or five beds in it. There was no light on. It took a moment before I realized that beside each bed an old man sat on a straight chair. One had his head in his hands. A younger man, whose legs were bandaged and who was half lying and half sitting in a sort of medical rocker, tried to speak but half choked. He was clearly out of his mind. However, he smiled, the only person in that room who did or who could.

Ginny called out loudly, "Here we are! Is there anyone home?"

Then an enormous woman filled the doorway, wiping her hands on her apron.

"Oh . . . well," she said, as if she had been taken by surprise. "My daughter is just making up Miss Spencer's room. But I guess you can go in now." She laughed. "We're up tight these days, no place to ask you to sit down."

I had had so many shocks by then that I felt quite numb and only wanted to be left alone as soon as possible. My heart started up and I was afraid I might faint. But it was a comfort to find that I had a room of my own, just big enough for a bed, an armchair, and a bureau. The bed was parallel to the window, and the window looked out, much to my astonishment, on a long field with tall trees at the end and, beyond them, gentle hills.

"Look at the view," Ginny said. "Isn't it marvelous?"

"What is that woman's name?" I asked in a whisper. I had the feeling already that even a whisper would be heard.

"Mrs. Hatfield—Harriet Hatfield. She is a trained nurse." (That is what Ginny said, but of course she must have known that Mrs. Hatfield's only experience had been as an aide in the State Hospital for two years.) "She and her daughter work very hard to keep things going here."

There was dust under the bureau and an old piece of Kleenex.

John disappeared for a time. They brought me a cup of tea and a cheap biscuit, which I didn't eat. They offered to help me unpack my two suitcases, but I managed to make it clear that I am not infirm. I set the photographs of my mother and father and one of me with John when I was fourteen and he was in college on the bureau, and three things I treasure: a Japanese bronze turtle, a small Swedish glass vase, and the *Oxford Book of English Verse.* I found my little pillow and lay down on the bed then. After a while I recited the Lord's Prayer three times. I do not believe this prayer is heard by the Person to whom it is addressed, but I find it comforting, like a rune, something to hold onto.

When John and Ginny left, he said, "We'll be seeing you."

After a while I slept. The rain drummed on the roof. I felt that for a time I must be absolutely passive, float from moment to moment and from hour to hour, shut out feeling and thought. They were both too dangerous. And I feared the weeping. Lately, since the hospital, I have cried a lot, and that may be one reason John felt I must go. Tears are an offense and make other people not so much suffer as feel attacked and irritable. When the inner world overflows in this way, it forces something entirely private out into the open where it does not belong, not at my age anyway. Only children are permitted tears, so in a way perhaps my being sent here is a punishment. Oh dear, I must not think about that now. Everything is dangerous that is not passive. I am learning to accept.

Harriet Hatfield woke me, not urgently, and pretty soon her daughter, Rose, came in with my supper on a tray. At least I do not have to eat with the others and watch them spill their soup. I can lie here and look out at the hills. Supper was cornflakes with milk and a banana that first evening. I enjoyed it far more than one of Ginny's "gourmet" concoctions. But then I could not sleep. I had to get accustomed to the noises, queer little creaks, the groans and snores in the big room where the men are. It seemed a terribly long night. When I went to the bathroom I bumped into a chair in the hall and bruised my leg. Perhaps John will bring me a flashlight when he comes. I will ask for note paper and stamps, a daily newspaper, and maybe a bottle of Scotch. It would be a help to have a small drink measured out each evening before supper.

•

43

That thought was a comfort when I wrote it several days ago. Now I know that good things like that are not going to happen. Old age, they say, is a gradual giving up. But it is strange when it all happens at once. That is a real test of character, a kind of solitary confinement. Whatever I have now is in my own mind.

In a House of
Wooden Monkeys

SHAY YOUNGBLOOD

Summer rain sounded heavy on the new tin roof. Loud whispers ran up and down the rough wooden pews. Father MacIntyre was getting impatient. He knew Moses would not come and he could not perform the ceremony if Moses was not there.

"Yate where is Moses? We have waited long enough." The Father said.

"He soon come Father. He know we waiting for he." The young woman answered, lowering her eyes to the fat brown baby she held close to her heart. She didn't seem to notice the impatience in the air, but her throat was as tight as a witch's drum and her spine tingled with the tension. On this most important day she and Moses had fought over the ritual to baptize the baby in Holy Water to protect it. Moses had raised his hand to slap her, a thing he had never done, and left before he did. She was in misery, but could not show it before all those who had come to witness.

The child in Yate's arms was restless and cried. Yate carefully opened her worn, white cotton blouse and offered her breast, full with milk to the child. She guided her tender nipple into her baby's mouth, it sucked noisily. Her clear brown eyes watched, her full dark lips smiled at her baby, the most happiness she had ever had in her young life, because she got to keep this one. She had lost two babies already.

Hill folk said Widow took her babies. The first one Widow drowned in a dream sack, told folk she dreamed Yate's baby would be born dead, and it was. The second time, Widow strangled her baby with the mother's string. Everyone knew Widow had done it. Widow was a toothless young woman who had come to Greenlove Mountain as a girl to live with her grandmother, a rootwoman, in a wood shack by the road. Her grandmother died shortly after she came and as she was strange and thought to be blessed of evil, no one would take her in. So she lived high up on the mountain. She got the name Widow by the birthmark shaped like a black widow spider she carried on her forehead and by her dark attitude and visions of death.

The third time Yate discovered that there was a child growing inside of her, she began to go to Greenlove Mountain church on sundays. The whiteman had come from England to teach her people about his god, who he said was the All Mighty and All Powerful one. He certainly was a rich god. He allowed the priest to dress in fancy velvet robes and white satin hats, to perform grand rituals with white candles set in heavy brass and drink French red wine, he called blood, from an inlaid golden chalice.

Yate burned offerings at the breaking of each day and went to the church services every sunday morning to pray to the whiteman's god, hoping his prayer and juju would be stronger than Widow's magic, this time. She prayed with a desperate passion to Jesus and she prayed to the Virgin Mary, whom she pitied, to save her baby. Baby Gillian was born in her Mama Etta's house, arriving lungs filled with fear and clenched fists beating the air that smelled so of blood. Yate cried, praised the Lord and her personal juju. She kissed the Holy Medal she wore around her neck. Moses, he laughed at her, shaking his dread locks from side to side at his woman's foolishness.

"It is Jah taking care of thee woman, you betta forget dis jesus nonsense." He said, lighting a bowl of herb, smoke and scent of it rising in the air between them. More had come between them because of her promise to the whiteman's god.

Moses was pleased at the birth of a living child. For two

years they had only stolen hours. Mama Etta had kept a sharp eye on her daughter, sending her to town school hoping to keep the young lovers apart. With the birth of Baby Gillian even Mama Etta could not hold Yate, they could live together as man and wife. Mama Etta poured rum into the earth and slit the throat of a baby goat.

For as long as Yate could remember there were babies in Mama Etta's house. Soft, fat, warm, brown babies that cried when pinched, and laughed when teased in tender spots. Mama Etta was a rich woman, because she would always have someone to care for her. She had fifteen children to her credit. Her sons would provide for her and carry the family name to another generation and her daughters when educated would marry well and visit her often with many grand children to warm her lap. To Yate these things were important, to have someone to love you always, a man could leave you. To deliver a living, growing thing from her body was a miracle she wanted to bear. She knew that Mama Etta could not keep her from her man, even though he was a Rastaman, if she were to bear his child. She loved Moses enough, she could feel it in her heart and blood and limbs whenever he watched her undress at the river or touched her body with a reverence and ritual she marveled at when they made love on mossy patches of damp earth beneath the coolness of the waterfall.

Yate promised Jesus she would go up the hill to the whiteman's church everyday if her baby was allowed to be among the living, and so she did. When Baby Gillian was born alive and kicking, Yate invited all her friends and family, many of whom had never been to church, to come see her baby be blessed with Holy Water. Some came only for the spectacle, as they were suspicious of a man with only one god.

Saint Julien came because she was Yate's best girlfriend. They were friends and lovers long before she met Moses. Saint Julien's husband was at sea for many months of the year, it was only natural that she longed for hands and lips of passion on her breasts and on the soft spot between her thighs and warm arms to hold her through the endless nights her husband was away. So many men of the village loved the sea. She also could not have a baby by Yate to anger her husband. She often

47

wished that many things were not as they were, but when the men returned from the sea, the women turned from each other in that intimate way, back to their men. It had always been the way, from her grandmother's time and before.

The faithful of the congregation were waiting, hands pressed in respect for the ritual. This was to be the first christening in the church. Four families were present with new babies to be sprinkled with the priest's Holy Water. Father MacIntyre blew his nose into a white lace handkerchief and cleared his throat, as he did when he about to speak on some important subject in his sunday morning talks to them.

"I can wait no longer. Let us begin." The Father said.

"But my Gillian, will you bless her?" Yate whispered, tears reaching for the edge of her eyes.

The Father turned away from her tears and to those who had come for the ceremony. He was so cold his words chilled like ice.

"A man who would allow his child to be punished for his sins is not a man. If a woman is loose and without moral responsibility, she is the devil's sin and so is her child. In good conscience I cannot perform the rites for Yate's bastard child."

Angry looks flew above the injustice of his words. Up to this point there had been silence, but Mama Etta spilled herself into the room and stepped like a queen up to the altar, to her daughter's side.

"She is a daughter of the gods and loved not less. She ain't belonging to no rastaman, to no devil, no other woman, just me. I give her life and breath from between these thighs, something you can never do, because it is you who are evil and cannot bear a miracle. You are a no feeling wooden monkey and so are the people of this house." She spit in the dust before him.

Taking her daughter's arm, they made their way down the aisle and through the doors of the church. Father MacIntyre stood stiffly before the podium and watched helplessly as the pews emptied behind Mama Etta, Yate and Baby Gillian. The silent procession of those who had lost faith wound down the dirt path to the village.

Widow stood grinning in the doorway after most all had

gone but the Father. She said a few words that made no sense to human ears, shook some feathers, then squat to pee on the threshold. The remaining of the congregation watched in surprise as the Father seized his throat and choked himself to the ground, where he wallowed like a dog. Widow watched him some then turned to follow the others.

West With the Night

Beryl Markham

I have seldom dreamed a dream worth dreaming again, or at least none worth recording. Mine are not enigmatic dreams; they are peopled with characters who are plausible and who do plausible things, and I am the most plausible amongst them. All the characters in my dreams have quiet voices like the voice of the man who telephoned me at Elstree one morning in September of nineteen-thirty-six and told me that there was rain and strong head winds over the west of England and over the Irish Sea, and that there were variable winds and clear skies in mid-Atlantic and fog off the coast of Newfoundland.

"If you are still determined to fly the Atlantic this late in the year," the voice said, "the Air Ministry suggests that the weather it is able to forecast for tonight, and for tomorrow morning, will be about the best you can expect."

The voice had a few other things to say, but not many, and then it was gone, and I lay in bed half-suspecting that the telephone call and the man who made it were only parts of the mediocre dream I had been dreaming. I felt that if I closed my eyes the unreal quality of the message would be re-established, and that, when I opened them again, this would be another ordinary day with its usual beginning and its usual routine.

But of course I could not close my eyes, nor my mind, nor

my memory. I could lie there for a few moments — remembering wood and fabric moulded to her ribs to form her long, sleek belly, and I had seen her engine cradled into her frame, and made fast.

The Gull had a turquoise-blue body and silver wings. Edgar Percival had made her with care, with skill, and with worry — the care of a veteran flyer, the skill of a master designer, and the worry of a friend. Actually the plane was a standard sport model with a range of only six hundred and sixty miles. But she had a special undercarriage built to carry the weight of her extra oil and petrol tanks. The tanks were fixed into the wings, into the centre section, and into the cabin itself. In the cabin they formed a wall around my seat, and each tank had a petcock of its own. The petcocks were important.

"If you open one," said Percival, "without shutting the other first, you may get an airlock. You know the tanks in the cabin have no gauges, so it may be best to let one run completely dry before opening the next. Your motor might go dead in the interval — but she'll start again. She's a De Havilland Gipsy — and Gipsys never stop."

I had talked to Tom. We had spent hours going over the Atlantic chart, and I had realized that the tinker of Molo, now one of England's great pilots, had traded his dreams and had got in return a better thing. Tom had grown older too; he had jettisoned a deadweight of irrelevant hopes and wonders, and had left himself a realistic code that had no room for temporizing or easy sentiment.

"I'm glad you're going to do it, Beryl. It won't be simple. If you can get off the ground in the first place, with such an immense load of fuel, you'll be alone in that plane about a night and a day — mostly night. Doing it east to west, the wind's against you. In September, so is the weather. You won't have a radio. If you misjudge your course only a few degrees, you'll end up in Labrador or in the sea — so don't misjudge anything."

Tom could still grin. He had grinned; he had said: "Anyway, it ought to amuse you to think that your financial backer lives on a farm called 'Place of Death' and your plane is being built at 'Gravesend.' If you were consistent, you'd christen the Gull 'The Flying Tombstone.'"

51

I hadn't been that consistent. I had watched the building of the plane and I had trained for the flight like an athlete. And now, as I lay in bed, fully awake, I could still hear the quiet voice of the man from the Air Ministry intoning, like the voice of a dispassionate court clerk: ". . . the weather for tonight and tomorrow . . . will be about the best you can expect." I should have liked to discuss the flight once more with Tom before I took off, but he was on a special job up north. I got out of bed and bathed and put on my flying clothes and took some cold chicken packed in a cardboard box and flew over to the military field at Abingdon, where the Vega Gull waited for me under the care of the R.A.F. I remember that the weather was clear and still.

Jim Mollison lent me his watch. He said: "This is not a gift. I wouldn't part with it for anything. It got me across the North Atlantic and the South Atlantic too. Don't lose it — and, for God's sake, don't get it wet. Salt water would ruin the works."

Brian Lewis gave me a life-saving jacket. Brian owned the plane I had been using between Elstree and Gravesend, and he had thought a long time about a farewell gift. What could be more practical than a pneumatic jacket that could be inflated through a rubber tube?

"You could float around in it for days," said Brian. But I had to decide between the life-save and warm clothes. I couldn't have both, because of their bulk, and I hate the cold, so I left the jacket.

And Jock Cameron, Brian's mechanic, gave me a sprig of heather. If it had been a whole bush of heather, complete with roots growing in an earthen jar, I think I should have taken it, bulky or not. The blessing of Scotland, bestowed by a Scotsman, is not to be dismissed. Nor is the well-wishing of a ground mechanic to be taken lightly, for these men are the pilot's contact with reality.

It is too much that with all those pedestrian centuries behind us we should, in a few decades, have learned to fly; it is too heady a thought, too proud a boast. Only the dirt on a mechanic's hands, the straining vise, the splintered bolt of steel underfoot on the hangar floor — only these and such anxiety as

52

the face of a Jock Cameron can hold for a pilot and his plane before a flight, serve to remind us that, not unlike the heather, we too are earthbound. We fly, but we have not "conquered" the air. Nature presides in all her dignity, permitting us the study and the use of such of her forces as we may understand. It is when we presume to intimacy, having been granted only tolerance, that the harsh stick falls across our impudent knuckles and we rub the pain, staring upward, startled by our ignorance.

"Here is a sprig of heather," said Jock, and I took it and pinned it into a pocket of my flying jacket.

There were press cars parked outside the field at Abingdon, and several press planes and photographers, but the R.A.F. kept everyone away from the grounds except technicians and a few of my friends.

The Carberrys had sailed for New York a month ago to wait for me there. Tom was still out of reach with no knowledge of my decision to leave, but that didn't matter so much, I thought. It didn't matter because Tom was unchanging—neither a fairweather pilot nor a fairweather friend. If for a month, or a year, or two years we sometimes had not seen each other, it still hadn't mattered. Nor did this. Tom would never say, "You should have let me know." He assumed that I had learned all that he had tried to teach me, and for my part, I thought of him, even then, as the merest student must think of his mentor. I could sit in a cabin overcrowded with petrol tanks and set my course for North America, but the knowledge of my hands on the controls would be Tom's knowledge. His words of caution and words of guidance, spoken so long ago, so many times, on bright mornings over the veldt or over a forest, or with a far mountain visible at the tip of our wing, would be spoken again, if I asked.

So it didn't matter, I thought. It was silly to think about.

You can live a lifetime and, at the end of it, know more about other people than you know about yourself. You learn to watch other people, but you never watch yourself because you strive against loneliness. If you read a book, or shuffle a deck of cards, or care for a dog, you are avoiding yourself. The abhorrence of loneliness is as natural as wanting to live at all. If it were otherwise, men would never have bothered to make an alphabet, nor to have fashioned words out of what were only animal sounds, nor to have crossed continents — each man to see what the other looked like.

Being alone in an aeroplane for even so short a time as a night and a day, irrevocably alone, with nothing to observe but your instruments and your own hands in semi-darkness, nothing to contemplate but the size of your small courage, nothing to wonder about but the beliefs, the faces, and the hopes rooted in your mind — such an experience can be as startling as the first awareness of a stranger walking by your side at night. You are the stranger.

It is dark already and I am over the south of Ireland. There are the lights of Cork and the lights are wet; they are drenched in Irish rain, and I am above them and dry. I am above them and the plane roars in a sobbing world, but it imparts no sadness to me. I feel the security of solitude, the exhilaration of escape. So long as I can see the lights and imagine the people walking under them, I feel selfishly triumphant, as if I have eluded care and left even the small sorrow of rain in other hands.

It is a little over an hour now since I left Abingdon. England, Wales, and the Irish Sea are behind me like so much time used up. On a long flight distance and time are the same. But there had been a moment when Time stopped — and Distance too. It was the moment I lifted the blue-and-silver Gull from the aerodrome, the moment the photographers aimed their cameras, the moment I felt the craft refuse its burden and strain toward the earth in sullen rebellion, only to listen at last to the persuasion of stick and elevators, the dogmatic argument of blueprints that said she *had* to fly because the figures proved it.

So she had flown, and once airborne, once she had yielded to the sophistry of a draughtsman's board, she had said, "There: I have lifted the weight. Now, where are we bound?" — and the question had frightened me.

"We are bound for a place thirty-six hundred miles from here — two thousand miles of it unbroken ocean. Most of the

54

way it will be night. We are flying west with the night."

So there behind me is Cork; and ahead of me is Berehaven Lighthouse. It is the last light, standing on the last land. I watch it, counting the frequency of its flashes — so many to the minute. Then I pass it and fly out to sea.

The fear is gone now — not overcome nor reasoned away. It is gone because something else has taken its place; the confidence and the trust, the inherent belief in the security of land underfoot — now this faith is transferred to my plane, because the land has vanished and there is no other tangible thing to fix faith upon. Flight is but momentary escape from the eternal custody of earth.

Rain continues to fall, and outside the cabin it is totally dark. My altimeter says that the Atlantic is two thousand feet below me, my Sperry Artificial Horizon says that I am flying level. I judge my drift at three degrees more than my weather chart suggests, and fly accordingly. I am flying blind. A beam to follow would help. So would a radio — but then, so would clear weather. The voice of the man at the Air Ministry had not promised storm.

I feel the wind rising and the rain falls hard. The smell of petrol in the cabin is so strong and the roar of the plane so loud that my senses are almost deadened. Gradually it becomes unthinkable that existence was ever otherwise.

At ten o'clock p.m. I am flying along the Great Circle Course for Harbour Grace, Newfoundland, into a forty-mile headwind at a speed of one hundred and thirty miles an hour. Because of the weather, I cannot be sure of how many more hours I have to fly, but I think it must be between sixteen and eighteen.

At ten-thirty I am still flying on the large cabin tank of petrol, hoping to use it up and put an end to the liquid swirl that has rocked the plane since my take-off. The tank has no gauge, but written on its side is the assurance: "This tank is good for four hours."

There is nothing ambiguous about such a guaranty. I believe it, but at twenty-five minutes to eleven, my motor coughs and dies, and the Gull is powerless above the sea.

I realize that the heavy drone of the plane has been, until

this moment, complete and comforting silence. It is the actual silence following the last splutter of the engine that stuns me. I can't feel any fear; I can't feel anything. I can only observe with a kind of stupid disinterest that my hands are violently active and know that, while they move, I am being hypnotized by the needle of my altimeter.

I suppose that the denial of natural impulse is what is meant by "keeping calm," but impulse has reason in it. If it is night and you are sitting in an aeroplane with a stalled motor, and there are two thousand feet between you and the sea, nothing can be more reasonable than the impulse to pull back your stick in the hope of adding to that two thousand, if only by a little. The thought, the knowledge, the law that tells you that your hope lies not in this, but in a contrary act — the act of directing your impotent craft toward the water — seems a terrifying abandonment, not only of reason, but of sanity. Your mind and your heart reject it. It is your hands — your stranger's hands — that follow with unfeeling precision the letter of the law.

I sit there and watch my hands push forward on the stick and feel the Gull respond and begin its dive to the sea. Of course it is a simple thing; surely the cabin tank has run dry too soon. I need only to turn another petcock . . .

But it is dark in the cabin. It is easy to see the luminous dial of the altimeter and to note that my height is now eleven hundred feet, but it is not easy to see a petcock that is somewhere near the floor of the plane. A hand gropes and reappears with an electric torch, and fingers, moving with agonizing composure, find the petcock and turn it; and I wait.

At three hundred feet the motor is still dead, and I am conscious that the needle of my altimeter seems to whirl like the spoke of a spindle winding up the remaining distance between the plane and the water. There is some lightning, but the quick flash only serves to emphasize the darkness. How high can waves reach — twenty feet, perhaps? Thirty?

It is impossible to avoid the thought that this is the end of my flight, but my reactions are not orthodox; the various incidents of my entire life do not run through my mind like a motion-picture film gone mad. I only feel that all this has happened before — and it has. It has all happened a hundred times in my mind, in my sleep, so that now I am not really caught in terror; I recognize a familiar scene, a familiar story with its climax dulled by too much telling.

I do not know how close to the waves I am when the motor explodes to life again. But the sound is almost meaningless. I see my hand easing back on the stick, and I feel the Gull climb up into the storm, and I see the altimeter whirl like a spindle again, paying out the distance between myself and the sea.

The storm is strong. It is comforting. It is like a friend shaking me and saying, "Wake up! You were only dreaming."

But soon I am thinking. By simple calculation I find that my motor had been silent for perhaps an instant more than thirty seconds.

I ought to thank God — and I do, though indirectly. I thank Geoffrey De Havilland who designed the indomitable Gipsy, and who, after all, must have been designed by God in the first place.

A light ship — the daybreak — some steep cliffs standing in the sea. The meaning of these will never change for pilots. If one day an ocean can be flown within an hour, if men can build a plane that so masters time, the sight of land will be no less welcome to the steersman of that fantastic craft. He will have cheated laws that the cunning of science has taught him how to cheat, and he will feel his guilt and be eager for the sanctuary of the soil.

I saw the ship and the daybreak, and then I saw the cliffs of Newfoundland wound in ribbons of fog. I felt the elation I had so long imagined, and I felt the happy guilt of having circumvented the stern authority of the weather and the sea. But mine was a minor triumph; my swift Gull was not so swift as to have escaped unnoticed. The night and the storm had caught her and we had flown blind for nineteen hours.

I was tired now, and cold. Ice began to film the glass of the cabin windows and the fog played a magician's game with the land. But the land was there. I could not see it, but I had seen it. I could not afford to believe that it was any land but the land I wanted. I could not afford to believe that my navigation was at fault, because there was no time for doubt.

South to Cape Race, west to Sydney on Cape Breton Island. With my protractor, my map, and my compass, I set my new course, humming the ditty that Tom had taught me: "Variation West — magnetic best. Variation East — magnetic least." A silly rhyme, but it served to placate, for the moment, two warring poles — the magnetic and the true. I flew south and found the lighthouse of Cape Race protruding from the fog like a warning finger. I circled twice and went on over the Gulf of Saint Lawrence.

After a while there would be New Brunswick, and then Maine — and then New York. I could anticipate. I could almost say, "Well, if you stay awake, you'll find it's only a matter of time now" — but there was no question of staying awake. I was tired and I had not moved an inch since that uncertain moment at Abingdon when the Gull had elected to rise with her load and fly, but I could not have closed my eyes. I could sit there in the cabin, walled in glass and petrol tanks, and be grateful for the sun and the light, and the fact that I could see the water under me. They were almost the last waves I had to pass. Four hundred miles of water, but then the land again — Cape Breton. I would stop at Sydney to refuel and go on. It was easy now. It would be like stopping at Kisumu and going on.

Success breeds confidence. But who has a right to confidence except the Gods? I had a following wind, my last tank of petrol was more than three-quarters full, and the world was as bright to me as if it were a new world, never touched. If I had been wiser, I might have known that such moments are, like innocence, short-lived. My engine began to shudder before I saw the land. It died, it spluttered, it started again and limped along. It coughed and spat black exhaust toward the sea.

There are words for everything. There was a word for this — airlock, I thought. This had to be an airlock because there was petrol enough. I thought I might clear it by turning on and turning off all the empty tanks, and so I did that. The handles of the petcocks were sharp little pins of metal, and when I had opened and closed them a dozen times, I saw that my hands were bleeding and that the blood was dropping on my maps and on my clothes, but the effort wasn't any good. I coasted along on a sick and halting engine. The oil pressure and the oil temperature gauges were normal, the magnetos working, and yet I lost altitude slowly while the realization of failure seeped into my heart. If I made the land, I should have been the first to fly the North Atlantic from England, but from my point of view, from a pilot's point of view, a forced landing was failure because New York was my goal. If only I could land and then take off, I would make it still . . . if only, if only . . .

The engine cuts again, and then catches, and each time it spurts to life I climb as high as I can get, and then it splutters and stops and I glide once more toward the water, to rise again and descend again, like a hunting sea bird.

I find the land. Visibility is perfect now and I see land forty or fifty miles ahead. If I am on my course, that will be Cape Breton. Minute after minute goes by. The minutes almost materialize; they pass before my eyes like links in a long slow-moving chain, and each time the engine cuts, I see a broken link in the chain and catch my breath until it passes.

The land is under me, I snatch my map and stare at it to confirm my whereabouts. I am, even at my present crippled speed, only twelve minutes from Sydney Airport, where I can land for repairs and then go on.

The engine cuts once more and I begin to glide, but now I am not worried; she will start again, as she has done, and I will gain altitude and fly into Sydney.

But she doesn't start. This time she's dead as death; the Gull settles earthward and it isn't any earth I know. It is black earth stuck with boulders and I hang above it, on hope and on a motionless propeller. Only I cannot hang above it long. The earth hurries to meet me, I bank, turn, and side-slip to dodge the boulders, my wheels touch, and I feel them submerge. The nose of the plane is engulfed in mud, and I go forward striking my head on the glass of the cabin front, hearing it shatter, feeling blood pour over my face.

I stumble out of the plane and sink to my knees in muck and stand there foolishly staring, not at the lifeless land, but at my watch.

Twenty-one hours and twenty-five minutes.

Atlantic flight. Abingdon, England, to a nameless

59

swamp — nonstop.

A Cape Breton Islander found me — a fisherman trudging over the bog saw the Gull with her tail in the air and her nose buried, and then he saw me floundering in the embracing soil of his native land. I had been wandering for an hour and the black mud had got up to my waist and the blood from the cut in my head had met the mud halfway.

From a distance, the fisherman directed me with his arms and with shouts toward the firm places in the bog, and for another hour I walked on them and came toward him like a citizen of Hades blinded by the sun, but it wasn't the sun; I hadn't slept for forty hours.

He took me to his hut on the edge of the coast and I found that built upon the rocks there was a little cubicle that housed an ancient telephone — put there in case of shipwrecks.

I telephoned to Sydney Airport to say that I was safe and to prevent a needless search being made. On the following morning I did step out of a plane at Floyd Bennett Field and there was a crowd of people still waiting there to greet me, but the plane I stepped from was not the Gull, and for days while I was in New York I kept thinking about that and wishing over and over again that it had been the Gull, until the wish lost its significance, and time moved on, overcoming many things it met on the way.

The Long Night

Toni Cade Bambara

It whistled past her, ricocheted off the metal hamper and slammed into the radiator pipe, banging the door ajar. Glass was crashing in the apartment below, taking a long time finishing, as though happening in a slow-motion filming. Spatters of concrete and brick nearby, splintering of wood. The ping of a bullet on the fire escape. Storms of grit heaved up against the livingroom windows. Herds over the roof, bellowing. And something else. Pots and pans maybe, or cymbals as though dropped from two thousand stories. Out back somewhere a car stalling, coughing, sputtering, then, like the garbage cans being scraped against concrete, turning over.

"Don't kill 'em. Don't kill —" A barrage of shots and a radio suddenly up then mute.

She sat huddled in the dark, balled up tight, deep within the bathtub. Her hands were bleeding where the nails cut, fists as clenched as teeth, as mercilessly drawing blood. Her eyes fixed on the fissure in the porcelain just below the faucet, a split leading down to the drain.

My Lifeline. She opened her mouth to say it. The dark flooded in, but nothing came out. *I'll never,* she thought, *I'll never take another bath in this tub again. If I get through the night,* she added. *If I . . .*

Many wouldn't. Many hadn't. A student on the stoop still where death at eight o'clock had seeped into a hole in the back of his neck.

Heavy thuds on the stairs coming two, three, five steps at a time. Bells ringing. Bodies heaving against doors. She slammed her face shut and squashed herself into, under the faucet, down the drain.

"A mop and pail, for chrissakes!"

A door slamming with difficulty, meeting resistance. Banging. Bolts. "Go away. Please, please go away. We got lil kids in here. Please."

Heavy boots on the steps again. A menace on the landing. Grunt breathing at her door. A sudden body crash against the steel plating, wood, locks. She jammed her mouth down between her knees to keep from laughing or screaming, one. *A police lock to lock the police out.* Down the hall another weight against a door. Someone crying. Near the stair hushed growling.

"Shoot the lock of . . . gotta . . . mop . . . pail . . . so much blood."

"Suppose someone's home? We don't want . . ."

"What'll we charge em with?"

"Think of somethin'. . . . riot soon."

"Maybe . . . hate to get caught up here . . . take your badge off."

In the Schenley box marked This Side Up a cargo too precious to destroy, dangerous to transport, death to surrender up. If she dashed to the kitchen and skidded under the table, there might be time to. *To what? Why think of it now,* she thought, crushing herself closer to the drain and imagining instead her limbs scooting across the rooftops, broken field running over the skylights, past pipes like Carl had taught her, the leap to 417, then down two flights, the closet with the false wall, the black room they'd built. She'd wallpapered the closet herself, tap-tapping to be sure of a uniform sound. Wallpapered all the closets with the same quaint, floral pattern Carl's mother had sent all the way from Montreal.

"Open up. Police."

Wanted: The Killers of Lester Long/The Killers of Bobby Hut-

ton/The Killers of James Rutledge/The Killers of Teddy —
"Open up in there."
Do Not Embrace Amnesia. The Struggle Continues. Memory Is a Powerful —
"Shoot the fuckin' lock off, for chrissakes."
The Assault on the Begone Pesticide Plant Was an Assault on Guinea Pigism in Our Community. The People Spoke. The Attack on the Precinct Was an Attack on Lawlessness. The People —
A blast. Another. The door shoved brutally back against the carpet she'd never laid quite right.
Harriet Tubman's Work Must Continue. Support the —
And if I'm caught. She dared not think it. Caught in a bathtub. No place to flee but down. And they'd hound her into the pipes. The savage claw scratching against metal, clutching for flesh. *The box:* posters, photos, statistics . . . *all that work. Is the tablecloth long enough?* She pictured it somewhere behind her left eye where a throb had begun. *The box.* The addresses were under the camphor bar in the silverware drawer. Detective special, stolen from ballistics in the back coils of the refrigerator in a rat-poison box. In the sugar cannister the negatives of the campus agents. And in the safest place, tacked to the cork board in clear view, the number you called which for fifty dollars taped to a page of the main library encyclopedia yielded up a copy of your dossier. Fifty feet of useless footage sprang from her eye sprockets: hurtling herself through the dark to the kitchen with a torch. Or running full tilt at the ransackers with a lance.
"Get the light."
"Shithead, we'll draw our own fire. Flashlight."
"Where's the kitchen in this place?"
They'd tracked in a smell. It filled the rooms. It sought her out and gagged her. They'd find the box. *Africa Supports Us. Asia Supports Us. Latin Ameri —*
"Get the mop there."
The PRG Supports Us. The FLQ Supports Us. The FLN —
"No pail. Look for some bucket . . ."
They'll find the box. They'll look for me. The blows. The madness. The best of myself splattered bright against the porcelain. No. The best of myself inviolate. Maybe.

They'd ask about the others. Cracking her head against the faucet, they'd demand something ungivable, but settle perhaps for anything snatchable, any anything to sanctify the massacre in the streets below. And would she allow them to tear the best of herself from herself, blast her from her place, that place inviolate, make her heap ratfilth into that place, that place where no corruption touched, where she curled up and got cozy or spread her life leisurely out for inventory. Hurtle her into the yellow-green slime of her own doing, undoing, to crawl on wrecked limbs in that violated place, that place. Could she trust herself. Was she who she'd struggled to become so long. To become in an obscene instant the exact who she'd always despised, condemned to that place, fouled.

She would tell. They would beat her and she would tell more. They would taunt and torture and she would tell all. They'd put a gun in her eye and she would tell even what there wasn't to tell. Chant it. Sing it. Moan it. Shout it. Incriminate her neighbors. Sell her mama. Hawk her daddy. Trade her friends. Turn in everybody. Turn on everything. And never be the same. Dead or alive, never be the same. Blasted from her place.

My children will . . . but then I'll have no children, there'll be no room in that place to incubate children. They'd know. Growing there in the folds of that fouled place they'd know. And they'd ask. And their eyes would wipe me out.

"What's this?"

Rummaging in the refrigerator. Something sloshing to the floor. The ten-watt floodlight.

"Just get some papers to wipe our . . . look at my shoes."

Faucet running. Glasses slipping off the drain to crash against the pots.

"My God, my boots are full of blood . . ."

". . . footprints . . ."

My ancestors. Those breaths around me in sudden inexplicable moments of yes; welcome intrusions from some other where saying, yes, keep on. . . . They'll spit on me in the night.

"Let's get out of here."

Could she tell? Wouldn't her heart vault into the brain and stomp it out? Trained. In case of betrayal, self-destruct.

The bathroom door flung wide and a gust blew over her neck and back. That smell. A glob of light tumbled round the dark and settled somewhere. She could not look. Maybe she was the light. Balled up so tight, so hot in panic, so near death and another death yet, glowin', glowin' red/orange/yellow, glinting shots of shine around the arena in a suicidal beam. She would not look up. She would not look and meet those eyes. The eyes of the beast. Of the golden monkey that spits and kills.

"Here's a bucket."

The scrape of the bucket being dragged out from behind the toilet — scraping across her spine. The voice a boot on her neck. This was it, and what did she have. Heat behind the refrigerator. Heat in the Kotex box in the back of the linen closet. And she in the bathtub. With that smell. That reek that stopped her heart and forced her eyelids up. And then she saw him. Up too close to the screen, surreal. Jello-like around the edges like Superman taking off. Superman leaping into the bathtub to break her back. *No.* She would never tell. Strike. She would strike. Someone or three would go down in the go-down.

She'd made out a will. They all had. Long line of relatives and associates named executors of estate in case of funnytime death. Statutes of limitations had a way of running out when charges were brought against the police.

"Let's go."

The glob of light clicked off. The drip of the toilet splashing onto the tiles now. Door pulled in starts and stops shut. The heavy crashing thuds down the stairs. She listened. Tight up against the lifeline fissure of rust gone green, she swept the mind clean to hear the footfalls, to isolate them. Someone had stayed behind. Someone was waiting in the dark. Sly death crouched to pounce upon her life and wreck it. Crouched and waiting, impatient to tear her with savage teeth, her essence spilling out of place and oozing down the chin, the chest, the arm. Impatient he would creep across the carpet of leaves that covered the pit. And she would strike. She was poised for the attack. And with what would she undo him? A can of Ajax? A wire soap dish? *My Afro pick,* she decided, spotting it on the toilet tank. Seemed fitting. She almost wished someone were there. Silence. Stuck horns, screaming, scurrying of feet against the slush, but silence. Riffling of pages somewhere in the living room. Curtains fluttering in shreds. But silence.

Vibrations from the porcelain were drowsing her asleep. Not the same vibes as from other walls.

Drafts from school walls blew rudely in the young face awaking, as she stood in the corner under punishment from those early caretakers. Chill breeze quivering the nostril hairs where up against the wall the cast of twelve, assembled for some droll Punch and Judy show, awaited directions from those other caretakers. Or the accurately known vibrations from walls encountered deliberately blindfolded, when they learned to maneuver in the dark, to touchtalk pipes and rods out of their hiding places and assemble guns and radio sets by Braille. Trained to recognize obstacles by the length and chill of their breezes, so as not to bump and knock breath and blood out and leave a break in the chain, a hole in the network, a chink just large enough for a boot to kick through, a butt to muzzle in. The walls of the bathtub were different.

More like the vibes of the stone quarry of two summers before where she and Carl had worked for $1.10 an hour for the privilege of eating. Or like the walls of the grotto where she'd spent the only vacation of her life, wet, love-warmed and dazzled for a whole summer with Carl. Shouting foolishness in all the tongues of the sea, they swam underwater entangling four legs and surfacing, felt/heard their shouts glanceback off the grotto walls cool and hollow against their cheeks. That was last summer. The Carl of moss and fruit and bitten shoulders and the privacy of mosquito-net tents. The Carl before the call to Canada. The call into exile.

She stopped shivering at first light. That milk-of-magnesia-bottle blue, Carl had said. She looked at her hands, sticky and brown, pieces of nail like glass shards atop a brick wall. Pain shot straight through. Like in the days of intensive training when the hands would no longer open and shut by ordinary means. Hot water, Ben-Gay, the gun strapped in the hand with adhesive tape. The practice shots squeezed off, bringing tears down the nose on the inside, then pushed back again by the smoke. Chinese mustard, Carl had said.

It took all of ten minutes to wrap the hands around the edge of the tub and hoist herself up. That same tremor of hysterical laughter, stopped before, now erupted from her knees it seemed. Straddling a bathtub, a bucking-bronco bathtub, she could not stop it now. Lava poured from her mouth and flopped her head over onto the hamper, denting it while the lower half of her body was still being dragged up out of the tub like some crazed water creature pushing for the next stage.

"Oh my," she guffawed, like Carl's mother used to when Carl broke through her ladylike decorum with some wild tale. *Oh my, she'd said when she'd opened her door to find Carl's woman there and Carl already gone. Oh my, when Concordia Bridge flashed on the screen, fixing them in the middle of the rug. The tan station wagon speeding past the police barriers, a mere blur between television cameras, barely visible through snow and distance as it seemingly flew onto the island where the Cuban officials waited with the plane. She had dropped her bag on the rug and run to the television, the older woman already there turning up the sound.*

They'd traded the lives of two Canadian trade commissioners for the release of the West Indian students charged with kidnapping a dean, extortion, and untold damage to the university's two-million-dollar computer complex. For their release and safe passage to Algeria for the students and what was left of the cell. And she had come too late. Aboard the plane she'd learned that Algeria had refused them. In the cab, she'd heard a West Indian diplomat disinherit the fugitives. She had arrived at Carl's mother's in time for the televised getaway and little more.

Buzzy, Hassan, and Lydia barely being picked up by the cameras as they got out of the station wagon. The other Bloods she didn't know, mere coattails heading into a building. Then Carl, barely recognizable through the swirling snow, waving his last goodbye, as his mother patted the TV box as though it were only a photograph she was seeing safely souvenired in a snowball paperweight.

She was out of the tub now, slipping unsteadily. She'd thought she'd stand upright. That was the idea. But she found herself lunging toward the pockmarked windows like a stumble drunk. One rectangle of bullet-splattered frame led to the pavement below, where she wanted to be. But not like this, in a faint, leaning onto the fire escape slats in a swoon. But she did want to be below.

For the people would be emerging from the dark of their places. Surfacing for the first time in eons into clarity. And

their skins would shrink from—not remembering it like this—
the climate. Feet wary of the pavement for heartless jokes they
did remember. And their brains, true to their tropism, would
stretch the whole body up to the light, generating new food out
of the old staple wisdoms. And they would look at each other as
if for the first time and wonder, who is this one and that one.
And she would join the circle gathered round the ancient stains
in the street. And someone would whisper, and who are you.
And who are you. And who are we. And they would tell each
other in a language that had evolved, not by magic, in the
caves.

Things to Do

BINNIE KIRSHENBAUM

Mostly I was doing two things:
1. Planning my escape.
2. Making lists.

The lists were a New Year's resolution to grab hold, to keep my days from slipping by, to organize. A list demands action. You must accomplish before you can scratch off. A fully scratched off list, I thought, would bring me satisfaction. I could sit back and study it, marvelling at how much I'd done.

As lists are very clear and leave no lines to read between, writing out my daily reminders brought to me a revelation. This was not any kind of life. The need to escape it was as transparent as Poland Spring Water, which happened to be the third item on the grocery list. Yes, a list demands action.

The telling list was this one. It was dated January 14th.

Things to Do:
1. Wake up
2. Make coffee
3. Drink coffee/Watch Donahue
4. Make bed
5. Vacuum
6. Dust (if there's time)
7. Call Madeline

   8. Grocery shopping
      a. Chicken breasts b. Vegetable (broccoli)
      c. Poland Spring Water d. Paper towels
   9. Pick up Robert's shirts
   10. Prepare dinner/Watch People's Court
   11. Watch 5 O'Clock News/Wait for Robert

The very chilling fact about this January 14th list was that
it was identical to my lists from January 13th, 12th, 11th, and
beyond. Oh, there were slight variations. Mostly having to do
with the groceries. And with #9. I did not pick up Robert's
shirts every day. Some days I dropped them off.

On the 15th of January the list was again a twin, or a quad-
ruplet, or whatever sameness is when you get that high. Except
for two things. One was to get my mother a birthday gift.

   12. Possible Birthday Gifts
      a. Sweater b. Handbag c. Earrings
      d. Tango lessons

The other addition was #13.

   13. Leave

Leave. Make like a tree and leave. That used to be a favorite of mine. Along with make like a banana and split. To leave,
I mused, is to bloom, to unfold and sprout wings. To leave like
the heroines in the early feminist novels who left and bloomed,
but drably. Moths, not butterflies, they found themselves
planting zucchini at Plain Jane's Commune for Unkempt
Women. This was not how I wanted to go. Better to make like a
banana, a snappier way out.

One decision spawned a notebook of lists. Lists do that.
They branch off and make new lists the way amoebae repro-
duce. One reminder, one memory, a doubt each needed a list
of its own. I had to be thorough. There could be no rushing out
only to find I'd left something behind. That'd kill the exit.

The first thing I needed to know was where to go. This resulted in two lists: an *A* list and a *B* list.

   Where to Go *A:*
   1. To mother's house
   2. Start a Commune for a New Generation of
      Runaways
      a. Talk Madeline into leaving Henry.

I did not like this list for two reasons. One reason was it was too thin. The other reason was it was too ugly. I turned the page and wrote up the *B* list.

As long as I was going to run off, I ought to run off to someplace terrific. I thought it best to run to the sort of place featured in *National Geographic* or *Lifestyles of the Rich and Famous.* For this list, I consulted the Atlas.

The Atlas was in Robert's study on the shelf next to *Gray's Anatomy,* two books which had to do with getting around.

I carried this book of places to the kitchen table and flipped to the index in the back, jotting down the ports of call which struck my fancy.

Where to Go *B:*
1. Abruzzi
2. Andalusia
3. Arctic
4. Baghdad
5. Babylon
6. Balboa Heights
7. Barren Grounds
8. Belgravia
9. Beverly Hills
10. Black Forest
11. Burma

By the time I got to the C's, I was fully satisfied there was no shortage of hot spots a wife over the wall could go. That was one obstacle I could cross of the list. Some of the obstacles remaining were finding the courage to leave Robert, finding the courage to face the unknown, finding the courage to start fresh, finding the cash.

How Much Cash I Will Need
1. Plane ticket (one way) $600
2. Housing (incl. gas, electricity, phone) . $2,000
3. Food (until I land a job) $500
4. Odds and Ends $500

Although in some books this amount might have been pittance, to me it was practically 4,000 big, faraway dollars because I didn't have a sou I could call my own. This was because I did not have a job and also because Robert was a throwback.

71

I used to have a job. It was a job I didn't care for. I did paste-ups for a small advertising agency. This job did not challenge me and was merely a job in this era of careers.

When Robert and I had been dating a solid seven months, I spent one evening whining about the tedium of the paste-up business.

"Quit," Robert had said. "Quit and marry me. After we're married you can take all the time you want to look around for something you like better."

This was why I married Robert. I married Robert so I could quit my job.

Another reason I married Robert was because he was a doctor. I did not have a very good health plan and was afraid to cross the street for fear of being squashed by a car, a squashing which could have resulted in a coma. I had a phobia about going into a coma. I was scared that with my chintzy health plan, they'd pull the plug on me because they'd need my bed. Or my kidneys. They would not disconnect a doctor's wife. I married Robert so I could cross the street in peace.

When I wrote up my list as to all the reasons I married Robert, I saw I was a whore. I married him to be taken care of. Loving him was not on the list but complete dental coverage was.

Once I asked Robert why he married me, assuming he, too, had his reasons. "Because I love you," he said. I asked him why he loved me, what about me did he love so much. Robert had to think about that. Finally, he said, "I guess because of how much you love me." To me, that was like one of those algebraic equations which, in the end, cancels itself out.

Reasons Why I Think Robert Married Me:
1. I was there
2. I didn't appear to have much backbone
3. He believed temporary weakness to be a fixed state
4. He believed I loved him
5. He knows nothing about love
6. He thought I could be manipulated
7. While we were dating, I could be manipulated
8. He thought I'd be the sort of wife which was hard to find since Donna Reed went off the air

I might have gotten another job after quitting mine except that the day after we were married, we moved away from the city. Robert had a surprise which he said was for me. This surprise was that he'd wangled himself a position in a suburban hospital where he got to be a big cheese. For a wedding gift, Robert bought me a four-bedroom stone house in this same suburb.

Wedding Gifts I Would Have Preferred:
1. a string of pearls
2. an old shoe

When Robert drove me up to the house in the new BMW he bought himself as a wedding gift, I said, "Robert, this house is in the middle of nowhere. You know I don't know how to drive. I'll be stranded out here."

Robert promised he would teach me how to drive. He also pointed out that there was a shopping center within walking distance and that the other wives on the block all drove and would be delighted to take me into the center of town whenever I wanted. I had the feeling Robert had cleared this with the other husbands.

Promises Robert Made and Broke:
1. Teaching me how to drive
2. Spending more time with me and less at the hospital
3. Travelling
4. To add my name to the checking account
5. Making love to me more often
6. His marriage vows in general and specifics

If Robert and I had had a joint checking account I would have cleaned it out in a minute. This was no time to be scrupulous. But after agreeing to have my name put on the blue pinstripe checks, Robert changed his mind. "We don't need a joint account," he said. "I pay all the bills and give you money for everything you need."

"These are modern times," I said. "It's anachronistic that I have to ask my husband for money. I should have money of my own."

"Then why don't you earn some." Robert got a perverse bang out of cruelty stemming from situations he controlled.

73

A few nights later when he was feeling more kindly towards me out of guilt because he was again watching *Nightline* as opposed to making love, I brought up the subject once more. "Robert," I said, "I'd really feel better if I had money at my disposal."

"What do you want that I don't buy for you?" Robert asked.

Madeline frequently said Robert was as good as gold, to which I always said, "Too bad I can't trade him in for cash."

Madeline thought this was a joke I was making. She'd throw up her hands and say, "Oh, you're so bad," as if I were a child who'd made a cute sort of mess like getting into Mommy's cosmetics and emerging with lipstick on my eyelids. Madeline lived next door and was absent from school the year we learned about women being all they can be. Madeline thought we, she and I, had it made. Especially me. Madeline claimed to be green with envy over how much clothes and jewelry and appliances Robert bought me. Appliances I refused to learn how to use. "I wish Henry were half as good to me as Robert is to you," Madeline eyed my ten-speed coffee bean grinder. Henry was in banking and talked to me once about commodities as if he thought I was one.

"So," Robert said, "what is it you want?"

"Freedom," I told him. "I want money of my own for freedom. For spontaneity. Suppose," I explained in a way which had nothing to do with the facts, "I want to buy you a present. I don't feel right asking you for cash to buy you your own gift."

"You're very sweet," Robert kissed the top of my head.

Out of biology, I lifted my face and planted my lips on his mouth. My tongue made an attempt to probe when Robert pulled back. "I'm exhausted, hon," he said. "I put in a long day."

Other Excuses Robert Has Dealt Me:
1. I didn't spend my day sitting on the couch watching soap operas, you know.
2. My stomach is bothering me. Was that fish you made fresh? Or did you buy frozen fish again?
3. I've got some things on my mind.
4. I've got a rash. Nothing serious. Just an ingrown hair but it's irritating as hell.

5. Maybe in the morning.

There was a spot warm for #5 on the list of broken promises.

When we were first married Robert was after me to have a baby. "I think it's time we started a family," he said.

And I said, "Oh, you do?"

We did not have a baby because I was popping Ortha-Novum. Robert had no idea I was on the pill. I did not tell him and he did not think to ask. This particular escape hatch I kept in its ivory plastic container in my drawer under the stack of Hermes scarves.

Robert thought I did not conceive because I was a flop, a woman with parts missing. "I think you ought to come to the hospital and find out what's wrong," he said.

"Maybe it's you," I said. "Maybe you're shooting blanks." Completely, I relished the minute of doubt which flickered in his eyes before he got hold of himself. "Don't be foolish," he said.

That was the day Robert, by most standards, quit making love to me. I imagined he had his reasons.

Robert's Reasons for Witholding:
1. Why bother if I couldn't produce Robert Junior
2. Why waste it on a woman who once, even if it was just for a minute, questioned his potency
3. He might have sensed I wasn't always interested

Even though it had become statistically unlikely that I would get pregnant, I swallowed my pill daily anyway. I needed to play it very, very safe if I were going to fly the coop.

Things Robert Doesn't Know About Me:
1. That I was, and am, on the pill
2. That I am capable of deceit
3. That I plan to fly the coop
4. That I am skimming money off the top and socking it away
5. That I know about his lunch date on the sly

One point in Robert's favor was that, despite his unwillingness to grant me my own source of funds, he did not pinch pennies or keep tabs on household expenditures. When I, for example, upped the price of his laundry ten dollars a week,

Robert assumed it was inflation all over. Nor did it ever dawn on him to wonder why my sweaters were rinsing out in the sink when I hit him up for fifteen a week for dry cleaning these same sweaters.

Another way I accumulated money was to take twenty dollars a day for groceries and then clip coupons, watch for sales and buy generic staples and day-old bread. In this manner, I was good for sixty dollars weekly. Still, even at that rate, it would have taken me well over a year to raise bond. One more year, added to the year I'd been married, and I would have been a tamed elephant.

Tamed elephants filled the vacancy left by the car squashing. I got this worry from a documentary Robert and I watched one night. This documentary was about the domesticating of elephants in India where they turn wild animals into manservants and houseboys.

After locating a group of elephants, the men doing this dirty deed herded one elephant into a pen. The elephant clearly hated this. She crashed her body against the fence over and over, trying to break it down to free herself. She was giving it her all, so much so that she didn't notice the sneak who'd crawled into the pen with her. This sneak, slithering on his belly, tied the elephant up by the legs, the front legs together and the back legs together so this elephant couldn't move an inch. Elephants cannot hop. This was done at dusk. All the night the elephant thrashed and trumpeted, calling out against this indignity. The elephant made noises which were painful to listen to. I was rooting for this elephant to break loose and stampede the men to a pulp. Only she was roped together too tightly. These men knew their trade. When the sun came up, in the harsh morning light, the elephant was still. Quiet. She knew something she didn't know in the dark. She knew she'd lost. Her spirit had been broken. The sneak who tied her up in the first place had a word for this which I promptly forgot because it was too pathetic.

When that documentary was over, I was very depressed. Robert laughed and said, "You're so sensitive. I'll bet you used to cry over Lassie."

This could be filed in the list of things Robert doesn't know about me.

Robert's lunch date on the sly was a dermatologist from his hospital. I saw them together at a restaurant in town called Friar Tuck Inn where the waitresses dressed as serving wenches. The place was definitely Robert's speed. Robert and this tootsie sat at a window side table and mooned at each other. Even though that was my husband lunching, talking excitedly with another woman, I found it a delightful episode to watch. Funny, even, like it was a movie. Robert's dermatologist had bad skin.

I watched them long for one another across the salt and pepper every Wednesday when I came into town with Madeline who drove in to have her hair done. Madeline wore her hair in a wash and set style she could not manage on her own. This hairdo allowed me an hour and a half to spy on my husband and his pockmarked babe.

It was a small step in the imagination to take them from the Friar Tuck Inn and place them in a linen closet at the hospital where I pictured them tugging at their hospital whites, panting. It was a picture which made me feel safe. A wronged wife has every right to walk out. I was still after having my card punched. I needed validation. It wasn't enough that his sort of ways didn't turn out to be mine. So, I stretched Robert's lunches into tawdry affairs so I could get out from under.

I wrote out many farewell notes for practice drills. I equated a farewell note with a deathbed scene. I wanted something poignant and powerful. Yet, lovely in its way.

A Sampling of Farewell Notes:

1. I know about your lunch dates. I cannot stay married to an adulterer.
2. As you can see, I have left you. Good-bye, Robert.
3. I hate you, Robert. I do believe I've always hated you.
4. I only married you so they wouldn't swipe my kidneys.
5. You were breaking my spirit. In another lifetime, you were the sneak with the rope.
6. It wasn't just you. I had to leave. All of it.

When I asked Robert for $250 to take a painting class at the

Community Center he said, "That sounds good. I'm glad to see you're taking an interest in something. It's important to have hobbies." Often I expected Robert to introduce me as "the little woman."

Robert got out his Mont Blanc and wanted to know who to make the check out to. "The Community Center or the teacher?" he asked.

"I'm not sure," I said. This fit right in with Robert's ideas of my being a bubblehead ignorant of the ways of the world. "Why don't you just make it out to 'Cash' to be safe," I suggested.

Robert wasn't keen on that. He thought I might lose the check between home and the Community Center, which was four blocks away. "Then anyone who found it could cash it," he said. As if I didn't know this.

I asked myself what was I thinking when I married Robert.

Thoughts on My Wedding Day:
1. There's still time to back out
2. I must be out of my mind
3. People can change
4. No one could really be that smug. I can break him of that habit.
5. There's always divorce
6. I really hated that job
7. Nothing. I wasn't thinking anything.

I told Robert not to worry over my losing the check. "I'll put it in my sock for safekeeping."

The next morning I took the check to the bank where the teller asked to see my driver's license. "I don't have one," I said.

"Some other form of I.D. then?" she asked.

I did not have any I.D. As far as the bank was concerned I either did not exist or was a petty criminal. "I'm the man's wife," I said. "That is my husband's check."

The fool of a teller wanted to call Robert up for verification of this. "It's for your own protection," she said.

"I don't need any protection," I told her. "I need the money." I took the check back.

In the middle of the night I woke up feeling like I couldn't breathe. I'd had another one of those dreams. Next to me,

Robert was sleeping soundly. I watched his chest rise and fall with regular inhales and exhales. This made me so mad I slapped him hard. Good reflexes had me feigning sleep as Robert sat up with a start. "Who What?" he said. "Hey," he shook me. "You just slapped me."

"I did? Are you sure?" I asked. "I was sleeping. I guess I was having a bad dream. Sorry." I turned over, leaving Robert to nurse the side of his face.

Dreams I Have A Lot:
1. I am trapped in a box
2. I am trapped in a box underwater
3. Robert is choking me
4. Robert is choking me in a box underwater
5. I'm locked in a broom closet with no way out
6. I'm locked in a broom closet with an elephant

It wasn't just the bad dream which made breathing difficult. I'd picked up one of those whopping cases of the flu, some out-of-town variety which battered my bones and bruised my internal organs. I ached everywhere and ran a fever I was certain was going to leave me brain damaged. I'd never been sick with Robert before so I asked him to phone my mother or Madeline because I wanted sympathy and not some clinician with a chart. I wanted someone to hold my hand and mop my brow and feed me soup. "I can do that," Robert said. And sure enough, he did.

In the delirium of fever I wrote a list, a list as to why I should not run off.

Reasons To Stay:
1. Robert takes care of me when I'm sick
2. Robert takes care of me when I'm not sick
3. Robert pays all the bills
4. I never have anything to worry about
5. I don't even know what's out there
6. As long as I'm here, I'm not afraid of dying
7. I haven't had a job in over a year

When my fever broke I reread this list which I kept intact except for the heading. I changed that to read: Reasons To Leave.

As the painting class ruse proved to be a bust, I needed to

come up with alternative plans for cash.

    Other Ways To Get Money:
1. Borrow from mother
2. Borrow from Madeline
3. Hock jewelry

Borrowing from my mother was chock full of obvious pitfalls. My mother was the stoic sort who thought happiness was akin to beauty; not everyone gets it so you take what you do have and use mascara.

I called Madeline on the phone and asked her if she had any money I could borrow. "Hang on," she said, "I'll look." Madeline came back and said she had seventeen dollars. "There's probably some loose change under the couch pillows I could dig out. Will that be enough?"

"No," I said. "I need more like a thousand."

"Uh oh," said Madeline. She thought I was pregnant and after a high-priced abortion. "Are you sure you want to do this? Have you discussed this with Robert?"

I told Madeline why I really wanted the money because that was easier than making something up. Madeline said I was out of my mind. "Give me one good reason to leave Robert," she said.

So I did. "Last night," I told her, "I bought two chocolate eclairs. From that new French bakery. After dinner I was doing the dishes and Robert wanted to know what was for dessert. So I told him there were two chocolate eclairs on the top shelf of the refrigerator. I did not think I had to tell him that one of those eclairs was for me. He ate both of them, Madeline. Without even asking me if I wanted so much as a bite."

Madeline thought I was making too much of this. "Come on," she said. "A chocolate eclair. You'd leave Robert over a chocolate eclair?"

"There's more," I said.

"Like what?" Madeline asked.

    Things I Never Told Anyone About Robert:
1. The eclairs were not an isolated incident. Robert always eats both desserts.
2. Whenever I offer an opinion, Robert chuckles softly to himself.

3. In the past four months Robert has made love to me less than six times.
4. Robert lunches with a dermatologist who has bad skin.
5. Before we were married Robert gave me a dose of the clap.

In light of the fact that he was, after all, a doctor, I found it quasi-unforgivable that he infected me with venereal disease. He should have known what was what.

Rather than apologize, which aside from the penicillin was all I was really after, Robert adopted the role of the accuser. "In my considered opinion," he said, "it was you who gave it to me."

This wasn't, but should have been, on the list of things I was thinking on my wedding day.

While Madeline was getting her weekly wash and set, instead of peering into the Friar Tuck Inn, I went to the local jewelry store. I had a treasure chest of necklaces and bracelets from this gyp joint; enough factory-produced ropes of gold to hang myself from. This jeweler, being the only game in town, cleaned up on husbands trying to buy clear consciences with 14kt. gold beads.

Before going inside, I took off my engagement ring and wedding band. They made no effort to stay on my finger and slid off like they'd been greased.

The jeweler offered me $800 for the duo. This was a lousy price and I told him so. He shrugged. "I don't deal in this sort of thing. My customers are already married. All I can do with these items is melt down the gold and reset the diamond."

"Melt down the gold?" I asked. "So this ring won't even exist?"

"That's right," he said.

I grabbed up the $800 and left the tokens of my marriage with this man who was going to melt them away. My wedding band might reincarnate as "Marcy" or "Sheila," a gold nameplate hanging from a thin chain.

Even though my passport had years left until it expired, I wanted a new one, one that didn't bear the stamp from an island in the Caribbean under French domain. Robert and I spent a long weekend there which was supposed to be a full week. We cut it short because we were bored. "I'm going out of my skull," Robert had said. "How many hours can you spend sitting by a pool without going out of your skull?"

"We could do something else," I offered.

"Like what?" Robert wanted to know. "Not the beach." Robert did not like sand. It got everywhere.

"We could go into town. It's supposed to be charming."

"These towns aren't safe," Robert said. "As a matter of fact, they are downright dangerous."

I wanted my new passport to bear my old name and newer looking me on the picture. I wanted to be rid of Robert's judgements as my mirror, reflecting the way I dress, wear my hair and speak my piece.

How I Am Up Front:
1. Shoulder-length blond hair worn loose
2. Never wear heels more than one inch (Robert is barely taller than me)
3. Very light make-up
4. Good, but not ostentatious jewelry
5. Good conversationalist but don't go too deep
6. About as informed as the 5 O'Clock News allows
7. A nice person although inclined to snap non-sensically

At Hair Fare, I found Madeline under the dryer reading last month's fashion magazines. She lifted the plastic helmet off her head and asked me what I was doing here. We were supposed to meet at The Teapot in a half an hour.

"I'm going to get a make-over," I told her.

The stylist tied a pink bib around me and asked if I had anything special in mind.

"Real short," I said.

"Are you sure?" She combed out my tangles. "Every time I cut long hair to short, they always cry on me. I don't want anyone crying on me."

"Real short," I repeated. "Like his," I pointed to the man who was feeling Madeline's curlers for dampness.

I had no idea my hair had weighed so much. I felt light, un-burdened the way I feel after a long day of shopping to come home and put the packages down. What was left of my hair, I had dyed black.

"Your blonde hair." Madeline was the one who cried. "Your beautiful, long blonde hair. Did you save it, at least?"

Other Ways to Change My Appearance:
1. Wear three-inch heels
2. A bold red lipstick
3. Jingle-jangly costume jewelry, such as earrings which are fruit bowls
4. Own up to what I think
5. Remove tail from between legs
6. Eyeliner (maybe)

I was going to claim, when Robert asked why I wasn't wearing my wedding rings, that I took them off because they pinched. In its way, this was true, but Robert never asked. I gathered he did not notice, having gotten caught up with the fact that he didn't take to my haircut any better than Madeline. Hideous was the word he used. "What's with you?" he asked. "Don't you have anything better to do with your time?" I suspected he was after me to dust more.

Robert had an allergy to dust. I rather liked the stuff especially when it grew to be dustballs. Dustballs reminded me of mini-tumbleweeds when they rolled out from under the couch. Robert picked one up between his thumb and index finger and dropped it in the trash. While washing his hands off from this adventure he said, "Maybe you can wear a wig."

The day my new passport arrived Robert wanted to know what the Atlas was doing in the kitchen.

"I was looking up places to go," I said.

"I told you, hon," Robert put on his apologetic voice, "I don't think I'll have time for a vacation this year."

"Maybe I'll go alone," I said.

Robert chuckled softly to himself.

I had $4,063. I counted it three times and then called Madeline. I told her to come right over. I took her into my bedroom and opened the closets and dresser drawers. "Take whatever you want," I said.

Madeline looked at me like I was a cross between the Good Fairy and a March hare. She wasn't sure if she were awake or not. "I'm serious," I said. "Take whatever you want. Take it all."

While Madeline was grabbing up cashmere sweaters and Hermes scarves, I told her my side of things because I wanted to tell someone. "It's just not what I wanted," I said. "I didn't know what I was doing and I tried this and now I know what I don't want. That's something. It's enough to go on."

Madeline wanted to know how I thought she'd look in the bottle green chiffon I wore last New Year's Eve. "With my coloring, I don't know," she held the dress next to her cheek.

I left Madeline in the bedroom to pick over her loot. I sat down at the kitchen table and wrote up a list.

Things To Do:
1. Drop off Robert's shirts
2. Lose laundry ticket on way home
3. Pack a light suitcase
4. Passport and money in inside pocketbook flap
5. Write farewell note
6. Staple farewell note to lampshade
7. Call for taxi
8. Gather courage
9. Gather suitcase
10. Make like a banana and leave.

Walking Steel

MERRIL MUSHROOM

Jess stood where the carpenter's helper had left her. As she watched him walk away, her belly churned with anxiety. *I might have known,* she wailed inwardly. *I might have known.* Then the sound of the first whistle sliced through her thoughts, cutting into her despair but not severing it from her, reminding her of the practical fact that she had ten minutes to get to her job site before the second whistle would blow to signal the official start of the work shift. *I can do anything,* Jess told herself for the zillionth time that week. *I am a strong, brave amazon and I can do anything.*

Jess tore her gaze away from the retreating back of the helper, looked at the edge of the cliff nearby, and her entire life of the past six weeks, since she first began working as a carpenter's apprentice on this huge construction project, passed before her eyes. "I thought I was doing pretty damn good," she muttered to herself, "getting used to it out here." She'd been the first woman hired in the program, hired straight from her job as an aide in a nursing home, hired as a single mother with two children to support. Jess was somewhat timid by nature, definitely not the "outdoorsie" type, and had been apprehensive from the beginning. Nothing had prepared her for her first day on the job, on the three-square-mile building site where four thousand employees in trades and labor all worked together in the field, with hundreds of pieces of machinery and heavy equipment pushing, hauling, lifting, roaring. And the mud, the dust, the noise, the heat, the men, the immensity of it all, the need to be strong and agile, which Jess was not.

During these weeks, Jess learned to not freak out when she had to work beneath loads swinging from crane cables overhead. She watched men climbing, hanging, working in places where a human being was never meant to be, and she wondered at their ability to do this. She decided that she, herself, did not have this ability, and resolved to do anything she had to do in order to be able to spend the entire four years of her apprenticeship standing on firm, solid ground.

Fortunately for Jess, the first crew she was placed with was putting up walls on a wide expanse of concrete flooring, so Jess was able to work on solid ground without having to find excuses. She occasionally caught a glimpse of the other woman in the area who had been hired shortly after Jess herself was hired. This woman, Sylvia, usually was on top of a steel wall, and every time Jess saw her, she was glad that this was not she, herself, atop that wall; and once again Jess thanked the goddesses that her own crew was working on the flat, secure floor.

Of all the possible sites where carpenters worked, one terrified Jess most of all; and she whispered a mantra of thanksgiving every time she passed this place in the course of going on errands for the journeymen on her crew. It was called the "reactor hole," and it was to be a circular room where a nuclear reactor would eventually rest. At this point, it was basically a huge pit in the earth into which was tied a mesh of criss-crossed reinforcing steel bars. Around these was poured concrete, layer by layer, until it would reach a thickness of sixty feet. Before the concrete could be poured, the steel had to be properly placed and tied by the ironworkers. Then the carpenters would build wooden walls to hold the concrete in place until it set. This meant working on a floor made entirely of criss-crossed steel bars an inch in diameter, unstable footing at best, bars far enough apart that a person who stumbled could probably slip through and fall, to be dashed to pieces on the rough concrete surface eight feet below. There was always a crew of carpenters working out on that steel, and every time Jess passed by where she could see them, she whispered her mantra in gratitude that this was not her crew; and then she hastened back to her own work site on stable, safe, solid ground.

But apprentices were scheduled to change crews every six weeks, and there was no way for Jess to stay where she had been. Right on schedule, six weeks to the hour after her first day on the crew, the carpenter's helper arrived and instructed Jess to get all her tools and follow him to her next assignment.

The farther away they went from the great concrete floor, the deeper her heart sank. *Oh, Lordess, I was hoping to get another placement on the ground,* Jess thought. *What if I get put with a crew working on top of a wall?* Then they were stopping at a place where Jess had never permitted herself to even dare to consider that she might have to work. They were stopping before the site of least expectations, the site of most trepidation; and the helper was exchanging words with a burly, heavily-tanned foreman who looked over at Jess and made a sour face, then turned his back, walked to the edge of the nearby cliff, stepped over the edge, and descended out of sight.

"That was Ray," the helper told Jess. "He's a good old boy." Then he turned on his heel and left Jess alone at the edge of the cliff overlooking the reactor hole.

Oh my Goddess! thought Jess, staring desperately around. She hoped against hope that maybe she was mistaken, maybe her new crew was really working elsewhere and the foreman just happened to be here by accident. *No, don't think about accidents!* she quickly admonished herself.

Jess walked to the edge of the cliff and looked over. The men were clustered on a ledge below, pulling nail aprons and power tools from the long, green gang box, buckling on their pouches and slinging tools over their shoulders. Ray stood among them, frowning deeply. He looked up, saw Jess. "Well, c'mon," he hollered, then turned his back on her. *Just what else I need,* Jess groaned inwardly, *a good old boy.*

A rickety wooden ladder with widely-spaced rungs rested against the rock face, its top step a good two feet below the edge where Jess stood. She swallowed hard. *Must be thirty feet down!* Sweat rolled over the side of her face, down her neck, and into her collar. She remembered the day she'd first seen one of these wooden ladders which the carpenters made to use as they needed. She had immediately promised herself to never lay foot on one of those rickety, homemade potential hazards — a promise she'd managed to keep until now.

Now it seemed as though Jess had no choice. She stared about, but didn't see any other way down. Below, the men were milling around, waiting for the second whistle. Taking one moment at a time, Jess studied the situation. There were no places to hold onto the ladder there at the very top. As she wondered what the best position would be to begin her descent, she suddenly realized that she would, in fact, do this thing. A sense of pride and relief swelled through her. She was preparing to actually descend the ladder! She would not fail. She would not lose her job. She would not humiliate herself in front of all these men.

As her wandering eye swept the ledge where the men were standing, Jess suddenly noticed yet another ladder which appeared to go down yet another level, and even as she looked, the second whistle blew. The men moved toward the lower ladder and, one by one, began to descend; and Jess suddenly realized that she'd better get down that first ladder before the entire crew vanished from sight. She felt a sudden panic at the thought of being left behind. She backed up to the edge of the cliff, leaned forward, and stepped over, feeling her foot meet the second rung down on the ladder. She leaned farther forward until she was resting against the wall of the cliff, stepped onto the third rung down, and grabbed the top run with clammy hands. *Whew, that was every bit as bad as I thought it would be! The rest of this has got to be easier!* She shifted slightly to free the pouches of her tool belt which had gotten caught on the rungs, breathed deeply, and tried to slow her pounding heart.

By the time Jess reached the bottom of the ladder, the crew was gone. She hurried to the edge where the second ladder rested, looked over, and suddenly felt faint. In her intense focus on descending the first ladder and her subsequent self-congratulations on this achievement, she hadn't thought about where she was. She'd forgotten about the place of steel where there was no floor."

Below her, the men were struggling across the thin bars, balancing precariously, teetering from side to side as they placed their feet, trying their best to keep their stability, while as far as Jess could see was an ocean of squares outlined in metal with middles that dropped off into nothingness. Far and wide stretched the steel Jess had so dreaded every time she had passed this place in the weeks before. As quickly as she could, she descended the second ladder, holding on tightly to the rungs, trying to keep her tool belt from getting caught, trying to remain steady and not knock the ladder from its place in her nervous haste.

Maybe they don't really have to go across the steel, Jess told herself convincingly, as she tried to hurry without losing her grip and falling to certain death. *Maybe they are really going somewhere else to work and are just taking a short cut over the steel, and I can go the long way around somehow on the flat, stable concrete floor.* She reached the bottom of the ladder and turned.

Near her, on the ledge, stood a journeyman carpenter. He was playing out an electric lead for the welder, while in the very center of the non-floor, journeymen were setting boards down on the steel, placing sawhorses on the boards, pulling electrical cords across the bars and setting up saws and drills. Other men were carrying boards out and making a pile of them. Jess stared. She felt sick. She could not for the life of her imagine how these men were going to work without a floor to stand on; and she could even less imagine how she herself would work there, never mind how she would even be able to *get* there. *I can't do this!* Jess thought in a panic. Desperately, she grabbed at the journeyman. "Where are we supposed to be working?" she demanded.

"Yonder," he pointed across the steel to that place of her worst fears. He stared at her. "Better c'mon, now," he drawled. "They ain't much for working with a woman on this crew, and they won't like you shirkin.'" The cord he was holding pulled tight, and he stepped out onto the bars.

"Wait!" Jess couldn't bear the thought of losing the only human being who had given her what amounted to a kind word in her terror. "Um, isn't there any other way to get there?"

"Nope."

89

"Couldn't I go around, somehow?"

The journeyman shook his head, walked a little farther out on the steel.

"Can't I maybe go underneath," Jess called, "you know, on the concrete, and then climb back up out there?"

The journeyman kept walking, did not look back at Jess, and she was left alone.

I don't know how to do this. Jess was on the verge of tears. *I can't. I'm too afraid. My knees are bad. What if I fall? A person could really get hurt falling around this place.* She stared at the huge spaces between the thin bars and the rough concrete so far below. *I could fit right through there if I fell. I'd smash myself up really badly on that concrete. I'll get dizzy. I'll lose my balance for sure. My knees are bad — they'll give out on me.* Her shoulders sagged, and she felt weak all over. *I can't do this.*

Suddenly Amazon Jess emerged and stood before herself. *You may as well climb back up that ladder and walk off this job site and go back home again if you are going to let your fear rule you.*

The frightened Jess was suddenly brought up straight in embarrassed defiance. *What do you mean?*

I mean you either have to get out on that steel or go home right now and never come back.

But, but, but, Jess thought back at herself, *surely there's something else I can do here. I mean, I need this job. Maybe I can get transferred to another job site or even to another trade apprenticeship, somewhere I won't have to climb or walk steel. Somewhere that I will be able to work on solid ground. Surely some other arrangements can be made.*

No, Amazon Jess said, *it wouldn't make any difference. No matter what field you ended up in, you'd still have to climb, and you'd still have to walk steel. What it all boils down to is you either put up or shut up; you either find some way to get out on that steel and do your job, or you give it all up right now, go home, and crawl back to your safe little minimum wage job on safe, solid ground.*

Angry with herself now, Jess stared across the steel. The men were all at work, cutting boards to fit between the bars of the floor, building a bulkhead to separate off the next concrete pour. About midway to that spot, a ring of vertical steel extended. *If I can only get to that,* Jess thought, *I could hold on to it and get much closer to where the crew is before I have to let go again.*

Maybe I can even keep holding on. She felt safer at the prospect. Tentatively, she took one step onto the steel. The bar moved beneath her foot, and she got such a rush of fear that she thought she would pass out. She shifted her foot slightly, stepped out until her arch was resting where the bars crossed. Bearing most of her weight on the sole of that foot, she raised her other foot off the ledge, separating it from the security of solid rock floor, brought it up even with the first foot. Straddling two spaces, Jess brought both feet even with each other, leaning her weight onto her soles which rested on the raised intersections of steel. Fixing her sights on the vertical steel before her, she murmured to herself, "I can do it. I can do anything. I am a strong, brave amazon and I can do anything!"

And she did.

A Window on Soweto
(an excerpt)

JOYCE SIKAKANE

Detention

I was detained on May 12, 1969 at about 2 a.m. We heard
knocking and woke to the flashing of torches outside and shouts
of "Police! Police! Open the door!" We all got up — my mother,
myself and my two brothers — and the police came in. There
were three white policemen, one white policewoman and an
African policeman, all in plain clothes.

They demanded Joyce Sikakane and I said it was myself
and they produced a warrant of arrest under Section 6 of the
Terrorism Act. They said they wanted to search the house.
They were all brandishing their guns about and so they searched the house and took away whatever documents and personal
papers — all my letters for example — they wished. The policewoman was guarding me the whole time.

After about two hours they told me to get dressed, as I was
still in my nightie; I did so and was escorted to the car. I was
afraid to wake Nkosinathi who was still sleeping, so I left him
without saying goodbye.

On the way out of Soweto the car dropped off the African
policeman in Meadowlands. I remember him saying "Thank
you my baas, you caught the terrorist. I hope you get the information you want out of her."

We drove off to John Vorster Square (Security Police HQ) where another policeman got out, and then on again. When I asked where we were going, the only reply was that I was being detained under the Terrorism Act. I was terrified: I didn't see myself as a terrorist and didn't know why I should be detained under the Terrorism Act.

I was taken to Pretoria Central Prison. They knocked on the big door, the guard looked out and then opened the gate and I was led in. First we went to the office; they spoke to the matron and papers were signed. My engagement ring was taken from me — I was upset about that. Then we crossed the prison yard to another part of the prison. In the yard were about a hundred African women, some with babies on their backs, some sitting on the ground, some with vegetable baskets full of onions, pumpkins and so on, whom I could see were vendors who had been arrested for illegally selling vegetables in the street. As I came into the yard, the policeman shouted to the women to shut their eyes. This was because I was a Terrorism Act detainee, to be held incommunicado, which meant no-one should know who or where I was. I was taken past and up some stairs, where the two policemen escorting me greeted another man as Colonel Aucamp.

He told the matron to take me to a cell. And I heard her ask, "Is she a condemned woman?" as I was shown into a cell with a bright blinding light that made me see sparks.

Aucamp immediately said "No, no, not that one, I made a mistake." So I was taken out and led along to the common shower room, where there were lots of women prisoners, some naked under the showers, some undressing, some waiting their turn. The matron told me to undress, which I did, and got under the cold shower. I could tell the other women knew there was something special about me, being under escort and alone and jumping the queue like that.

After the cold shower I picked up my paper bag of clothes — the matron told me not to dress — and I was led to a cell. It was narrow and high, situated in what I later discovered was the isolation wing. The outer steel door was opened and then the inner barred door; I went in and the matron locked first one and then the other.

So there I was, in this tall narrow empty cell, gazing around. There was a small high hole covered with mesh, for ventilation. And it was very cold: May is the beginning of winter in South Africa and we had already had some frost. Suddenly I heard women's voices coming from outside in the yard, talking. I was horrified to hear them talking about their love affairs inside prison — the experienced women telling the freshers what to expect, how some were chosen as husbands and some as wives, and generally describing the whole scene to them. It gave me a real fright, standing there naked. I at once got my paper bag and put my panties on!

When I looked around at the contents of the cell all I saw was a damp sisal mat, rolled up, and three grey blankets, also damp and smelling of urine. That was all. I just sat down on the mat and waited.

It wasn't until 7 o'clock that evening that the cell door opened. There was a white wardress and an African woman prisoner in prison uniform, who shoved a plate of food through the door, along the floor, together with a galvanised bucket. All the time the wardress stood between me and the prisoner, so I should not be seen. Then they left, locking the doors behind them. But I heard them open the next cell and then I knew I wasn't alone: if the next cell was occupied I wasn't the only woman detainee.

From then on the pattern of prison life was always the same. In the morning at about 7 a.m. the cell door was opened, the shit bucket and empty plate taken out and a plate of porridge and cup of coffee put in. There was a bucket of sometimes warm water too, to wash oneself and one's underclothes. Lunch was usually about noon, though it could be earlier — on Sundays it was about 10:30 — and consisted of izinkobe or dry mealies — corn kernels — which had been boiled but were still dry and hard. There was a beverage too, some sort of drink, which the prisoners used to call puza'mandla — drink power! Then at about 2 p.m. came supper, which was soft maize porridge with one or two pieces of meat, possibly pork, in it. That was all until the next day.

For the first few days I didn't eat anything. I was frightened, angry, depressed, wondering why I had been detained, scared of what might happen, and crying most of the time. By the third day, I had cried all my tears out. At least, I think it was the third day. Two huge policemen, with layers and layers of chin, came for me. I asked where they were taking me and they said, to give an account of your sins.

I was driven in a big Cadillac, with a policeman on either side of me and two more in front. We went to the Compol building (police HQ) in Pretoria. Knock, knock again, the police escort identify themselves and we drive in.

Down some corridors to an office. It looks like any other office except it has these wooden partitions. Right facing me is a stone sink and then there's a desk and a few chairs. I can see it's a work room. All along the walls is this wooden partitioning, covering the windows but capable of being drawn back. It kind of encloses the room, insulates it from outside. And just off this room is a sort of gym closet with punch bags — and a huge African policeman with fierce red eyes standing there. While I was being interrogated policemen kept trooping in to practice boxing on the punch bags.

Interrogation

There was a constant stream of policemen, about fifteen or twenty, coming into the room, as if they were going on stage. They were brandishing guns, holding documents, smoking cigarettes, greeting me, some scowling at me. They all looked different, some like bulldogs, some like Alsatians, some like timid cats. Some of them behaved with great politeness, like perfect gentlemen. I think this performance was just put on to confuse me, for the next thing was Major Swanepoel coming in. He is the most sadistic and most feared of all the police interrogators; several people have died as a result of his "questioning."

"Have you heard of Major Swanepoel?" he said. "I am Major Swanepoel." All the other policemen gave way to him, treating him very deferentially. Then interrogation began.

They fired questions and statements at me; all of a sudden they were all talking about me and my personal life — all my experiences, which they seem to know better than I did! As they did so they incidentally revealed the extent of their informer network: I found they knew about all sorts of incidents in my career—the story about the Malawian air hostesses being allowed to stay in an all-white hotel, for instance, that I had been working on when I was detained. I also discovered, from things they said, who else had been questioned: Winnie Mandela, wife of ANC leader Nelson Mandela, and Rita Ndzanga, for instance. They had interrogated many other people I knew, and from what they knew I could see they had been tortured to extract the information.

From me they wanted confirmation: that certain things had been done, that I had knowingly participated, and whatever else I could add. From what they know one has to judge what to admit and what to hide and what one might not manage to hide—because it flashes into your mind what risk to others is involved, and also the possibility of being tortured yourself and whether the type of information you have is worth dying for. I knew that in our case what we had been doing was something that would not, in any other country, be considered "terroristic": we were involved with the welfare of political prisoners, helping to make arrangements for families of prisoners to visit their husbands or parents. And so why not admit it? Yes, I did that—so what? We hadn't been involved in anything connected with violence or arms—that would have called for other methods of interrogation. As far as I was concerned they were more interested in getting information about the underground communication network.

The interrogation lasted right through until the following day. They took turns, and took breaks. I was just standing there. I would be tired, I would squat down, I would jump about a bit. I was shown the bricks—the torture bricks on which the men detainees are made to stand. The questioning went on, without food, without anything, till the following morning. Then I was taken back to my cell.

It was about ten days before I was taken again for interrogation. This time it lasted for three whole days because this time they were concerned with taking a statement. Under the Terrorism Act a detainee may be held until a statement to the satisfaction of the Commissioner of Police has been given, and the purpose of the interrogation is to obtain such a statement which can then be used against you or someone else. They still ask questions: anything you admit goes down on the statement.

This time my interrogation took place on the third floor of Compol building, and the interrogators were Major Botha and Major Coetzee. They were trained and experienced political officers. Oh, they were courteous gentlemen, but I could sense hatred—they hated every bit of me. But they had to get what they wanted from me.

They put the proposal that I should be a state witness, giving evidence for the state against the others. I asked why should I do that? and they said, well, you're young, you're an intelligent girl, you have a fiancé outside the country. If you are afraid to give evidence because of what your organization will do to you, we can always give you another name and find a job in one of our embassies abroad—say in Malawi or London, where you can join your fiancé!

All the time, because of what they wanted out of me, they were at pains to explain that they were not against Africans or black people in general. They were only against communists. They argued that people like myself, young, intelligent, pretty, etc., were being misled by communists. They, on the other hand, were offering me a chance. I found this insulting. How could they sit there, admit that apartheid was a repressive system, which they did while maintaining that racism occurred all over the world. What hypocrites I said inside me to say communists had misled me into wanting to change the system. I didn't need any communists to tell me apartheid is evil. I know. Nor would I join the enemy camp for the sake of self preservation.

So I told Major Botha and Major Coetzee I was not interested in their offer. They said in that case you are going to be here a long time. Others had given evidence, they said. If you refuse we have lots of other evidence we can use, the others are willing.

In the end they took a statement. Under the law it's supposed to be made of one's own volition—but I wondered how, under the circumstances of indefinite detention under the Terrorism Act, anything can be called of one's own volition. I came to the point when I agreed to some of the things they said—

well, if you say that, yes, it's so.

After they had taken the statement Major Coetzee said "Well, Joyce, we think you should think seriously about our offer. We will transfer you to another prison, so you can think over the offer." They they repeated their offer of a job in London. I didn't bother to reply yes or not, I just kept silent. And I was taken back to my cell.

The Chipko

SALLY MILLER GEARHART

Garland was squatting over a shallow hole in the carpet of pine needles, contemplating the woes of the human species and trying to face her own possible impending death. Shitting was not only good civil disobedience protocol—in case they brought in sonarbowel units; it also called up in her the creatively philosophical, and particularly so now that dying seemed such a sudden and extreme reality. As usual, she had begun her morning contemplation with the immediate material circumstances: the dark pre-dawn sky, the cool woods, the nearby preparations for a violent confrontation, her own present— rather strained—position in the scheme of things. And as usual she had leapt immediately to broad overarching universal concepts (good-and-evil, motion-and-rest, being-and-nothingness) that forced her this time to take refuge in "Hamlet." She pushed her sphincter muscle hard trying to force out the dregs of yesterday's rice and sprouts, then tightened it again beginning the series of clean-up contractions. The Prince of Denmark accompanied her. ". . . Their cur. Rents turn. A wry. And lose. The name. Of ac. Tion." She uttered the last words aloud and, wiping herself with a sheaf of broadoak leaves, she rose triumphantly to pull up her pants and step to the side of the hole. There was just enough light to guide her proper covering of her

99

accomplishment. She made her formulary bows: one of gratitude to the Receiving Mother and one of appreciation to her body for its miraculous processes.

She picked her way carefully back to the temporary camp that crowded the small meadow. Beyond it and over a rise lay the gentle hillside that they would be defending in a few hours. She could make out now the slow-moving forms of other early risers—or un-sleepers—pulling themselves erect, bulky shadows trying to tiptoe through still-filled sleeping bags. The group had grown, she noted, even during the night. The expanse of bedrolls covered the whole eastern end of the clearing and extended itself well into the trees.

As she watched the camp come to life she wondered how many times in this world's history it had been women who had awakened early on the day of a battle and stood in a quiet dawn to dread or hope or remember or wonder. For there were mostly women and children here for this chipko, just as there had been twenty-five years ago when the first whole forest had been saved by such a demonstration. Most of the weave-schemes called for the ultimate protection of anyone under twelve, but a surprising number of six- and seven-year olds had refused to be banished from the action; Garland wasn't convinced that either they or their mothers knew how nasty this confrontation was going to be.

"So are you any good with dogs?" Ellen was behind her, holding out to her a mug of something steaming.

"Okay. No better than the next person. Why?"

"They heard we were spiking trees. It's not true but they're royally pissed anyway. So they're bringing dogs today. Maluma just found out. Said to pass the word."

"I heard it was going to be whirley-birds." Garland sipped her tea and then set it aside to stretch her back and her legs. "Have they ever used air support here?"

"No. And I doubt that they will. The only thing they could drop that would wilt us and not the loggers is mace bags and even Champion International's not going to spring for gas masks for all those loggers." Ellen flung tea dregs onto one of the clumps of low-growing feeder grass and rested her cup on a stump. "I don't know what could stop helicopters. Unless maybe the flying furies could scare the bejesus out of them."

Garland looked up. She didn't know Ellen well enough to discern a joke in her manner. "You believe in them? Women who can fly?"

"I'd like to. Wouldn't you?"

"When we heard about this chipko we sent word about it to some women in Western Michigan. Never heard back from them. There are supposed to be flying furies down there."

"Well, if there are flying furies anywhere it would be in Western Michigan. I think it's one big fantasy, myself. I only talk about them to keep my spirits up."

"Yeah," Garland said. Then she drew her oakheart fighting stick from its six-foot cotton sheath. "I'm not sure I'm ready for this," she mused. "The only chipkos I've done were mild compared to what they described last night. Nobody got hurt bad, much less killed."

"So the bluffs have been called and the peaceful parts are over. The jacks are more desperate. They're pushed to feed their kids. 'I'm just following orders, ma'am,' as he pulls his starter cord. They won't use the battery-driven chain saws, you know. Too quiet. Not enough snarl. The gentlemen we'll be seeing today get their contrachipko training from the N.R.A. Here, let me show you the routine."

She took up her own long inch-round stick, silently addressed it by name and then assumed an alert-rest fighting stance. She moved swiftly then into a series of quick sword-strikes with high blocks. Bending almost to a squat she established an internal pattern of low reverses and knee-breakers and then climaxed with a wide shoulder-high backhand sweep. She ended in the classic absorption stance with her stave extended at head level in the Embrace of the Enemy. The seducement of that energy drew even Garland off-balance and in toward Ellen's center.

Garland bowed and spoke silently to her stick, addressing it by name, and stroking its familiar smoothness. "Obeah, Fear-Striker, you are wood to protect wood today." She crossed a whole ocean and half a continent to remember the quiet island grove where the stick had its origin. What a contrast to today's wholesale cutting! There there had been public prayers, rituals, consultations (inter- and intra-species) before any tree could be cut. And when the moment came, what tears were there, what lamentations! Then finally what celebrations of the new trees planted in the shadow of the fallen! She stepped behind Ellen. "Once more, por favor."

They spent the dawn rehearsing the stickmatrix's moves, those precise coordinated attacks designed to rob woodcutters of their machines without seriously injuring the woodcutter. The stickmatrix was the only element of chipko strategy that could be called offensive. Characteristically it went into action only after a tree (or a person) had actually been touched by a faller or a saw. But its preliminary kata, done in unison at the first moment of real threat, was distinctly aggressive and often formidable enough — like the maw of a great whale, some suggested — to give even the largest saw a sputter. More than one crew of leggers had succumbed, before any blow was struck, to the vision of twelve women (the Goddess made thirteen, and the sticks made them seem like a legion) advancing toward them in a wave of mysterious open power. It was this kata that Garland practiced with Ellen until dawn became sunrise, and until some unnamed figure refilled their cups with a strong nightshade tea for the last time.

Close to a hundred women and children, with a few men, were exiting the meadow and slipping into the woods over the rise, a peace-obsessed army, moving almost noiselessly to the shelter of an oak grove. There they relieved the night watchers and the changing body of scouts who reported from both directions along the dirt road on low-rev motorcycles or on the bicycles that sacrificed speed for silence.

The Weavers, the main body of the company, took their assigned places on the perimeter of the cutting site, just across from the clearing on the other side of the road where a yellow crane, its boom towering upward, sat on a large flatbed. Another flatbed held a Number 8 Cat. On the ground, a smaller bulldozer waited patiently to do its task. It was there in the clearing that the trucks would draw up to discharge the logging crews. The Weavers, in groups of friends, lovers, or families, surrounded sets of trees, intertwining their anger, their passion, their love, their stubbornness. From that phalanx rose a protective shield that extended toward the as-yet empty road.

A group that had come to be called the Stillers mingled with the Weavers but differed in their task. They were to reach out mentally to the oncoming fallers, calming anger, damping wild and otherwise unpredicted actions that individual men often resorted to. Garland had once seen a logger, crazed by his thwarted attempts to cut the women's fighting sticks, actually turn his revved chain saw on one of his fellow loggers. Stillers had saved the near-victim's life in that instance—and perhaps that of the attacker. The Stillers certainly didn't give the impression that they were participating in the confrontations. Usually they hovered behind the Weavers looking very tranced-out. Most chipkos, however, and for that matter most operative non-violent groups, refused these days to do an action without some Stillers, so much had they come to depend upon them.

Both Stiller and Weaver maintained maximum flexibility in their positions so that they could accommodate any shifts in the direction of the attack. And both Stiller and Weaver were ultimately committed to the oldest strategy of all, if it came to that: hugging individual trees, there to stay until that tree's life was no longer threatened.

Moving back and forth among them all was Maluma, a strange kind of military genius, clad quite practically in boots and soft cotton from toe to chin and wearing from her chin up a wild headdress of brightly colored birdfeathers. "Though maybe that's battle dress, too," Garland reminded herself. Maluma quizzed her lieutenants on plans and counterplans, carried babies from one parent to another, hugged or joked with her troops as occasion allowed, and recited with one or another of them: "I protect these trees. I protect myself. I protect my comrades. I protect him who attacks us. I will not be moved." Over the decades those words had become chipko Weavers' haunting chant.

Garland had forgotten that she was going to die today. Instead she was fascinated all over again by the steadiness, the assurance, of these weaponless warriors and their leader. Her own adrenalin was already lifting her high, making her feet move up and down in soft stomps of anticipation. Deliberately

103

she closed her eyes. "Broad. Low. Easy. Slow," she told herself. Obeah pulsed with her as she retarded her rhythm.

An old Yamaha geared down over its driver's shouts that eleven pickups and jeeps plus panel trucks and a string of larger rigs were less than nine minutes away to the west, an estimated thirty loggers. And more could be expected from the east. There was a stir among the waiting Weavers and Stillers, a lift to the beginning day, and a murmur in the tops of the oak trees. As she stepped through roadside briars Garland found herself scanning the early morning blue above the clearing. Her mind conjured a skyful of pairs of Amazons flying side-by-side, a war-cry on their lips, descending upon the forest. "Hope springs eternal," she muttered grimly.

Clarion was collecting fighting sticks for the blessing, her actions now shot through with a sense of immediacy. Thirteen women were gathered around her, more than those needed for the katas, but not enough to form a semi-matrix. The three extras would probably stand with the Weavers as replacements for the matrix when it was moving as a unit. They would join actively when the matrix broke for any individual fighting.

Garland failed to calm her racing heart as she entered the ring of women next to Ellen, adding her own stick to the ones that Clarion was holding on end in the center of the circle: fifteen wooden staves of varying lengths, hues, textures, and degrees of use, each with stories to tell, each marked in some indelible way with the identity of the woman whose spirit extended through it. Garland looked around the circle, trying to match staves with women.

She joined her hands to the battle sashes of the women beside her and her voice to the rising incantation. They called up the rage of the earth, the suffering of every beaten woman, the death of every witch and that of her familiar, the agony of burning faggots, the strength of the roots, trunks, limbs, buds, leaves, and fruit of every tree from alpha to omega. They upturned the gathered rods and set them vertical again, then addressed their destined paths according to the four directions, eight planes, and seven modes of swiftness. They sang for the moment of Quickening in the conflict, the moment at which they would know that the birthing of victory, however pained, would be sure and sweet. They thanked the wands for their protective power, prayed that any injury they brought would heal around a seed of change, and reclaimed their weapons with a shout that Weavers and Stillers joined.

The sound of the first motor came just behind the last three scouts, two of them cyclists. "The dogs are in the panel trucks," one reported, drawing her bike behind the line of Weavers. A wave of consternation passed over the gathering. One woman and two small crying girls withdrew to the top of the hill. The women in the stick matrix assumed a first form position standing with their staves at rest.

Trucks of all sizes began pulling into the clearing or parking on the roadside. The sheriff tumbled out of one pick-up, a journalist with a tape recorder from another. Enthusiasm was pouring out of the cabs like the home team from the locker room at playoffs. A man in a grey workshirt with rolled-up sleeves lurched out of the lead truck. He took off his Big Tar cap and shifted his clipboard to wipe his brow.

"Who's in charge?" he called out, stepping toward the trees he wanted to cut. When only silence greeted him he motioned to one of the other drivers. "Roy!" Then to the lines of humans standing between him and his livelihood he said, "I want to talk with your head woman. And don't give me any of that equal stuff. Somebody's got to be responsible."

Maluma pulled away from the Weavers and advanced toward him. Growling trucks and slamming cab doors drowned out what they said to each other. Garland saw the big man gesturing toward Roy, and Roy speaking to Maluma. Maluma shook her head. One of the men kicked a chain saw on. A burst of raucous laughter charged the air. "Guys, cut it!" shouted Grey Shirt. The chain saw died. Maluma turned and walked back to the lines of Weavers.

Grey Shirt raised his voice in the growing silence. "This is your last chance, all of you. We have to get to these trees and we have a court order that backs us. I'm asking you once to leave quietly. Go back home and have some breakfast." Pause. "I'm asking you twice: please leave so we can cut the timber." Pause. "This is the third time: you have to leave peaceably so we can do our job."

105

No one moved, including Grey Shirt. Then he jerked his head toward the men behind him and sliced the air with his clipboard. The loggers broke into action. Doors to the panel trucks were flung open and pairs of large fighting dogs began straining on leashes in front of strong men. Chain saw motors tore into the silence. With remarkable timing, more trucks heaved into view from the east side of the hill. They too spilled out waves of shouting men with saws at ready, motors revving, chains flashing in their endless circling. Now from both edges of the cutting site dogs were goaded into snarls and rough barks. They converged on the human barrier confronting them and filled the morning with fury.

Garland felt rather than saw the wave of activity surging toward her. Then she was lost in the swirl of the matrix as it began its move, internally at first, and then with concentrated overt focus. A contingent of women with spinning wands danced in unison onto the road, intoning a barely audible hum. Startled woodsmen and their dogs hesitated and then drove forward again toward the matrix only to halt when the women broke into a concave double semi-circle of raised sticks: the Embrace of the Enemy. For a second the chaos of barks and motors ceased. The forest and all its occupants stood in tiptoe anticipation. Then in the throat of the matrix the hum grew to full voice, a ki-ay growing louder, and louder still, threatening at last to split the silence. Just short of its climax, one of the fallers shouted, "Don't fall for it, men! It's a trick! Move! Move! They can't sustain it! Move, I tell you!"

The spell broke, and with its shattering a new roar of cacophony descended. Garland was dimly aware that the chaos sounded different but before she could decide the reason a sixteen-inch chain saw whipped up and toward her. She sidestepped, driving Obeah's far end into a soft solar plexus. Her attacker doubled over at an angle precisely designed to let her slip her stick into the brake guard and lever the machine out of his hands. To her left Ellen delivered a knee-breaker to the advance of another logger, this one reaching with outstretched blade to a forward standing juvenile oak. All around her a set-to raged. Men shouted, saws roared, Weavers chanted, dogs — no, there were no dogs barking! That was the difference! Dogs, in fact, had simply stopped moving. They sat or lay in the road in an almost reverent silence, regarding the women. No amount of hauling or kicking could stir them. Dobermans, Shepherds and Pit Bulls, expensively and ruthlessly trained to be ferocious, were refusing to attack. Garland noted a single exception: one Shepherd was actually wagging its tail and attempting to drag its leasher toward the loud-chanting Weavers.

Fallers who were not angrily and futilely urging stolid animals into action were shouting twice as loud, squaring their shoulders twice as stiffly, and advancing with redoubled determination toward the scattered matrix and beyond it toward the oaks. In a shift of strategy, two of them would force a Weaver from a tree, holding her helpless or at times immobilizing her with ropes while a third attempted a jump cut on the rough old trunk. He would be foiled by another body that immediately wrapped itself around the tree. And again: pull her away, rev the idle, step to cut, and find another body inches from the blade. And again and again throughout the forest.

Garland, with other stick-fighters attempting to stave off the onslaught of men with saws, looked when she could toward the Weavers and their attackers. In an instant before he attempted again to cut, she saw one faller trying by force of long experience to keep his blade from nearing human flesh. His face rang a host of changes—contempt, braggadocio, conflict, fear, anguish, frustration, and finally rage and dogged determination. He brought the spinning chain a centimeter from a bare shoulder and then jerked it high above his head as he shrieked, "Get her AWAAAAAAAY!"

A constant flow of chanting Weavers was appearing from nowhere to replace those dragged back from the trees. Those dragged back, once released, flung themselves around yet other trees. Garland found herself praying that the good luck would hold, that they would continue to see no blood, that the fallers would give up . . . that the figure stalking toward her with raised and revved saw would go for her outflung stick and not for her belly button.

The man in fact went for the stick, a wild concentration propelling him onward, an ugly smile marring his face. Garland pushed her breath into Obeah, focusing entirely upon the slow drawing of her attacker around, around, and yet further around until she saw his intent to charge. At that moment she swung the stick behind her, twirling tightly and executing the perfect veronica. The logger lunged and stumbled. Then with a frantic scream he toppled to the ground, twisting so that he saved his chest but not his forearm from the still fully-throttled spinning chain. Garland got the blood full in her face, and shocked herself by licking and savoring its saltiness before she dropped upon the ignition switch to kill the motor.

The man was shrieking, and jerking in uncontrolled spasms that flung his truncated limb repeatedly against her breast. She determined to ignore what lay before her eyes: a shirtsleeve that couched a severed wrist. Instead she grabbed the flailing stump and secured it against her. Then with her full torso she covered him and blocked out the noise and chaos that pounded around them. Gently she held the unresisting body below her and pushed slow extensions into it. The body eased. Garland eased. She looked up then to call for help only to discover above her the forms of two large men. Without conscious thought she reached for her stick. She stopped her motion as one man shook his head. "We'll take him," he said.

"You need to stop the blood," she said, shifting to her feet.

He nodded. "We'll take him," he said again.

In the rising mid-morning light, in the interstices of a two-stroke heartbeat and over the inert body of one fallen in the fray, three people searched each other's faces for signs of understanding. Then one of them, partly to hide the rising of very inappropriate tears, turned her back and plunged toward the jungle of sound where lines were clearly drawn and friends and enemies were more easily identified.

Garland had just joined an embattled Clarion and two other stick fighters in their defense of a tree called Big Mama Oak when she realized that there had been a distinct change in the whole encounter. Her heart sank when she saw that the battle had shifted, and why. The men, almost as many now as those who opposed them, had begun imprisoning the non-resistant women in huge army trucks so that very slowly the number of those who returned to protect the trees was dwindling. Garland could see a cordon of guards surrounding the trucks. They beat down with ax handles and threatened with aggressive chain saws the heads and arms that poked through the high cloth covering of the truckbeds. "Come on!" Garland shouted, pulling Clarion toward that scene.

They clashed head-on with two men trying to force Maluma into a truck. Garland rejoiced to see that Weaver and Stiller tactics had changed now from pure passive non-resistance to an active effort to get back to the trees. She rejoiced a second time when Maluma released a wild cry that stunned her keepers and gave Clarion a chance to thrust her stick across one man's Adam's apple, thus pinning him against the side of the truck. At the same moment Garland brought Obeah down on the knuckles of the other faller and twisted the lower end of the stick upward to wedge beneath his jawbone. From there she levered him off the ground and into a feet-over-head spin that landed him unconscious several yards away.

Clarion and Maluma were trying to get near the long bolt that imprisoned the people in the truck and Garland was about to throw an attacker who had conveniently grabbed her stick. But all of them froze like statues at the sound of a collective shout of joy. It ascended from a wedge of loggers slowly approaching Big Mama Oak. Already the twenty or so remaining Weavers and Stillers were being seized and tied by groups of men. However hard they struggled in their new-found active resistance they could not break free or reach their beloved trees. Toward the center of the grove the remaining members of the matrix fought a losing battle against a sheer mass of men who moved calmly over them, disarming them, securing them to trees with their own battle sashes.

Intoxicated by such promise of success the men in the wedge were laughing now, pushing forward behind a confident logger who led the way toward the old oak. "Take the big old one first, Pierre! Let 'em see her fall!" "Watch, ladies, watch. She'll make such fine panelling for your house!"

As Garland leapt forward, large men closed in on her, surrounding her and her companions. As she lost her stick she managed to duck her chin and avoid a neck lock. She relaxed into a low energy-gathering stance and with all of Mother Earth beneath and within her she raised her hands in front of her face, dragging with them the protesting arms of the man who held her from behind. She knelt, and with a surge of power swept her assailant over her head and into the path of another oncoming man, thus leaving her own arms free to receive and dispatch her third attacker. But there was a fourth. And a fifth. And a tenth.

She broke beneath their weight and sank to the ground. With what she knew would be her last free breath she hurled a curse at the cordon of men approaching the unprotected tree. As the mass of logger flesh descended on her breathless body she discovered a chink that gave her a view of the ultimate defeat.

She saw Pierre raise his chain saw. His company of men cheered. He placed its blade close by the bark of the old oak—knee-high, so the Cat could later have a purchase on the stump. The men cheered again. He revved the motor and began the slanting bite into the wood.

A rock the size of a fist struck the chain saw from Pierre's hands and drove it into the dirt. The cordon of loggers was peppered with a rain of human bodies. The men fell back, overwhelmed by a sudden foe.

From out of nowhere a war-cry split the air. And Garland felt her burdens lift. As man after man was pulled from atop her, as breath after blessed breath went coursing through her hungry lungs, she craned her neck upward toward the mid-morning sun.

The sky was full of women.

Mrs. Morris Changes Lanes

ZOË FAIRBAIRNS

The names of some of the bikes—Footpad, Puma, Ripper, Axe—aroused deep anxiety in Mrs. Morris, and the tone in which the salesman asked if he could help her sounded more like an accusation of trespass. She would prefer him to order her from the showroom rather than press her to buy. She hadn't even chosen a color yet. Some shades were definitely unacceptable. Black was difficult to see at night and red suggested anarchy and toughness.

"I'm just looking," she said.

The Puma was a 700 and the Footpad a 650. The Ripper and the Axe came in various sizes, if size was indeed what those numbers referred to. They might be quantities. Quantities of what? Was it good or bad to have a lot of them, or were they just reference numbers like bus routes? Was it just a matter of design that dictated foot-brakes on some models, hand-brakes on others, or was it more important than that? Where did the petrol go? What kind of petrol?

"Was it for yourself?" the salesman persisted.

She was glad of the opportunity to explain. "They've cut my buses down to one an hour."

"These," he said, "are very popular with the ladies."

It was called a Polka Pop 49. It was lilac in color, and had wheels like old sixpences. An enormous shopping basket was attached to the front, and there was more luggage space at the rear. It looked as if it could be carried home under someone's arm. it looked as if, once there, it should be placed on the table at a children's party, covered with candles, and sliced.

"It has an electric start."

"Very nice."

"And it won't start unless the brake's on."

"Off, you mean?" said Mrs. Morris.

The salesman looked puzzled. "No, I meant on. It's a safety feature."

Mrs. Morris still didn't understand. "Why would I want to move off with the brake on?"

"Dear oh dear oh dear," said the salesman, giving her some leaflets. He wandered off to chat happily with a knowledgeable new customer who appeared to be about the same age as Mrs. Morris's son, and ought to be at school.

Mrs. Morris read the leaflets and spent a considerable amount of time observing motorcycles on the road. One day she approached a Hell's Angel who was parking his Throbber 1100 in a car park, and he was kind enough to give her a good deal of advice.

She went to another showroom

"Was it for yourself?" the salesman began. "Because these are very popular with the —"

"I have heard," said Mrs. Morris, "that these Polkas guzzle oil and you're always having to change the spark plugs."

"Well, I wouldn't say —"

"It's no more than you'd expect with a two-stroke engine, is it?" said Mrs. Morris. "Show me a four-stroke, 50 cc's."

"There's this one," said the salesman.

"Electric start, I see," said Mrs. Morris. "Not always reliable, are they? Is there a kick start back-up?"

"Yes," said the salesman.

"Automatic transmission?"

"Yes."

She asked a few more questions and then she said, "Fine. Now I'll need L-plates and a crash helmet."

"Were you planning to ride it away now?"

"No," said Mrs. Morris. "I would like you to deliver it to the town hall on Sunday morning."

"If it doesn't arrive," thought Mrs. Morris as she waited in the car park of the town hall on Sunday morning, "I can always pretend I'm here in an administrative capacity. Or," she added to herself as more of her fellow students, average age nineteen, turned up, "or that I am a parent, come to watch."

She was surprised to find herself the only person without a motorcycle. Everyone else had ridden here with no apparent difficulty, and Mrs. Morris wondered why they were bothering to take training at all. She also wondered whether she was the only person to have read the Motorcycling Safety leaflet which said that your first ride should be a properly supervised training ride, and that the shop should, therefore, deliver the machine to the training area. Certainly the youth who drove up with her shiny new Handy Rider in the back of his van had a slightly resentful air, as if he did not expect to have to do this kind of thing on Sunday mornings.

He set the bike on its stand and asked her to sign for it. He smelled of coffee, as if his breakfast had been interrupted. Mrs. Morris remembered with a pang the pile of pancakes she had left in the warm oven at home and thought of the family sitting round to enjoy them. Pancakes were a treat.

"*Where's* she gone?"

"To church, she said."

(Mrs. Morris wasn't happy with this, but it was all she could think of.)

"She doesn't go to church. I think she's got a lover."

"She does at Christmas."

"It's July and she was wearing trousers. It's a lover, I tell you."

"Perhaps. Mrs. Morris sidled round her Handy Rider, viewing it from all angles. For now she felt a little shy.

The instructors were arranging orange and white cones in lines and shapes in the car park. Mrs. Morris had often seen similar cones on busy roads, marking off the sites of accidents.

113

"This is the figure of eight," said an instructor called Dave. "And this is the slalom. Find your own speed, don't hit the cones, pick them up if you do and try not to put your foot down. One at a time now, off you go."

"Er, David," said Mrs. Morris, approaching him on foot.

"Yes, my love."

"That's my moped."

"And a very nice moped it looks too."

"Could you show me how to start it?"

He looked at her in amazement. She pulled off her helmet, hoping her grey hairs would provide sufficient explanation.

"You do drive a car?" he said suspiciously.

"No. Only a push-bike," said Mrs. Morris. "I'm a family joke." The youngsters were sailing round the cones. What was she doing here?

Dave seemed to be asking himself the same question. He went to consult his colleagues about it, having first said, "Wait there." Where did he think she would go?

"I think a spot of one-to-one tuition is called for," he said, returning.

She was grateful but she said: "What about the others?"

"Don't you worry about them. Now, before we learn to start, we learn to stop. This is the front brake and this is the back brake. Be sure and apply the front brake a fraction of a second before the back otherwise the wheels may lock, particularly if you're travelling at high speeds."

"But I wouldn't."

"Wouldn't what?"

"Travel at high speeds. This is a moped, it only does thirty."

"Dangerous, that," said Dave.

"What?" gasped Mrs. Morris.

"To look at it, you'd think it had more poke. If a motorist overestimates how much acceleration you've got, you could be in trouble. Ever think of getting one of those Polka Pop Pop things?"

"They look like toys," said mrs. Morris.

"Exactly, so there's no danger of motorists taking them seriously. Never mind, what's bought's bought, this is your throttle. You move it slowly towards you for more speed. If you take your hand off it it slows down automatically, like the dead man's handle on a train."

Mrs. Morris rode her moped across the car park. Dave had to walk quite fast to catch up. "Didn't hurt, did it?" he grinned.

"Oh!" breathed Mrs. Morris, her cheeks burning, hair escaping from her helmet. "Oh!"

"Now you can have a try at the cones. Get yourself a pair of gloves for next time. Even cheap ones'll save you a layer of skin if you come off."

Steering round the first cone was exhilaratingly easy. But she misjudged the second. Realizing she was not going to get round without hitting it, she put her foot down but forgot to decelerate at the same time. The asphalt came up to meet her.

She lay beneath her Handy Rider. Dark drops of liquid spattered the ground. Blood? No, petrol. The engine had stopped running too, so the bike was obviously damaged. It might even be a write-off, and her insurance was only Third Party, Fire and Theft, so she would not be able to replace it. Ah well. Buying it had been as good a use as any for her nest-egg, a brave try that had taught her something about herself — or rather, confirmed what she had long suspected. There were some people in the world who were meant to travel under their own steam, and others who were meant to accept lifts and use public transport. Mrs. Morris belonged to the latter group. She tested her limbs one by one, preparatory to getting up. They seemed to work. Her hands were not even grazed.

She hauled the bike upright. Dave grinned, arms folded. He did not help her.

"It works," he said.

"What does?" She tried to glance unobtrusively at her watch.

"The Automatic Impact Cutout on the engine. You were just testing it, weren't you?"

"No," said Mrs. Morris.

"Yes," said Dave. "You're not hurt."

"But shouldn't I get the, er, alignment checked, before I ride it again?"

"Get on," said Dave, "and ride round those cones."

"The mirrors are bent."

"Good. Let them stay bent. They're the most dangerous part of a motorbike, in my opinion. The mirrors."

"Why?" said Mrs. Morris, with great interest. "What if I want to see behind?" At least while they were discussing mirrors, she wasn't having to ride.

"If you need to see behind, look behind. Get your head on a swivel. Keep looking behind. I'll show you what I mean. If I hadn't forbidden you to use mirrors, how would you use them?"

Mrs. Morris recognized a trick to get her sitting on the bike again. Reluctantly she got on, but she kept her feet on the ground and the keys in her pocket. Dave stood behind her, and told her to adjust her mirrors until she had them the way she thought she wanted them. She had a feeling she was being set up.

"I'm a car," he said. "Coming along behind you, wanting to overtake. Can you see me?"

"Yes."

"I'm getting closer. Can you see me now?"

"Yes."

"Now?"

"No."

"There you are then. I'm in your blind spot. According to your mirror, I'm not here. Suppose you decide now to pull out or turn right. Whoomph!" He drove his clenched fist into his palm with a loud smack. "Our time's nearly up. Ready to ride home?"

"What?" said Mrs. Morris. "Pardon? I couldn't even stay on in the car park."

"That was nothing. Ride it home, go on, if you leave it here you'll never see it again."

If it gets stolen, she thought, *I'll get my money back.*

"It probably doesn't work any more," she said.

"You hope," he jeered. "All right, I'll make a deal with you. Ride three perfect figure-of-eights, now, and I'll take your bike to my place and look after it for you till next week. And *next* week, *you will ride it home.*"

It worked perfectly.

"I want to see the whites of your eyes," said Dave, the

116

following week, preparing her to ride round a block of left turns. "I want those mirrors bent so that you can't use them, and I want to see you turn round and *look*. I'll be driving behind you so you're quite safe, but forget it's me. Pretend it's a lunatic. Pretend everyone else on the road is a lunatic."

Pretend! she thought, chugging round the block. People hooted at her and whizzed by. She approached the corner. She wobbled as she looked behind but the sight of Dave's car steadied and reassured her. She flicked on her left indicator. In the time it took her to do this somebody might have sneaked in, so she looked again. She made her turn.

"Fine," said Dave. "Two things. You're a bit unsteady."

"I can't help wobbling when I look behind."

"And you're riding in the gutter."

"But people get annoyed if they can't overtake."

"You own that thing," said Dave, "and you're licensed to ride it. It's taxed and insured, you pay income tax — "

"Well, my husband does," said Mrs. Morris.

" — and you have as much right to your bit of the road as a bus, the Prime Minister's Rolls or a tanker full of phenol. Is that understood? You can do some right turns now."

Mrs. Morris set off with gritted teeth. Word perfect on her Highway Code, she knew that the correct procedure before turning right was to position yourself just to the left of the middle of the road. That meant pulling out in front of the following car.

Still, as long as she knew that the following car was driven by Dave —

But it wasn't!

She had only shot a quick glance over her shoulder (to save wobbling) but she knew it was not Dave. Dave's car was green and this one was red.

Why had Dave abandoned her?

He wouldn't do such a thing. It must be her fault. She must have taken a wrong turning and lost him. But she hadn't taken any turnings yet. Soon she must: at the T-junction ahead she must go right, with a strange red car following her.

She forced herself to think calmly. Her memory of the red car was that it had been sufficiently far away that she could

117

safely signal and pull out. But that had been when she looked
. . . it might have put on speed since. Her mirrors, their stems
bent as instructed by Dave, told her nothing. She looked again.
The red car was still a fair distance away, but was it getting
nearer? How could she tell with the quick look which was all
her need to remain upright allowed her? To be on the safe side
she decided to let it overtake her first. But it didn't. What was it
waiting for? The driver couldn't know that she meant to turn
right, she hadn't signalled yet. The junction was almost upon
her. *She must signal her intentions.* She flicked on her right indicator but still she dared not pull out. She had no idea how the
red car was progressing, or whether the driver had finally lost
patience and was making a dash for the junction, and she dared
not risk losing her balance at a corner by looking again.
"Sorry," she muttered, changing indicators, "I meant left." And
she turned left. The driver of the red car came left too, giving
her a wide berth, a friendly beep and a wave as he went by. She
realized then that he hadn't been impatient at all; he'd seen her
L-plates and had been waiting for her to do what she wanted.
But how could she have known that?

Mrs. Morris stopped by the road. She wiped her brow and
thought for a long time. She knew exactly what to do. The
question was, when would she do it?

Dave's familiar green car went by and pulled up ahead of
her. He got out and approached her with an irritable expression, *"Now* what are you doing?"

"Sorry, Dave, I lost you and then I lost my nerve."

"What are you doing with those mirrors?"

"Adjusting them," said Mrs. Morris. "I've decided I'd like to
use them after all."

"I've told you not to use them! There's no point in you coming on this course if you're just going to go your own sweet way.
The mirrors are the most dangerous—"

"Not for me," said Mrs. Morris.

Dave stared.

"Dave, I'm sure your advice is very good advice, a life-saver
in fact, for some people. Those youngsters who look as if they
were born on motorbikes must be taught caution. But I'm so
cautious it's taken me forty years to get this far."

"Yes, and if you want to live another forty, you'll do as you're told!"

"Dave." She patted his arm. "If I ever have an accident, do you think it will be caused by my reckless riding?"

"You obviously weren't listening when I told you about the blind spot," he grumbled, watching her adjust her mirrors. "You can't eliminate it so there's no point in trying."

"Here's what I have in mind," said Mrs. Morris. "I'm riding along and I want to turn. I look in my mirror and if I see anything even slightly dangerous I'll postpone the maneuver."

"You'll never get to where you want to go."

"I shall. I might be late, but the buses were always late anyway. Now, if the road appears to be clear, *then* I'll look round. As a sort of final check. But in the meantime the mirrors will give me a general picture and increase my confidence. And I won't lose my balance."

"Perhaps you'd like my job."

"No, you're a very good teacher, Dave."

"Thank you."

"It's just that you've been teaching me the wrong things."

For the rest of the session, the mirrors were not discussed. He put her on roundabouts, left turns, right turns and straight on. He stood glaring on the central island. She used her mirrors in the way she had planned, but as long as she glanced over her shoulder as well, he made no comment.

"You going to ride that thing home today?" he inquired.

"I think so," said Mrs. Morris.

"See you next time, then," he grinned. "Be brave."

It was something that he said *be brave,* and not *be careful.*

Brave! Compared with what she'd said to him, the dual carriageway and the three-lane roundabout ahead were as nothing. She'd actually looked him in the eye and said *you've been teaching me the wrong things!* But he *had* been. He'd been so busy telling her to look behind that he'd neglected to mention what for. He'd stated the obvious—that you shouldn't pull out when something was in the act of overtaking—but who would, for heaven's sake? those eager youngsters might, but not Mrs. Morris. He'd been teaching her as if she were an entirely dif-

119

ferent person. He hadn't mentioned, in all his fussing over the different ways of looking behind, that if, however you looked, you *saw* something, it didn't necessarily mean that you had to abandon the maneuver, as Mrs. Morris had abandoned her right turn when she saw the red car. The fact that a vehicle was visible in your mirror might, on the contrary, mean that it was safe to proceed, for if it was in your mirror it followed that it was not in your blind spot! And if it stayed in the same place in your mirror, it followed that it was not accelerating. And if you watched it for several seconds in your mirror you would see whether or not it was signalling, a poing you might miss with a swift glance. And there was another point he had not made with regard to her own signalling: that a signal was a declaration of intent, not a request for permission.

Her mirror was clear. She glanced behind and moved off. The roads were quiet. She tried not to think about the dual carriageway ahead, and the three-lane roundabout that lay unavoidably between her and her home. "No two roundabouts are alike," Dave's voice warned in her head. There he went again. It was probably the right thing to say to a youth on a Throbber, but what Mrs. Morris needed to remember was that the same Highway Code rules applied to all roundabouts, and everyone had learned them, and no one wanted to die, and no one wanted to kill Mrs. Morris.

Before she reached the dual carriageway, there was one more thing she had to do. She stopped at a call box and phoned home.

"It's Mum," she said.

"Hello, Mum, where are you?"

"Nowhere. I want you all in the front garden in fifteen minutes."

"What for?"

"What for, what for? Why don't you do as you're told, for once?"

There wasn't much traffic on the dual carriageway, but what there was was moving fast. Twice she considered moving into the right lane in preparation for the roundabout, but abandoned the idea having spotted something coming at speed in her mirror. She almost resigned herself to staying in the left hand lane, going left at the roundabout, going round the block and trying again, but the thought of her family waiting, impatient but expectant and all unbeknownst, for the most astonishing spectacle of their lives, spurred her on.

They wouldn't wait for ever.

They'd say, *oh, it's just Mum being silly again. She's probably bought herself a new dress. We can admire it just as well inside.* And they'd go in.

I will let one more car overtake me, she thought. *And then I will signal to announce that I intend to pull out and then I will do it.*

They've no business going so fast near a roundabout. I have a perfect right to change lanes.

Flinching from the imagined impact of a fast-moving car in the rear of the Handy Rider, Mrs. Morris pulled out to the right and took the roundabout exactly as the Highway Code said she should.

The rest of the journey was like falling off a log.

Riding a moped, she chuckled to herself. *It's like falling off a log! This is ME!*

She turned the corner of her road and saw her family standing in the garden.

She checked her mirror, glanced behind, signalled left and came to a smooth halt by the curb. They seemed not to notice. She switched off her engine. They were still staring along the road. She took off her helmet.

"Hello," she said.

For a long time nobody spoke.

Then her son stepped forward and inspected the controls on the Handy Rider.

"Hey, Mum, can I have a go?"

"No," she sighed. "You have to have lessons."

Her Wild Barbarian Heart

MARTHA SHELLEY

She's naked. The upholstery of the car scratches her thighs. The driver is wearing a black turtleneck under his jacket, young and expensively casual. They're in an apartment house garage, he lives upstairs, she's known him for years though his face is generic and his name skitters off into darkness. He pushes the remote button. A motor throbs. The garage door slides along its tracks, opens to disgorge them, then a squad of men with Uzis step out of the shadows, surround the car and drag her out while her friend sits silent and helpless behind the wheel . . .

Heart in her throat, Sandy forces an arm out from under the blankets and fingers the night table lightly till she finds her glasses. The room snaps into focus: posters, a vase of feathers and Indian combs, shells on the dresser, amulets that make it safe to contemplate weirdness. Not the gunmen—she has a special dream category for them along with axe murderers and S.S. officers. But what friend drove the car, who is this man so close she'd let herself sit naked beside him?

Then she remembers, today's the tournament. Slippers on, robe on, kitchen light, kettle. Carefully she spoons out yogurt and granola, wondering if she stuffed enough carbs last night. Last week they'd talked about carbohydrate loading after class, after Sensei volunteered four of his students for the competition. Next Sunday, he told them.

She remembers her stomach turning over. She smiled and said, "Next Sunday, 1993?"

He smiled right back. "You'll be too old and decrepit then."

"What do you think I am now?" she complained. But she knows he's right. She is 45, starting judo again at an age when others are finding gentler ways to play.

Sandy finishes her tea. Her stomach is crawling up her spine and she pads into the living room and flips through her records till she finds the Black Watch Regiment. She sets the needle down at "Scotland the Brave." Monster speakers — her lover Bettina's speakers — shake the floor beneath her, drums command her pulse and she sings with the bagpipes' wailing:

Bom Bom da Rum dum dum dum

marching through valleys shrouded in sulfurous smoke, the rhythm of cannon fire driving opponents across the judo mat, burning the fear away and the glowing center of her roars I WANT TO WIN. Win with a foot sweep, hip sweep, shoulder throw, seeing them fly through the walls on all sides —

"Would you mind turning the volume down?" Bettina asks.

"Oh. You're up already."

"No, I'm standing here sound asleep, watching you fight your way across the highlands at 7:00 a.m. on Sunday morning. I hope the neighbors find this equally amusing."

"Okay, okay. I gotta leave in 15 minutes anyway." Sandy grabs her jacket, wallet, keys. She's galloping down the stairs when Bettina calls after her, "Hey, don't forget your judo gi."

It really is called The Martinez Boys' and Girls' Club, she thinks. The words on the building are carved in solemn granite, as if it had never been just The Boys' Club all through her growing up. They won't know what it means to be left out, she muses, joyous and wistful at once.

In the gym the youngest kids are on the mat already, two pairs of boys on either side, a couple of girls in the middle. She watches the girls avidly. The one with thick ringlets keeps pinning the pony-tailed girl who always wriggles out in time, and finally the referee gives it to Ringlets by decision.

My hair was like that at her age, Sandy thinks.

In first grade she wears it tied with bits of ribbon and every day Joel down the street catches her on the way to school, pulls her braids till she cries, or else yanks up her dress. She dreads passing his house. Even when Mama complains to Joel's mom it doesn't help. Then one day he reaches out to grab at her and she turns and whacks him over the head with her lunch box, and he runs in circles crying as she hits him again and again, howling delicious revenge chasing him all the way home.

She scans the audience. Sensei over on the right, next to him Big Mike doing stretches and Mary bundled up in a sweatsuit under her gi, drinking tea from a thermos. Somebody calls her name and it's Joan from New York, her friend for the last 15 years, Joan the anthropologist who thinks judo is rather like an Aztec sacrifice but has shown up anyway to cheer her on.

"What do you think?" Sandy asks.

"It's very hard to take," Joan says. "I almost have to physically restrain myself. The mother in me keeps wanting to run up and separate those kids. I want to scold them, 'Children, children! That's not the way to solve your problems!'"

Sandy laughs. "But it's not real violence. It's very controlled, very ritualized. So they don't hurt each other. It's just another organized sport, like—"

"Kill him! Kill him!" A woman in the front row rises to her feet, screaming at her son.

"—just like the Little League."

"I see," Joan says.

No she doesn't. They never do. Mom said judo was ugly and that woman therapist said I was hostile. And Cynthia with all her talk of non-violence, keeping two lovers on a string and finally dumping us both for a man. They sit in the Artemis Cafe and blather about the Great Mother as if She is only the Breasted One at Ephesus and not also the Hunter, the puma Her daughter as well as the deer.

Then she thinks, Joan is here. She's got a heart condition and she's freaked out but she came to support you. She puts her arm in Joan's and they sit together silently, then Joan disengages. "I know there must be underlying order," she says, "but it seems so chaotic."

"What do you mean?"

"Just look."

Sandy tries to see it through Joan's eyes. A cavernous gym, a noisy mob, some in street dress and some in white pajamas with belts of various hue. Pajama-people wander through the crowd chatting with their friends, lounge in the ante-room or tape their toes together, do exercises (but not in unison). Three mats in the center, a three-ring circus of scuffling children and grownups yelling commands in Japanese. A restless kid does cartwheels, a sound system bounces announcements off the naked walls.

"And you seem so calm. An island of serenity," Joan says.

"Only because I didn't eat enough to throw up."

"Well, do you know who you're going to compete against?"

"No idea. I haven't seen many women white belts. And if I have to go against the brown belts, I'll get creamed."

Sandy registers and changes into her gi, stretches, jogs in place till Mary offers her tea, saying, "Don't wear yourself out before the match. It's important to keep your heart calm."

A surprise from skinny Mary, Mary who is finally going to her first tourney. Week after week Sensei would pin her to the mat, hold her down and yell at her, "C'mon, struggle, get out! You wanna be on the bottom all your life!" Sandy's cheeks flamed at his words. She didn't know if he meant to target her, too, but they stung, they sting even now, an evocation of her life's defeats, love and friendship betrayed, the politics of her generation cashed in for a fix or a steady gig.

She lies down and shuts her eyes. *The bagpipes start up again and her pulse races till she can hardly breathe and she forces herself to remember the Marble Mountains, she is floating on Wild Lake still a little chilly in July, inhale and bob up, exhale and sink, sunlight pouring orange and pink through her closed lids . . .*

"Hey, look who finally showed up," Mary says.

Sandy raises her head.

"The party didn't end till two o'clock," Alonzo says, shifting from one foot to another, swinging his gi by the belt. "I just got out of bed an hour ago."

"Well, I hope it's not too late for you to register."

"They'll take my money," he says confidently and disappears into the crowd.

Floating . . . a sweltering night in July. They're cruising up the Hudson, a boat party thrown by a women's magazine. Naively she expects to mingle with feminist writers but this is business, writers are decoration and the real guests are advertising men. She tries to drown their vibes in double scotches, rocking to the music with her lover, reveling in her own sweat and the big brass moon . . .

Someone objects to their dancing together. Later she finds out he'd been standing there maybe 15 minutes muttering obscenities and then he selects the shorter of the two, steps out in front of Sandy sneering

"Why don't you go hang yourself?"

and she knocks the drink from his hand, slams into him and he goes backwards down the metal staircase and is saved falling into a couple ascending from the lower deck. She's grateful that he hasn't broken his neck and she won't go to jail. But the savage in her is roaring with delight, awakened after years of schooling and smiling, only regretful that he hasn't broken his neck, isn't lying in a pool of his own blood. In the morning she swears off liquor, but the magazine bans her from future parties.

Then she punches the next guy who hassles her on the street and ends up with two black eyes, and she swears she'll take up karate.

"Oh, that poor kid," Joan says. "He's really scared."

Sandy rolls over on her side and sees a small boy standing on the mat, weeping uncontrollably. His opponent is waiting, the ref and the judges are waiting. His teacher takes him aside, hugs him and whispers in his ear. Then the boy wipes his face with his sleeve, goes on to win by a throw.

"Kids are so up front with their feelings," Mary says. "They don't stuff 'em down the way we do."

She lies back and thinks about slowing her breathing, inhale count four, exhale count six, inhale six, exhale eight. . . .

She's coming home after her first karate lesson. A long walk across lower Manhattan, the light descending from periwinkle to indigo and she hears someone walking behind her. She cocks her head a little, not breaking stride, checking him from the corner of her eye. In one hand he's clenching a stick thick as her thumb. The other grips a heavy chain with a German shepherd on the end of it. He throws the stick along the street, loosens the chain. Dog fetches the stick. Keep walking. There's nobody else on the street, nothing else to do.

She hears the stick coming again just as it smacks the back of her legs. She turns to face him, takes the stance she has learned in class that day. One hand up, one down. It is all she knows. Tonight I will live or die on 14th Street, she thinks, and a strange calm comes over her.

He draws to a halt, tightens the chain on his dog. His eyes bug out.

"Oh. You know karate," he says, and hurries away.

A burst of applause breaks her reverie. Somebody just got a throw, she thinks. A good clean throw. The audience loves it; it's the best way to win. She sits up too late, of course: the contestants are bowing, walking off the mat.

The music is starting again and she looks up at the ceiling to calm down, looks at the lake, the mountains where every summer she stumbled into poison oak and every winter hiking the East Bay Parks . . . *Why did I do that?,* she thinks, *walking blindly into weeks of pain? And why when Marilyn left me did I go after Cynthia, even when she said she was a taker I kept giving, even when she had another woman I kept wanting. And when she left me too I lay in bed blowing dope for days, not wanting to get up, thinking I was destined to be a world-class loser.*

Her eyes fill, the ceiling lights blur and shimmer. *She is in the dojo, in a line of students sitting on their knees. "What I love about judo," Sensei lectured, "is that you get thrown. You're crushed, you're beaten, utterly defeated. But you get up and do it again, a hundred times, a thousand times. And still you get up." And you did,* she thinks, *you got out of bed and went back to judo. You learned not to be there when the blow came. And you go to the mountains every summer and you haven't had poison oak in the last three years, not since you moved in with Bettina.*

That's what I need to tell Joan, she thinks, but before she can speak they're calling her name and Mary's. She jumps up and hurries across the gym to present herself. They tell her to sit by the timekeeper's bench.

The music begins again and her heart starts to race. With an effort of will, she shuts the tape. The music is her talisman, she'll turn it on when the match begins and she won't be afraid.

Her name again. She looks up, startled. "Me?" The timekeeper nods and she leaves her glasses on the table. The audience disappears into a multicolored fog. It's just Sandy and Mary and the referee.

She bows and the bow is peace, a split second of deepest tranquility.

"Hajime!"

Now it's just the two of them. She doesn't want to fight Mary, doesn't want to beat someone from her own school.

They are evenly matched in the dojo, Mary's superior technique offsetting Sandy's extra 30 pounds, a question of who loses concentration first. *The music is gone. There is nothing in her but wanting to win, searching for that opening, the unguarded space to lead Mary into a fall. It isn't Mary anymore, it's The Opponent and they are both down on the mat and Sandy is on top of her, in for a pin, all the weight focused on the neck like Sensei says, sinking into the earth and holding, holding, holding . . .* Then the ref is tapping her on the shoulder and it is done.

She gets up and bows. She can hardly look at Mary as they walk off the mat.

She leans against the wall behind the timekeeper's table, panting, unable to slow the beating of her heart. Don't let them call me right away, she pleads, to no one in particular. At least one match in between to rest.

Three sets of men go on, then they call Sandy's name and someone named Marguerite, a girl of 18.

Marguerite stares at her, horrified. "Why do I have to fight this one?" she demands. "She weighs 150 and I'm only 106."

"It doesn't matter to me," Sandy says, thinking she'd be relieved to get dressed and go home. But what about the brown belts?

"You have to fight the women in your ranking," the timekeeper says to Marguerite.

"Don't throw me hard," the girl pleads. "I hurt my back this week."

Then why are you here? Sandy thinks, but she keeps silent.

"Throw her fast and get it over with," Mary whispers impatiently.

Sandy is waiting for the ref to start, wondering if she can throw the girl without hurting her, and then thinking Let her take care of her own back, not giving a damn, wanting even to hurt, willing to do what she must to win.

Marguerite fights like a wrestler, she's bent over and going for the knees and Sandy thinks *tomoe-nage* but she's afraid to try sacrifice throws, she's never done them well and doesn't want to end up on her back. She tries to lead the girl into a foot-sweep but they stumble down to the mat instead and Marguerite thrusts her fingers in Sandy's face and the ref calls a foul. Then they're up, circling each other and getting nowhere and down again and Marguerite tries to choke her but Sandy just pulls her hands away and settles in for the pin. Someone is counting, 27, 28, 29, 30, *ippon!*

"Good job," she tells Marguerite as they're leaving the mat, "I couldn't get close enough to throw you." But inside she's sneering, What a whiner. She didn't deserve to win. And then she's ashamed of her thoughts, and then confused.

"What next?" she asks the timekeeper.

"That's it. You took first place."

"But what about the brown belts?"

"They're too advanced. You stay within your rank."

Back with her classmates. Sensei offers his congratulations. She laughs with the driver in her dream and holds out her trophy. "This is the first time I won something for being overweight. Sitting on a kid half my size. Or maybe I deserve it for dragging my ancient ass on the mat."

Mary offers her a cup of tea. "Your hands are trembling, too," she observes.

"Of course," Sandy says. She can change now, take off her gi and her kneepads and stuff them in the shopping bag with her first athletic trophy, a tin man on a plastic pedestal. She laughs at it. She's glad the day's over, doesn't ever want to go through this again. I'm getting too old for adolescent games, she thinks. But the wild barbarian heart of her is singing, Next time, wait till next time. I'm going to win by a good clean throw.

The Great Shakedown

JUDY FREESPIRIT

Fifteen. I think that's about the time I started the great shakedown. When I was fifteen years old I found a copy of a book my mother had taken out of the library, and began reading it. It was entitled *King's Row* and in it I found, for the first time, the word for what my father and I had been doing for the past ten years. The word was "incest," and seeing it written on the page made me feel overwhelmingly relieved. If there was a word for it, I must not be the only person in the world who had done it.

I cried off and on for several days after that, and finally decided I would put an end to the game which by this time had escalated to include penile penetration and pre-ejaculation withdrawal. I had been taken advantage of, and I knew it. But I needed to figure a way to finish it for good.

The next time my mother was out and my father approached me I pulled away teasingly and said, "I feel like I'm being used. I think you ought to pay me for my services. After all, if you didn't have me you'd have to pay a prostitute." To my surprise my father never even hesitated before asking, "How much do you want?" I had to think fast. "Ten dollars," I said and he smiled a little as he pulled a roll of bills from his pocket and peeled off a ten, handed it to me then took my hand and led me

130

to the bedroom.

The next time I asked for fifteen dollars, then for twenty dollars. When I reached twenty-five he balked.

"That's too much. I won't pay."

"OK," I said, "then go to a prostitute."

Much to my relief that was all there was to it. I'm not sure why, but I wouldn't be surprised if he was relieved to have the whole episode finished as well. He never tried it again, except for one time about five years later when I was home from college. My mother was in the hospital for a hysterectomy. He came into my room after I was in bed and looked directly into my eyes.

"I'm really lost without your mother," he told me. "Won't you make me happy just this one time—for old time's sake. I won't ask you again."

Even though I refused him and sent him away, I almost felt sorry for him. That was the very last time he ever mentioned it.

When I was twenty-one I married Felix. Shortly before our wedding I told him about my sexual relationship with my father. He seemed upset about it, but he obviously didn't know what to do and, as was his way, he never mentioned it again. When I alluded to it on rare occasions during the next fourteen years, he seemed uneasy, but never said anything and I never pressured him. I think I must have figured that it was not such a big deal. I was good at that denial business and so was Felix.

I also told several male shrinks over the years as I struggled through individual and group therapy, trying to sort out my unhappiness, which was pervasive in spite of my "perfect" marriage. But they weren't any help. Then I found Robert. He was a psychologist and former minister who I met at the height of what was sometimes referred to as "the Human Potentials Movement" in the late 1960s. Robert ran marathon therapy sessions which each took place over an entire weekend.

At my first marathon there were ten men and women. My most vivid memory of that event took place toward the end of the weekend, as we were all sitting in a circle on couches, chairs and large floor cushions. I was in a chair, sitting on the opposite side of the room from Robert. I don't remember how the subject came up but at one point I mentioned that my father and I "had a sexual relationship" and the room became electric.

"And how do you feel about that," Robert asked as he leaned forward and looked directly into my eyes.

"Well," I said, trying to look cool but feeling very nervous, "it was a long time ago. I don't know that I have any feelings about it. I guess I've worked it through."

"What about your feelings toward your father," he pursued.

"Oh I don't feel very much about him. Mainly I just feel sort of sorry for him. He didn't do anything really violent. I mean he didn't hurt me or anything."

"And you've never felt angry at him in all these years?" he asked.

"No. I'm not angry at all."

"I want you to put your father into this room and talk to him," Robert was saying, as I receded down a long cone shaped tunnel which seemed to be sucking me backward. "What do you want to say to your father?"

"Hi Dad," I said, giggling. "I don't know what else to say. I don't really have anything to tell him."

"Tell him how you feel about what he did to you."

"I can't do that, Robert. I don't feel anything."

I knew he wanted me to be feeling something and I wanted to please him, but I was cold as a rock and feeling like everything around me was getting dark. I could hardly get any air at all into my lungs. Why didn't he just go on to someone else? Why was he pushing me this way?

"You don't feel anything? Not anything at all?" His voice was getting louder.

"No, nothing," I insisted. "Should I be feeling something?" Now I was beginning to be angry at Robert, but I didn't want to tell him.

Then the most extraordinary thing happened. Robert stood up. He was a full six feet four inches in height and wearing a plaid flannel shirt, blue jeans and cowboy boots which made him even taller. His face was stern and his fists clenched as he started to walk slowly across the circle toward me. He kept walking until he was standing directly over me. His face was red, his bottom lip quivering and his eyes brimming with tears as he shouted, "I HATE YOUR FATHER FOR WHAT HE

DID TO YOU. I HATE HIM. DO YOU HEAR ME? I HATE HIM FOR WHAT HE DID TO YOU." Then his shoulders slumped and his whole body became wracked with sobs as the tears streamed down his face. I just sat there watching him in stunned silence as several of the group members rose and went to him. As they held him he wept aloud in anguish.

Several months later Felix and I were together at another of Robert's marathons, in another livingroom with a different group of people. By this time I had begun to recognize a great many feelings and had come to terms with some of them. Felix was skeptical, but he had seen dramatic changes in me that made him curious to see what happened at these sessions. I was talking again about how my childhood sexual experiences with my father had affected me.

"I don't think it's had much of an effect," I was saying. "I mean I did hold in my anger at him, but now that I've gotten in touch with that and expressed it, I think things are fine. Really."

"Do you mean that?" Robert prodded.

"Well, maybe I do feel a little held down because of it. I mean I probably could be doing more with my life. I feel somehow like I've been held back . . . held down. I don't know how else to put it."

Robert was sitting on the floor in front of the fireplace. "I'd like you to come and lie here on the floor in front of me," he told me.

I walked to where he was sitting and lay on my back on the carpeted floor with my feet toward him.

"Now," he said, "I'd like all the men in the room to come and sit around Marsha." I heard them moving toward me and felt the floor vibrating beneath my body as they surrounded me.

"OK, now I'd like each of you to put your hands on Marsha and hold her down."

Felix was holding my left arm. I could see that Robert had one of my ankles in each of his big hands. Other men held my right arm, my shoulders and my thighs. There must have been about six of them, and for a few seconds I just lay there thinking how silly this was. Then, the thought occurred to me that I had two choices: I could just stay as I was in this passive position or I could try to get up. In a split second I decided I was going to get up. First I attempted to raise my arms, but they were pinned firmly to the floor.

"Let me up," I said as I tried to raise my feet. I squirmed but I was held firmly on the floor. "Let me up, goddamn it," I shouted as I struggled to get free. Then suddenly something in me exploded and I was fighting with all my might as sounds roared from my mouth. "I'LL KILL YOU, YOU HEAR ME, I'LL KILL YOU" I shouted from deep inside in a voice I had never heard before. "LET ME THE FUCK UP YOU MOTHERFUCKERS OR I'll KILL YOU. I'LL KILL YOU. I HATE YOU. GODDAMN YOU I'LL KILL YOU!"

This probably went on for only a few minutes, but I was totally soaked with sweat when I finally stopped struggling. The men around me were all breathing heavily and looking dazed. Felix said, "I didn't know, I didn't know, I didn't know," over and over again.

"OK," Robert said, "you can let her go now." I could feel them all move away from me as I lay there panting. After what seemed to be a very long time I slowly sat up. I could feel Robert looking at me but I couldn't look at his face.

"What do you want now?" he asked me.

"I don't know."

"What do you want?" he repeated.

I felt like a child again. Finally, I raised my head and looked at him. The numbness was returning and I both welcomed and dreaded it.

"I'd like you to hold me," I said very softly.

He opened his arms and I crawled up to him and was immediately surrounded by his big body. Then he rocked me gently as I sat there, curled up in his arms. He made no sound, but I could feel his rib cage quivering with sobs, and when I finally rose to move back into the circle, my hair was wet with his tears. He had cried for me. Once again Robert had done what I had been unable to do for myself. I would be forever changed.

The Steps Involved in Falling

Teresa Noelle Roberts

The clear sky is like crisp blue cotton overhead. It's a sunny day, but the air is cool, with an insistent, pleasant breeze. The lone climber pulls herself onto the rock ledge, brushes off her hands on her thighs, and looks back at where she came from. Below her, the creek gleams in the sun. The last time she climbed here, in the fall, the creek was just a trickle, but that was a winter ago. Today, its roar followed her halfway to this ledge.

She gulps water from her canteen and tries to catch her breath. She didn't stop to rest at all during the climb — stupid of her, expecially since she's climbing alone. She hasn't done anything that foolhardy since she was fourteen and she climbed this same mountain, this same rock face, by herself. Back then, the climb had really been too difficult to do on her own, and she'd been filled with a wild bravado born of panic; the next day, she'd had to leave Vermont and go to New York City, prep school, her aunt and uncle's flat, skyless world. Now this peak is an old friend, easy compared to the climbing she's done in her four years in Colorado. Still, she sees in herself that fourteen-year-old, tempting the fates with her daring. Or should she call it cowardice? The prospect of New York City seems to have this effect on her.

Don't think about it. Drawing a deep breath, she throws her head back to gaze at the brilliant blue above her. The wind stings her sweaty face, but it feels good. Antiseptic in a cut.

Nervously, she pushes one strand of fair hair out of her eyes. She'd have thought that it would be easier to control now that it was short, but she can't get used to how it waves and rebels now in the damp Manhattan spring. She runs her fingers through the mop, feeling the sweat and grime caked there from the long, humid day. The hair flops back down into her eyes. She gives up and begins to look around the room, studying its dinginess, the paint peeling off the far wall. It is airless here on the fourth floor, even with all the windows open and the rain falling in a gray, relentless stream outside. The unpleasant odors from Avenue D are reaching them without being carried by a breeze. Maybe by the end of the summer, if all goes well, some of the neighborhood will smell like flowers. As she stands up, she thinks lovingly of mountain air. It amazes her that it can be this warm before gardens have even been planted. But they should have been planted by now. The delay has been cleaning the field of cement and rusted metal, used needles and garbage.

Vertigo. Pure luck that, so close to the edge, she hadn't pitched forward into the roaring stream below. She peers down, half expecting to see her own broken body somewhere down the mountain. Of course, she wouldn't have fallen straight into the creek bed. The rock ledge juts up only about twenty feet. At the foot of the ledge, where she would have landed, is just a gradual slope, covered with grass. Well, grass and rock. You might survive a fall like that, but not without getting hurt. She inches back from the edge.

Closing her eyes, she forces herself to think about falling. The horror of feeling herself slip. Digging her fingers into the rock as if that could save her. Clawing at the air. The hideous smack that she might not hear when her head struck rock. Or maybe not. Maybe she'd just break a few bones. They say you can hear them snap. The long hours of waiting as the sun set and the small animals rustled nearer, for a rescuer she knew wouldn't come because, contrary to habit and good sense, she hadn't told anyone where she was going. It could be days before someone found her, days before she died. All the while they'd be waiting for her in New York.

She realizes she's shaking. She isn't sure why, though: *falling* or *New York*.

She looks at the room full of people. Almost all of them are dark-skinned. Most of them are older than she is, or at least seem older, sharper. A few weeks ago, they were all strangers to her, but now she can pick out familiar faces, people who have been interested in the community garden from the first. This evening, though, there are newcomers, people made curious, probably, by the work going on in the vacant lot. Some of the new people look bored already, but most of them watch her with a mixture of cynicism and hope, wanting her to say something useful or at least entertaining, but not really expecting it.

She's struck again, as she has been so often, by her own unspeakable arrogance in thinking she has something to offer to these people who know the poor streets of New York like she knows her favorite mountains. *This isn't your world*, she tells herself. *You may know about organic gardens, about green growing things, but you don't know what green growing things might mean to people who live here. You don't know much about anything.*

She looks down at her hands, small and square, but strong, and still scratched up from her last climb. She does know something about something, though she doesn't know yet if it's something she can share with the people she's meeting through the Community Gardens Project. She suspects they'll be teaching her more than she teaches them. For now, there are things she can explain to the newcomers, at least. That she can do.

She repeats to herself the steps involved in not-falling. Recognizing the vertigo. Breathing deeply to steady herself. Inching back to safety. Laughing, then and only then, at her panic. Reviewing with herself the steps involved in falling.

"We're going to need a lot of help to get this garden going," she says. "There's still plenty of garbage in the lot, and once

137

that's carted out, we have to prepare the soil. Does anyone know where we can get a lot of dead fish or manure?" A few people laugh, either with her or at her. Somebody yells that it's not so funny; they used stuff like that for fertilizer back in Puerto Rico and it worked. Someone suggests the fish markets downtown. An old woman mentions that police horses, the ones they use in the parks, have to live somewhere, and wherever there are horses, there's bound to be, er, fertilizer. At that, somebody else makes a rude suggestion about possible uses for cops, and she finds herself laughing. She doesn't remember, now, why these meetings scare her.

She isn't normally this nervous. She has faced the danger of falling for years now, knowing that some risk is involved in each climb. Perhaps it's the fact that she didn't tell anyone where she was going that makes her uneasy, or the idea of going to the city to start her training for the Community Gardens Project, or both. She wonders if the people she'll meet will understand at all when she talks about the mountains. As she thinks, she brushes a strand of hair, escaped from its braid, off her face. The dirt on her hand leaves behind a streak of war paint.

A wiry woman holding a baby starts to ask her a question, but breaks down, at a loss for words in English, and finishes in Spanish. She answers in Spanish. She speaks slowly, but is surprised by how easily the words come to her. She must have learned something at the University of Colorado besides how to climb in the Rockies. Perhaps, with practice, speaking Spanish will come as easily to her as finding a place to grip on what looks like a sheer cliff.

It's time for the ceremony she came here to perform. She opens her pack and dumps out an odd collection of objects: back issues of a wilderness magazine; a topographical map that has spent too much time in the rain; a stack of resumés; a high-necked blouse she'd worn on job interviews when she still thought she wanted a "professional" job; a pair of hiking shorts; a book of matches from a truck-stop outside of Boulder; a pair of scissors. She begins with the paper items, weighting them with twigs so they don't blow away in the brisk wind. Soon they are blazing merrily.

The blouse lingers in her hand. At her first interview with the Community Gardens Project, they'd asked her why someone who'd grown up on an organic farm in Vermont and who'd avoided New York except for her brief and miserable stay in prep school would want to bring gardens to the slums of the city. She'd answered that living in the country had taught her important things, and people who didn't have mountains or forests or farm fields needed something green to learn from, too. They gave her a second interview anyway, and then she had a sensible answer ready, about the Fresh Air kids they used to get on the farm, about the principles of organic gardening, about her parents' 1960s idealism, which they'd passed on to her. She still thinks her first answer is true. She also knows there is another motive for her going: she has been in nature so much that if she doesn't force herself to get away for a while, she may take it for granted. She needs a new challenge.

Does she really want to go to the city? She knows her motives aren't pure, they aren't altruistic. She's doing it to grow herself, not primarily to benefit others, although she's happy it may do that too. She never wanted to be a yuppy. But there are other ways to test herself. She could still back out, even though her training starts in thirty-six hours. She has choices that fall somewhere between this and her old, safe job, leading hiking parties outside of Boulder.

The blouse is still in her hands. She takes the scissors and cuts it in half. At least she knows what she doesn't want.

A teenager volunteers to get his friends organized to keep a watch on the young garden. "I don't know shit about gardening," he says, "but I know nothing's gonna grow around her unless it's got a lot of friends." He smiles significantly. She realizes she hadn't even thought of vandalism. Good thing that kid did, because of course the new garden, all neatly laid out, would be a temptation to vandals. Ignorance is dangerous. She needs to learn this place, or she will be as unsteady here as that young man, so confident here, would be on a rock face high above the ground.

The interview blouse is blazing away. She puts the scissors to the hiking shorts, but doesn't cut. They are still good gear, good memories, and besides, she won't be in New York City forever. She folds them up, puts them back into the pack, and settles down to watch her little fire. Gazing into the flames, she wonders if it requires new strategies to avoid falling off subway platforms or out of high, open windows. Does the warning of vertigo still come when you're surrounded by skyscrapers?

A Saturday in August

TERRI DE LA PEÑA

Approaching the grassy area near the Venice Pavilion, Alicia Orozco immediately noticed that she stood out among the other women registering to march in the ERA Walkathon that bright August morning. First of all, she was the only Chicana in sight. Secondly, anticipating warm weather, she had worn a ruffled tube top to complement her trim white shorts and matching sandals. Everyone else was sportily attired in green ERA T-shirts, baggy shorts, and scruffy jogging shoes.

Self-consciously, Alicia moved into the milling crowd of registrants, searching for the table designated for "L through O" entrants. In line, she glanced around, searching for a familiar face, though not really expecting to find one.

The week before, she had read a *Los Angeles Times* article about the walkathon which would raise funds for the Equal Rights Amendment. Considering herself a feminist though she had never belonged to any organized group, she had decided, instead of lying on the beach reading, to make this weekend's moments in the sun worthwhile.

At work, she had timidly secured some sponsors for the event, knowing if she pledged herself to walk in their behalf, she would not be able to talk herself out of attending. By no

141

means an extrovert, Alicia constantly had to resort to such tactics to pry herself out of her cozy apartment; otherwise, she would spend most of her time there alone, her dark head submerged in a book. Her participation in this event was one of many efforts to push herself into an active social life. Most of the young women she had grown up with either had married or moved away. Shy by nature, she had trouble making new friends.

After paying her registration fees and turning in her pledges, Alicia ambled among the participants. Many of them were the outdoorsy type, robust women with ruddy complexions. Others seemed like refugees from suburbia, their giggling children and stalwart husbands in tow. And, inspiringly, a sprinkling of elderly women stood out, their wrinkled faces a pleasant contrast in that swirling Venice sea of youth.

Pausing before one of the many tables set up to sell ERA T-shirts and buttons, Alicia considered a purchase, hoping to blend in; she already felt ridiculous in the frilly tube top.

"I'd buy one if I were you. Otherwise your shoulders'll be scorched. You have ten hot kilometers ahead of you."

Stiffening, Alicia at first did not turn her head, loathing the possibility of seeming indecisive enough to prompt a stranger's comments. However, she was curious to glimpse the owner of that slightly sing-song East L.A. accent; after all, she had not come to walk alone, but to make friends. She certainly had not counted on meeting another Chicana.

"What size do you think I should get?" Alicia at last met the other woman's eyes. She found herself confronting a lanky Chicana in an oversized "ERA NOW" T-shirt that nearly reached her bony knees. Alicia wondered whether the young woman wore shorts underneath that loose shirt.

"They all run big."

"I can see that," Alicia admitted slowly.

Grinning, the thin Chicana unfolded one of the shirts placed upon the table and held it against Alicia. "This one looks fine."

"Okay. I'll take it."

"Get a button, too," her new acquaintance advised. "One of those huge ERA ones."

Taking out her wallet, Alicia paid for a button and a T-shirt. Together, the Chicanas moved away from the table.

"I didn't see you here last year. This your first walkathon?"

"Yes."

"You here by yourself?"

Alicia nodded. "I don't know anyone who'd be interested in something like this."

"Same problem, more or less. We're the biggest minority in California, so how come you and me seem to be the only Chicanas here?" She extended her lean hand. "I'm Marti Villanueva."

"Alicia Orozco." Abashedly, she took that outstretched hand, surprised at the vigor in Marti's grasp. Eyes downcast, Alicia noticed Marti's limbs were sinewy, the legs of an experienced jogger, her calf muscles prominent.

"You from around here?" The difference in their heights caused Marti to slump a little to catch Alicia's modulated voice.

"West L.A."

"I'm from the Eastside, but I've lived in Venice a couple of years. I like it out here." Marti gestured towards Alicia's purchase. "You going to put that on?"

"Where are the restrooms?"

"Just pull the shirt over your head and slip off the tube. We're all women here. You can forget your hang-ups."

"What?" Alicia frowned at that last comment.

"You're shy, right? I picked up on that real fast."

"I'm not used to taking clothes off in front of other people."

"It's just a T-shirt," Marti responded in exasperation. "Look, the johns are over there." She pointed in their direction. "But save yourself a trip. I'll stand in front of you and, once you put the T-shirt on, you can start working off the tube. Or leave it on, if you want. The thing is, you'll get reall hot wearing a tube and a T-shirt."

At Marti's somewhat bossy tone, Alicia began to question the wisdom of ever speaking with this self-appointed mentor.

"I'd rather do it in the restroom."

"Suit yourself. I was just trying to help out." Marti shrugged, watching Alicia flounce away.

•

143

Because of the restroom lines, Alicia did not emerge until more than fifteen minutes later. By then, the walkathon rally was underway, featuring local politicians, feminists, and celebrities. Spotting a scarecrowish figure frantically waving in her direction, Alicia hesitated. However, knowing she would soon be on her feet for ten kilometers, she decided to take advantage of Marti's offer.

"I saved you a seat," Marti announced. "Soon's this kick-off's over, we'll start the walk. I can hardly wait. I get high on this kind of stuff."

Marti's teeth gleamed against her coppery complexion. Her ebony eyes were almond-shaped, topped by level unplucked eyebrows. Her somewhat aquiline nose gave her thin face a touch of dignity. She was not pretty by any means, yet the combination of her spindly figure, compelling eyes, and hawkish nose made her unforgettable.

Alicia wondered what Marti thought of her. Undoubtedly, she considered her a nonassertive wallflower type, afraid of her own shadow. Quiet and small-boned, Alicia realized she often gave that impression, but she had a quick temper in spite of her shyness. She was not afraid to lose it either, though she sometimes was embarrassed at the extent of her anger.

"So tell me about yourself, Alicia," Marti began when they finally had started moving northwards towards Santa Monica, strolling in the midst of hundreds of feminists.

"I'm a medical transcriber at the University hospital."

"Sounds boring."

Taken aback, Alicia was momentarily silent. "Actually, it's very informative, but it can be monotonous at times." She felt more at ease focusing on Marti. "What kind of work do you do?"

"Phone company stuff. I'm an installer. Couldn't stand being in an office all day. I need to move around a lot." She absently kicked a couple of pebbles out of her way; they scattered haphazardly. "Every time I'd have an office job, I'd get fired for goofing off. People distract me, you know? I work a lot better by myself. But sometimes I miss talking to somebody." In profile, her gaze was reflective. "Whenever I feel that way, I go to a NOW meeting or to a women's bar. That perks me up for a while at least. Ever been to a women's bar?" She asked abruptly.

"No. I don't drink."

"Figures."

"Pardon?" Alicia began feeling flustered by Marti's brusque attitude.

"You're like a lot of Westside Chicanas—uptight. There's nothing wrong with having a beer once in a while."

"I don't like the taste," Alicia reluctantly admitted.

"Not even with comida Mexicana? There's nothing like a cold beer with a couple of tacos y frijoles. You ought to try it sometime. Maybe after the walk we could have dinner together, huh?"

"If we're still speaking," Alicia thought. Aloud, she said, "I might be too tired." She realized that was a poor excuse.

"It's a great way to wind up the day," Marti retorted, undaunted. "Man, I'm sure going to be craving a beer after this is over. It can be a long haul in this heat. You should've worn better shoes, Alicia."

"I'll be fine. I walk around the campus a lot in these."

"Ten kilometers at once in those flimsy sandals? Good luck." Marti smirked, her even teeth showing. Unself-consciously, she scratched one of her small breasts, rubbing it from side to side. Alicia felt embarrassed by her companion's actions.

"I may not be in as great shape as you, but I intend to walk the whole ten kilometers." She was irked by Marti's mocking tone.

"Or limp or crawl, right?" Marti laughed. "Hell, I believe you, Alicia. Your feet'll be sore for days, that's all."

"That's my problem," she said cooly, tossing her head in the opposite direction. Alicia wondered why she was not lying on the sunny beach instead of loping along with this rather obnoxious stranger.

"What made you come here, anyway?" Marti seemed to shorten her strides for the smaller woman's benefit.

"I want the ERA to pass."

"Yeah. What else?"

"I want to meet other feminists."

"Chicanas?"

"Preferably."

"Straight or gay?"

"What?" Alicia glanced at Marti, her eyes widening.

"You heard me. Straight or gay? Are you looking for friends or lovers?" Her ebony eyes were unwavering, studying Alicia's bewildered expression. "You don't have to answer that right away. I'll give you some time to think about it."

"I don't know if I want to ever answer that," Alicia muttered, once more mentally berating herself for agreeing to join Marti and being subjected to her constant interrogation.

But her thoughts did not linger on her companion. Alicia was distracted by the women walking before and behind them. They had begun chanting: "What do we want? ERA! When do we want it? NOW!"

Glad for the respite, Alicia enthusiastically joined the chanters, though her shouts were nowhere as raucous as Marti's bellowing. Thin fist raised, Marti punctuated each yell with a stabbing motion, her dark face vividly expressing her convictions. Staring at her in amazement, Alicia felt both awed and repelled by her companion's obvious determination.

After several minutes of sustained feminist chants and songs, the moving formation of women, each wearing green and white, shared an easy camaraderie. Women on all sides of Alicia and Marti broke into spontaneous conversation. For the first time that day, Alicia truly felt a part of the gathering: accepted. She relished the warmth and friendliness of the other women, though she certainly felt some reservations about the tall, thin one beside her.

"Oh, hey! There's Delia. Haven't seen her in ages. Be right back, Alicia."

Without a backward glance, Marti hurried off, leaving Alicia with a mixture of relief and loneliness. Striding along, she again pondered the wisdom of continuing to share Marti's company. Although Alicia had realized lesbian feminists would be present at the walkathon, she had never considered actually meeting one. Suddenly torn between her genuine desire to know Chicanas with similar interests and her admittedly childish apprehension about lesbians, she deliberated about staying or going home. The latter alternative was an easy escape, but would accomplish nothing. However, the first alternative, though risky, would serve as a learning experience, if nothing else. Silently, Alicia studied the pros and cons of the situation. At last, deciding to stay, she plodded along, the morning sun relentlessly beating on her dark head. Already she felt her calf and thigh muscles tightening; she knew she was not limber enough for this trek. Sighing, she glanced around and wondered when—or if—Marti would return.

After the first few kilometers, one of the NOW organizing committees had set up a "water stop" to allow the participants a few moments of rest and refreshment. Gratefully, Alicia accepted a paper cup of cool water from a smiling volunteer and stiffly seated herself on the low concrete wall separating the walkway from one of the beach parking lots. She sat alone, intently scanning the crowd for any trace of Marti.

"There you are." She eventually heard Marti address her. "I figured you'd be lagging behind."

"I'm taking a rest," Alicia retorted tautly, her ambivalent feelings returning.

Unfazed by the cool response, Marti joined her, spindly legs outstretched. "So am I. I didn't feel too comfortable with Delia. We used to be close, but her new lover can't stand me."

Alicia slowly sipped water and did not answer.

Marti ran her long fingers through her black hair. "I'm gay."

"I thought so." Alicia stole a quick glance at her.

"Does it matter?"

"For what?"

"For walking with you today. What else? You seemed pretty uptight when I asked you those questions. That's really why I left you alone for a while."

Alicia put down the cup and turned to face her companion. "To give me a chance to 'think about it'?"

Marti grinned. "Yeah. Look, Alicia, I'm not going to pounce on you. I just felt so happy at seeing another Chicana that I started talking to you right away. Sometimes, I feel so isolated, you know? I belong to NOW and know other femi-

147

nists, but it seems like I'm always the only Chicana. I get tired of being a 'token,' even though I know most of the other women don't see me that way. But I stand out, you know? In more ways than one." She tugged at her ear lobe, her candid black eyes never leaving Alicia's own. "If I bug you, tell me. I don't want to spoil your day."

"You aren't. Honest, Marti. I'm just—nervous—I guess." Alicia lowered her gaze. "I never counted on this."

For a few seconds, neither woman spoke.

Rising to her full height, Marti abruptly stretched from side to side, reaching down to touch her toes in their battered Adidas. "Coming?"

"Sure." Alicia's voice was soft.

"It's better to stay with the main group instead of splintering off. Sometimes there're creeps out here to harass us."

"Oh." Alicia's eyes rounded.

"Don't get scared. They just like to call us 'dykes' or whatever—you know, to try to intimidate us. The best thing to do is ignore them, but I usually feel like slugging them in the mouth," Marti added when Alicia fell into step beside her. "Don't worry, though. I won't."

"Marti—"

"Yeah?"

"Were you—involved—with Delia?"

"For a while. Till she met Sandy. I've been on my own ever since. It's been about six months now."

"Do your parents know?"

Marti uttered a terse laugh, distinctly unmirthful. "I haven't seen them in two years. My father threw me out. That's why I left the Eastside."

Alicia winced. "And your mother—what was her reaction?"

"She prays for me, but doesn't want to see me."

"I'm sorry," Alicia murmured.

"You had nothing to do with it," Marti said flippantly.

"I know, but I'm sorry anyway. I'm Chicana, too, remember? When I moved out, my parents practically had heart attacks. They couldn't understand that I needed my privacy. They believe a Chicana only leaves her parents' home when she marries—or dies."

"Or is a lesbian," Marti added. "Right. But what do you do that's socially deviant—have a lot of wild orgies at your place?"

Alicia giggled. "No! I go to school at night, and need time to study after work. I just couldn't hit the books at home—with the TV blaring and the kids playing and everything. It's really ironic, Marti. In my parents' eyes, I am socially deviant."

"They'd really think so if they saw you talking to me."

"I don't care." Alicia's voice was firm.

"I like the way you said that," Marti retorted, her tone mellowing.

A sultry breeze tossed Alicia's shoulder-length brown hair. Brushing it aside, she looked at Marti again. "I mean it. My parents are narrow-minded. I try not to be."

"So I'm your self-improvement project for the day? Is that it?"

"Marti, no!"

Marti viewed her with amusement. "I'm just teasing. You get uptight so easy."

"No, I don't," Alicia insisted.

"Sure you do. Cómo están sus pies?"

"Así no más."

"I might have to carry you the last five kilometers."

"No way."

Marti laughed, her dark eyes crinkling.

After a couple more rest stops, much animated conversation and exchanged confidences, the two Chicanas began forming a burgeoning friendship. However, as Marti had predicted, Alicia's sandaled feet throbbed painfully. She finally removed the sandals and walked gingerly along the sand, her sore feet a bit soothed. Marti strode beside her, as limber as she had been at the start.

Laughing over one of Marti's irreverent comments, Alicia hardly noticed when her companion and the others began to slow down. When Marti clasped her arm, Alicia looked at her questioningly.

"What is it?" she whispered.

"Can't you hear them? Listen."

A resonant chorus of angry male voices punctuated the festive summer air. "Seig Heil! Seig Heil! Kill the dykes!"

"Put on your sandals, Alicia. Fast." Marti's demeanor rapidly became somber. She craned her neck to see over the women ahead. "We'll all link arms and walk in formation when we go by those bastards."

Fumblingly, Alicia buckled her sandals. With no hesitation, she put her arm through Marti's, and several other women joined them in a solid line. Beside Marti, she felt safe, strangely moved by the intimate touch of her companion's thin yet soft torso pressing against her own. Unwilling to explore her disconcerting thoughts, Alicia instead focused on the feminists, noting how the ones in front had begun chanting again as they passed the threatening protesters. In seconds, all the women had commenced the chant, unified, psyching themselves for the possibility of male onslaught.

The actual confrontation proved more frightening than Alicia had expected. Clean-cut Anglo youths in beach clothes formed a milling gauntlet on either side of the walkway, shouting Neo-Nazi and woman-hating slogans. To view that shouting throng of otherwise innocuous-looking young men, their faces contorted with hate, terrified Alicia. Trembling, she clung to Marti and the woman on her other side, concentrating on the chanting and the tremendous sense of sisterhood encompassing the feminists. Despite her fear, Alicia felt triumphant at the unity displayed by the hundreds of women marching together.

Later at the rally site, listening to the concluding speeches, she lay on the grass while Marti carefully removed the offending sandals and gently massaged her feet. Alicia closed her eyes at her companion's warm and comforting touch.

"I live a couple of blocks away. Come over, Alicia, and you can soak your feet while I go pick up some comida Mexicana. Then we can sit around, have a couple of beers while we eat, and talk some more. What do you say?"

"Sounds like a great idea," she said lazily, her tousled head supported by her arms. Meeting Marti's wide grin, Alicia smiled contentedly. She knew she had found a friend.

Ruthy and Edie

GRACE PALEY

One day in the Bronx two small girls named Edie and Ruthy were sitting on the stoop steps. They were talking about the real world of boys. Because of this, they kept their skirts pulled tight around their knees. A gang of boys who lived across the street spent at least one hour of every Saturday afternoon pulling up girls' dresses. They needed to see the color of a girl's underpants in order to scream outside the candy store, Edie wears pink panties.

Ruthy said, anyway, she liked to play with those boys. They did more things. Edie said she hated to play with them. They hit and picked up her skirt. Ruthy agreed. It *was* wrong of them to do this. But, she said, they ran around the block a lot, had races, and played war on the corner. Edie said it wasn't *that* good.

Ruthy said, Another thing, Edie, you could be a soldier if you're a boy.

So? What's so good about that?

Well, you could fight for your country.

Edie said, I don't want to.

What? Edie! Ruthy was a big reader and most interesting reading was about bravery—for instance Roland's Horn at Roncevaux. Her father had been brave and there was often a

151

lot of discussion about this at suppertime. In fact, he sometimes modestly said, Yes, I suppose I was brave in those days. And so was your mother, he added. Then Ruthy's mother put his boiled egg in front of him where he could see it. Reading about Roland, Ruthy learned that if a country wanted to last, it would require a great deal of bravery. She nearly cried with pity when she thought of Edie and the United States of America.

You don't want to? she asked.

No.

Why, Edie, why?

I don't feel like.

Why, Edie? How come?

You always start hollering if I don't do what you tell me. I don't always have to say what you tell me. I can say whatever I like.

Yeah, but if you love your country you have to go fight for it. How come you don't want to? Even if you get killed, it's worth it.

Edie said, I don't want to leave my mother.

Your mother? You must be a baby. Your mother?

Edie pulled her skirt very tight over her knees. I don't like it when I don't see her a long time. Like when she went to Springfield to my uncle. I don't like it.

Oh boy! said Ruthy. Oh boy! What a baby! She stood up. She wanted to go away. She just wanted to jump from the top step, run down to the corner, and wrestle with someone. She said, You know, Edie, this is *my* stoop.

Edie didn't budge. She leaned her chin on her knees and felt sad. She was a big reader too, but she liked *The Bobbsey Twins* or *Honey Bunch at the Seashore*. She loved that nice family life. She tried to live it in the three rooms on the fourth floor. Sometimes she called her father Dad, or even Father, which surprised him. Who? he asked.

I have to go home now, she said. My cousin Alfred's coming. She looked to see if Ruthy was still mad. Suddenly she saw a dog. Ruthy, she said, getting to her feet. There's a dog coming. Ruthy turned. There *was* a dog about three-quarters of the way down the block between the candy store and the grocer's.

It was an ordinary middle-sized dog. But it *was* coming. It didn't stop to sniff at curbs or pee on the house fronts. It just trotted steadily along the middle of the sidewalk.

Ruthy watched him. Her heart began to thump and take up too much space inside her ribs. She thought speedily, Oh, a dog has teeth! It's large, hairy, strange. Nobody can say what a dog is thinking. A dog is an animal. You could talk to a dog, but a dog couldn't talk to you. If you said to a dog, STOP! a dog would just keep going. If it's angry and bites you, you might get rabies. It will take you about six weeks to die and you will die screaming in agony. Your stomach will turn into a rock and you will have lockjaw. When they find you, your mouth will be paralyzed wide open in your dying scream.

Ruthy said, I'm going right now. She turned as though she'd been directed by some far-off switch. She pushed the hall door open and got safely inside. With one hand she pressed the apartment bell. With the other she held the door shut. She leaned against the glass door as Edie started to bang on it. Let me in, Ruthy, let me in, please. Oh, Ruthy!

I can't. Please, Edie, I just can't.

Edie's eyes rolled fearfully toward the walking dog. It's coming. Oh, Ruthy, please, please.

No! No! said Ruthy.

The dog stopped right in front of the stoop to hear the screaming and banging. Edie's heart stopped too. But in a minute he decided to go on. He passed. He continued his easy steady pace.

When Ruthy's big sister came down to call them for lunch, the two girls were crying. They were hugging each other and their hair was a mess. You two are nuts, she said. If I was Mama, I wouldn't let you play together so much every single day. I mean it.

Many years later in Manhattan it was Ruthy's fiftieth birthday. She had invited three friends. They waited for her at the round kitchen table. She had been constructing several pies so that this birthday could be celebrated in her kitchen during the day by any gathered group without too much trouble. Now and then one of the friends would say, Will you sit down, for god-

153

sakes! She would sit immediately. But in the middle of someone's sentence or even one of her own, she'd jump up with a
look of worry beyond household affairs to wash a cooking uten-
sil or wipe crumbs of flour off the Formica counter.

Edie was one of the women at the table. She was sewing, by
neat hand, a new zipper into an old dress. She said, Ruthy, it
wasn't like that. We both ran in and out a lot.

No, said Ruth. You would never have locked me out. You
were an awful sissy, sweetie, but you would never, never have
locked me out. Just look at yourself. Look at your life!

Edie glanced, as people will, when told to do that. She saw
a chubby dark-haired woman who looked like a nice short
teacher, someone who stood at the front of the schoolroom and
said, History is a wonderful subject. It's all stories. It's where
we come from, who we are. For instance, where do you come
from, Juan? Where do your parents and grandparents come
from?

You know that, Mizz Seiden. Porto Rico. You know that a
long-o tim-o, Juan said, probably in order to mock both languages. Edie thought, Oh, to whom would he speak?

For Christsakes, this is a party, isn't it? said Ann. She was
patting a couple of small cases and a projector on the floor next
to her chair. Was she about to offer a slide show? No, she had
already been prevented from doing this by Faith, who'd looked
at the clock two or three times and said, I don't have the time,
Jack is coming tonight. Ruth had looked at the clock too. Next
week, Ann? Ann said O.K. O.K. But Ruthy, I want to say you
have to quit knocking yourself. I've seen you do a million good
things. If you were such a dud, why'd I write it down in my will
that if anything happened to me, you and Joe were the ones
who'd raise my kids.

You were just plain wrong. I couldn't raise my own right.

Ruthy, really, they're pretty much raised. Anyway, how
can you say an awful thing like that? Edie asked. They're
wonderful beautiful brilliant girls. Edie knew this because she
had held them in her arms the third or fourth day of life.
Naturally, she became the friend called aunt.

That's true, I don't have to worry about Sara anymore, I
guess.

Why? Because she's a married mommy? Faith asked. What an insult to Edie!

No, that's O.K., said Edie.

Well, I do worry about Rachel. I just can't help myself. I never know where she is. She was supposed to be here last night. She does usually call. Where the hell is she?

Oh, probably in jail for some stupid little sit-in or something, Ann said. She'll get out in five minutes. Why she thinks that kind of thing works is a mystery to me. You brought her up like that and now you're surprised. Besides which, I don't want to talk about the goddamn kids, said Ann. Here I've gone around half of most of the nearly socialist world and nobody asks me a single question. I have been a witness of events! she shouted.

I do want to hear everything, said Ruth. Then she changed her mind. Well, I don't mean everything. Just say one good thing and one bad thing about every place you've been. We only have a couple of hours. (It was four o'clock. At six, Sara and Tomas with Letty, the first grandchild, standing between them would be at the door. Letty would probably think it was her own birthday party. Someone would say, What curly hair! They would all love her new shoes and her newest sentence, which was Remember dat? Because for such a long time there had been only the present full of milk and looking. Then one day, trying to dream into an afternoon nap, she sat up and said, Gramma, I boke your cup. Remember dat? In this simple way the lifelong past is invented, which, as we know, thickens the present and gives all kinds of advice to the future.) So, Ann, I mean just a couple of things about each country.

That's not much of a discussion, for Christsake.

It's a party, Ann, you said it yourself.

Well, change your face, then.

Oh. Ruth touched her mouth, the corners of her eyes. You're right. Birthday! she said.

Well, let's go, then, said Ann. She stated two good things and one bad thing about Chile (an earlier visit), Rhodesia, the Soviet Union, and Portugal.

You forgot about China. Why don't you tell them about our trip to China?

I don't think I will, Ruthy; you'd only contradict every word I say.

Edie, the oldest friend, stripped a nice freckled banana she'd been watching during Ann's talk. The thing is, Ruth, you never simply say yes. I've told you so many times, *I* would have slammed the door on you, admit it, but it was your house, and that slowed me down.

Property, Ann said. Even among poor people, it begins early.

Poor? asked Edie. It was the Depression.

Two questions — Faith believed she'd listened patiently long enough. I love that story, but I've heard it before. Whenever you're down in the dumps, Ruthy. Right?

I haven't, Ann said. How come, Ruthy? Also, will you please sit with us.

The second question: What about this city? I mean, I'm kind of sick of these big international reports. Look at this place, looks like a toxic waste dump. A war. Nine million people.

Oh, that's true, Edie said, but Faith, the whole thing *is* hopeless. Top to bottom, the streets, those kids, dumped, plain dumped. That's the correct word, "dumped." She began to cry.

Cut it out, Ann shouted. No tears, Edie! No! Stop this minute! I swear, Faith said, you'd better stop that! (They were all, even Edie, ideologically, spiritually, and on puritanical principle against despair.)

Faith was sorry to have mentioned the city in Edie's presence. If you said the word "city" to Edie, or even the cool adjective "municipal," specific children usually sitting at the back of the room appeared before her eyes and refused to answer when she called on them. So Faith said, O.K. New subject: What do you women think of the grand juries they're calling up all over the place?

All over what place? Edie asked. Oh, Faith, forget it, they're going through something. You know you three lead such adversarial lives. I hate it. What good does it do? Anyway, those juries will pass.

Edie, sometimes I think you're half asleep. You know that woman in New Haven who was called? I know her personally. She wouldn't say a word. She's in jail. They're not kidding.

I'd never open my mouth either, said Ann. Never. She clamped her mouth shut then and there.

I believe you, Ann. But sometimes, Ruth said, I think, Suppose I was in Argentina and they had my kid. God, if they had our Sara's Letty, I'd maybe say anything.

Oh, Ruth, you've held up pretty well, once or twice, Faith said.

Yes, Ann said, in fact we were all pretty good that day, we were sitting right up against the horses' knees at the draft board—were you there, Edie? And then the goddamn horses started to rear and the cops were knocking people on their backs and heads—remember? And, Ruthy, I was watching you. You just suddenly plowed in and out of those monsters. You should have been trampled to death. And you grabbed the captain by his gold buttons and you hollered, You bastard! Get your goddamn cavalry out of here. You shook him and shook him.

He ordered them, Ruth said. She set one of her birthday cakes, which was an apple plum pie, on the table. I saw him. He was the responsible person. I saw the whole damn operation. I'd begun to run—the horses—but I turned because I was the one supposed to be in front and I saw him give the order. I've never honestly been so angry.

Ann smiled. Anger, she said. That's really good.

You think so? Ruth asked. You sure?

Buzz off, said Ann.

Ruth lit the candles. Come on, Ann, we've got to blow this out together. And make a wish. I don't have the wind I used to have.

But you're still full of hot air, Edie said. And kissed her hard. What did you wish, Ruthy? she asked.

Well, a wish, some wish, Ruth said. Well, I wished that this world wouldn't end. This world, this world, Ruth said softly.

Me too, I wished exactly the same. Taking action, Ann hoisted herself up onto a kitchen chair, saying, ugh my back, ouch my knee. Then: Let us go forth with fear and courage and rage to save the world.

Bravo, Edie said softly.

Wait a minute, said Faith . . .

157

Ann said, Oh, you . . . you . . .

But it was six o'clock and the doorbell rang. Sara and Tomas stood on either side of Letty, who was hopping or wiggling with excitement, hiding behind her mother's long skirt or grabbing her father's thigh. The door had barely opened when Letty jumped forward to hug Ruth's knees. I'm gonna sleep in your house, Gramma.

I know, darling, I know.

Gramma, I slept in your bed with you. Remember dat?

Oh sure, darling, I remember. We woke up around five and it was still dark and I looked at you and you looked at me and you had a great big Letty smile and we just burst out laughing and you laughed and I laughed.

I remember dat, Gramma. Letty looked at her parents with shyness and pride. She was still happy to have found the word "remember," which could name so many pictures in her head.

And then we went right back to sleep, Ruth said, kneeling now to Letty's height to kiss her little face.

Where's my Aunt Rachel? Letty asked, hunting among the crowd of unfamiliar legs in the hallway.

I don't know.

She's supposed to be here, Letty said. Mommy, you promised. She's really supposed.

Yes, said Ruth, picking Letty up to hug her and then hug her again. Letty, she said as lightly as she could, She *is* supposed to be here. But where can she be? She certainly is supposed.

Letty began to squirm out of Ruth's arms. Mommy, she called, Gramma is squeezing. But it seemed to Ruth that she'd better hold her even closer, because, though no one else seemed to notice — Letty, rosy and soft-cheeked as ever, was falling, already falling, falling out of her brand-new hammock of world-inventing words onto the hard floor of man-made time.

The Field is Full of Daisies and I'm Afraid to Pass

MAUREEN BRADY

Two ripe fruits, plump, ready, whole. This was our state when we met. Our bodies came together, fit, everywhere. We felt ourselves sail. We were on a strong sea. Our fingers danced to a new moon, and it seemed as if our feet would not come down to touch the ground. We felt too full to have a future.

The field is full of daisies, and I'm afraid to pass. I planned to go to work that day. This was part of a larger plan, my five year plan, which arrogantly assumed a long future. Reaching the flats, I waited for the woman in the car ahead of me to pass the truck. Waited and waited with the road stretching long and straight ahead through the meadow. Then decided to go. Then her car came moving into mine, into my side. I moved over and over and finally off the road and soared and thought I was gone.

We had just come back from Maine. From beach walking, loving in the tent; from watching the waves wash against the crevices and butts of the rocks. Then I lay flat on my back at the side of the road, the top of my head open. "Please, call this woman, Judith." I told the man. "Please, tell her to come." I gave the phone number. "Who is she?" he asked. "She is Judith . . . my very best friend." I closed my eyes. Willed my body only to struggle to clot the blood — not against the man. To live to come back to control.

The wheel went out from my hands. Spun and spun with my hands chasing. Spun and spun back the other way. I saw the field, the road, the field. No sound. Sight, no sound. The field. The road. Out of control. Often I'd read that in the newspaper, never quite sure what it meant. The car went out of control. Alone. No sound. The steering wheel, a broken toy. Here goes, I thought. Here goes. There must have been some noise, but I didn't hear it. I ducked my head before it hit the windshield, didn't even hear that.

"Can you get out?" a man, calling me. My deaf ears came out of the silence. His voice sounded far away, muffled. Who was I? Where was I? I was a person squatted rightside up on the roof of the back seat of a car, upside down. The field was full of daisies. The man was outside. I was birthing consciousness. I was fully innocent.

"Why don't you open the door?" I asked.

He was bent over so that his head was nearly upside down. "I can't. Can you get out?"

Don't rush me, I said to myself. Don't confuse me. My mind stuck on a cartoon of a character who had received a blow to the head and saw symbols floating in disarray. I noticed the blood driping on my new briefcase — soft brown leather, pleasing to caress — also on the roof of my new car — blue interior, five payments made out of thirty-six. Such was the environment I was being born into. I looked above me for the source of the blood, finally felt the top of my head.

GET OUT, I told myself, panic overtaking dismay. Tried to roll the window down, which was actually up. JAWS OF LIFE they call the machine that comes to bite open the wrecked car. I'd seen that in the paper, too, always imagined the victim being mouthed between iron jaws. Didn't want that, would rather have the soundlessness. My head began to scream pain. I stuck it through the window and crawled out. The man helped me to stand up and I felt thoroughly stunned, as if I had no history. "I have no idea what happened to me," I said.

160

"I saw," he said. "WOW. I saw through my rear view mirror." He watched my face. "Let's lie you down." He walked me a few feet from the car and put me down in the grass. "My head," I said. "My head is coming off." That's when I told him to call Judith.

I once studied neuroanatomy by dissecting a brain. I tried to remember the stiffness of its substance, a texture like tofu, but all I could imagine was an intestinal mush seeping from the hole in my skull. My eyes were closed. The woman kneeling beside me said, "Please, please open your eyes. Please be okay. Please be okay." The hysteria in her voice worsened my headache. I opened my eyes. She sighed. "Oh God, didn't you see my blinker?"

My memory moved into focus with her words. "You never put your blinker on," I said. "Never. I watched. I waited." I closed my eyes. I heard the man tell someone else to take her away. "Watch her, she's upset," he said.

SHE'S UPSET, my body responded. She's upset because I might die.

The first time Harold came to see about restoring the chimney, he was dazed with the loss of his daughter. All the time he measured, I followed him around and listened as he spoke out of the side of his mouth. "I ain't right yet, you know. I just can't figure why her. I take it you heard about what happened." I nodded, asked where the accident had occurred. "Over to the curve just before the lake road. Nobody saw. Nobody knows what happened. Emergency squad picked her up, carried her in to the hospital, her jabbering all the way. I got the call on the CB. Wife and I rushed in. She was dead by the time we got there." He stood back in the yard and contemplated the chimney for a long time, desolate.

I could feel my face swell as if it were a marsh that water was trickling into. My lips were swelling to numbness and my eyes wanted to puff shut. It was hard to move my attention from my head and face, but when I remembered Harold's daughter, I decided to take a survey of my organs. I tried to think myself on a route around my abdomen, to feel for the sensation of bruising, rupture, hemorrhage. My heart beat harder as I thought of Harold's daughter chattering her fear as she rode to the hospital. Places on my legs burned, but I couldn't feel anything except panic where my liver should be, my pancreas, my stomach, my gall bladder, my intestines, my spleen. As soon as I thought about my blood pressure, I felt faint. I told the man, who brought a stool and elevated my legs. "I'm an emergency tech," he said. "I guess I'm lucky," I said. "Am I still bleeding?"

Why don't we teach comforting as an emergency technique? As the time stretched out, I felt I might die for the lack of it. "Have you called Judith?" I asked. "What did she say?" someone asked. "About calling the girl, Judy." "Judith," I said, with enough venom that they drew back from me. The waiting time was exhausting. I felt with each new minute I had to call up deeper reserves from within.

The emergency tech decided to wrap my head to try to stop the bleeding. He instructed another man to straddle me so he could stoop and lift my head with full support around my neck. I didn't like his position; the enormity of his shoes at my sides felt humiliating. After they finished wrapping me, I talked to them a little. The blood on my face was hardening sticky and these two men took turns fanning away the flies that came to light on me. They kept looking off down the road for the ambulance, while I listened in the other direction for Judith. Enough time had passed that she would be arriving any minute, I thought, and then I would be able to relax and stop comforting myself. I could feel others who had stopped and gotten out of their cars to come and view me, watching, but I didn't let my eyes move to them. My rescuers were restless. They reminded me of my father, waiting for my mother to soothe the one of us who had caught her finger in the car door, pacing and jingling the change in his pocket as if life had stopped and would not resume until the crying was over and we could pull out of the driveway.

The emergency tech asked how old I was.

"Thirty-five."

"You married?"

"No."

"Tsk, tsk, tsk. What's a pretty girl like you doing without a husband?"

I couldn't believe I had to have this confrontation lying beside the road, losing my blood through my head, my face feeling more and more like a sponge, my nose merging with my upper lip. I opened my eyes, made my voice steady, said, "I never wanted to be married."

"Sometimes I get too nosy," he admitted, looking down the road again.

"Yes," I agreed, closing my eyes. I regretted having already complimented him on his bandaging technique.

The Sheriff's deputy came, asked me questions and tested me for a sense of humor. Why do people think that humor gives comfort? And for whom? When I felt most like a cartoon character, I wanted least to be treated as one. They had failed to call Judith. I wanted to scream. They had waited for the Sheriff to come and decide if my request should be honored.

Finally, the ambulance. A skinny stretcher, metal tubing and hard mat. I would know if I had broken my neck, wouldn't I? My writing teacher who was quadraplegic said he'd felt his limbs melt away right after the accident. My legs burned in spots, my right thigh, my left shin.

As the road dipped, my stomach dropped an infinity, the feeling just past the top arc of the ferris wheel. I was dizzy. The man accompanying me looked scared, slightly dazed, enough that I was afraid to tell him I felt dizzy. I asked him where he worked instead. He'd just come off the night shift at the paper mill, gone to bed for the morning when the call came.

In the E.R. the nurses worked rapidly, covered me with a sheet, stripped me of my clothes. One inspected my body with cool eyes while the other began shaving my head along the scalp wound. The scrapes of the razor jaggedly cutting the hair nauseated me, and I shook with chills. "A blanket, please." Can't you see I'm cold. They covered me with another sheet and left.

An official woman arrived, wanting to ask some questions. "Fine," I said, glad for someone to talk to. Name? Address? In-

surance coverage? To think that I took comfort in these questions. I wanted her to stay. She scribbled on her clipboard and
was gone. The room was large, stark, and the clock eyed me —
10:05. I had lived an hour. Where was Judith? Why should
someone, anyone, ME, have to stay alone in that large, stark
room, supervising her own LIFE until the doctor arrived?

10:15. I could not bear the isolation, but how to call out?
All my years of working in a hospital as a physical therapist,
wearing a white uniform, hearing patients call out to me,
"Nurse, hey nurse," usually wanting the bedpan. Always, I'd
resented the depersonalization of the term as well as the inac-
curacy. But if the nurses had introduced themselves, I didn't
remember. Finally, I called, "Nurse." I asked if she could call
my home and she brought a phone and dialed for me. My
brother, who was visiting that week, answered. I tried to explain the accident without making it sound horrible, without
ruining his vacation. Judith was on her way. I closed my eyes
and pictured her and tried to send her messages to drive carefully. When we first fell in love we commuted on weekends between New York City and Saratoga Springs. I remembered the
urge to fly, the milestones of thruway rest stops marking the
closing of the gap, the Friday nights of touching and touching,
confirming our feelings were not just fantasies we had conjured
up in our separation, saying, "Our lives have been building to
this all these years."

She was not there and then suddenly she was — holding my
hand, kissing my face, her eyes brimmed with tears, her presence filling the vast, stark room. I could see in her eyes how
battered I looked. They were the first eyes that expressed a relationship to me.

Just then, almost as if they'd been waiting for her too, they
whipped me off to X-ray. "Easy," I said, "No hurry," but they
left my stomach in the E.R. Judith walked beside the stretcher.
The pad they had covered the wound on my head with went
flying. The attendant picked it up off the floor and fitted it back
to my head. Again, I saw in Judith's eyes an honest response, a
large wound. I moved to instruction on the cold, hard X-ray
table for dozens of X-rays. My skull, my neck, my back, my
legs. I thought of an article I had read which described the

aging effects of ordinary diagnostic X-rays. I should be pro-testing this, I thought. I should permit only one view of each part. But I went on moving to instruction.

Trauma. The doctors would say my trauma took place in the car, then secondarily on the operating table as they cleaned out and closed up my scalp wound. But I saw a clear line of de-marcation between trauma and comfort, and every act, every gesture, every spoken word fell into a place on one side of this line or the other. There is no neutral territory in an open wound.

Trauma: I asked the surgeon to position my neck carefully when he put me under. "Here's the anesthesiologist, tell him," he said. "Doesn't he have a name?" I asked, wanting accounta-bility. I felt them look at each other across my body. I was sur-prised at my power to threaten them, given my weakened state.

Trauma: 10:05. Leaving me with only the clock to watch over me.

Trauma: They didn't call Judith when I asked them to.

Trauma: Cold sheets, no blankets in the E.R.

Trauma: The scrape of the razor.

Trauma: The man wanting to know why I'm not married. The big shoes at my side; the flipping, the upside down, the wheel spinning, the field, the road, the silence, the here goes—no time.

Comfort: It would have been a painless death.

Trauma: The pain in my head screamed with an intensity that obliterated the possibility of completing a thought. Several times it occurred to me to ask the doctor: could I have some-thing for the pain? "I have a question for you," I said repeat-edly, then couldn't remember what it was. I said stupid things when doctors and nurses asked me how I was, like "Glad to be here."

Comfort: That euphoria—still not sure I would live, would have memory, intelligence, clarity, but sure how much I want-ed my life *to be*.

Trauma: That night after the surgery I told the nurse I wanted to look in a mirror. "I think maybe you should wait a few days," she said, her voice officious, stern. "It's still me," I said. "I think I'll recognize myself."

Comfort: I looked. I touched all over my swollen face with my cool hand. My head was fully wrapped in a white, gauze turban. I admired the colors of my black eyes, the deep purple lines. I recognized the feelings fluttering in my belly: a deep vulnerability, a need for tenderness to touch every part of me. I held my cheeks and wept. I held the split open backs of my knuckles, then I held my neck. Then I felt the hot burning in my right thigh and spoke to my femur with pride in the strength and resilience of my bones.

I Used to Like
the Dallas Cowboys

DIONNE BRAND

I used to like the Dallas Cowboys. Steel gray helmets, good luck gray, bad luck blue, skin tight, muscle definitioned thighs. I'd prepare for Sunday's game, beer and my pillows at the ready. Rushing to the kitchen between commercials, burning the chicken or the boiled potatoes, depending on whether there was money, or making split pea soup, scraping up the last grain of garlic and the onions growing stems in the dark corners of the cupboard below the sink. I'd neglect the dishes from the night before or the week before, depending on the week, set up a phone line with Tony or Jo as the case may be, put the bottles of beer in the freezer, if I had beer, and wait for the game, sit through the pre-game or the highlights, have a fifteen minute nap, time permitting. This was after I'd just risen from an eight hour sleep, most of which was devoted to regenerating the body after dancing and drinking till four in the morning. Whatever liquor wasn't danced out had to be slept out. Naturally sometimes even sleep would not produce the miracle of waking up without a vicious headache and feeling waterlogged, but I had prepared for this by putting the television near to my arm.

Seems a while now, but back then, I used to really love the Dallas Cowboys. It's funny what things occur to you lying in a corridor at 3 a.m. in the morning in the middle of a war.

Which is where I am now. The sky is lit bright from flares and there's a groaning F16 circling the sky like a corbeau. The flares give off the light of a red smoky dawn, except for their starkness which makes you feel naked. The air, seeping through the wood latticework, smells chemical. A few minutes ago, before the flares went up, the cat, who lives in the house whose corridor I'm huddled in, ran, screaming and scratching over my back. She had heard the incoming planes long before they hit the island again, on this second day . . . night of the war. Having no sixth sense like hers, the rest of us dove for the corridor only when the flares went up and we'd heard the crack of the F16's through the sound of speed. I wasn't asleep. Just waiting. Amazing, how your mind can just latch on to something, just to save you from thinking about how frightened you are. It reaches for the farthest thing away . . . That's how come I remember that I used to love the Dallas Cowboys.

The Cowboys shone, the Dallas sun glancing off their helmets. They weren't like other football teams. They were sleek where the others were rough, they were swift where the others were plodding, they were scientific where the others were ploughboys; they were precise where the others were clumsy mudwaders; they were slim, slender where the others were hulking, brutish. Even their linebackers had finesse. Not for them the crunch and bashing of the Steelers, the mud and squat of the Raiders; they were quick clean, decisive. Punters trembled before the upraised arm of Harvey Martin, linebackers dreaded his embrace. Too Tall Jones had too much oil, too much quickness for a defensive lineman, too long a right arm. It was ecstasy when Hollywood Henderson intercepted a pass or caught a running back for a loss. But most of all it was Drew Pearson, Tony Dorsett and Butch Johnson who gave you a look at perfection of the human, male, form.

Mind you there were a few from other teams, like Lynn Swann, who was with Pittsburgh. He was as graceful as the rest of his teammates were piggish. Sometimes, I think he flew. He was so lithe, I think, everyone on the field stopped to watch him, this bird of beauty among them, so tied to their squat bodies and the heavy ground. He should have been with the Cowboys really.

The Cowboys were fine. They had a move which befuddled their opponents while it raised something in me that . . . It was when they were waiting for the quarterback's call; hunched over, they would rise in unison for the quickest of moments and then settle in for the count again. The look of all those sinewy backs rising and falling was like a dance. A threatening dance. It reminded me of 'the breakdown' which we used to do every Thursday, Friday and Saturday night at the Coq D'Or.

Rufus Thomas started it with his song "Do the breakdown" and we just got better and better, perfecting the bend from the waist and the shudders to the left and right. Some of us added variations in the middle or with the hips and the motions of the crooked arm as the weeks went by, till the next new dance; but everything about Black dance was there, in the breakdown. So when the Dallas Cowboys did the breakdown, it really sent me. I was their fan, the moment I saw it.

Seems like I made a circle with my life. Then, I was in Toronto. Now, I'm back here on the island, not the one I came from in the beginning, but close by. Speaking of circles, there is . . . was a revolution here and I came to join. Correction, revolutions are actually not circles but upheavals, transformations, new beginnings for life. I'm graying by the minute in this corridor. I feel feverish. That is a circle, ending where you began. The war outside is ending the revolution. We have nothing to listen to since the radio went off at 9 a.m. on the first day of the war, only the crack of the F16's over the house.

Rufus Thomas . . . tata ta tata tata pada ta pada pada boom . . . do the breakdown . . . That was in nineteen seventy or seventy-one. Seems a long time ago now, considering. That's when I first went to Toronto. I was sixteen. I went to school. I partied. I learned to like football. Not Canadian football, American football. Actually it was Sundays. Sundays. I had never liked Sundays. Back home everything stopped on a Sunday. The shop was closed; people didn't walk on the street, except in quiet penitence and their Sunday best; and worse, the radio no longer blared calypso and soul music but Oral Roberts' "the hour of decision."

Canadian football was too slow, the downs were too few and the ball seemed to be perpetually changing hands from one incompetent lot to the other, blundering up and down the field. American football, on the other hand, now . . . Well come to think of it, it was all the build-up, the pre-game assessment of the players, who was injured and who wasn't. You would swear that this was the most important event to take place in history—the tension, the coach's job on the line and the raw roar of winning. When my team lost, I cannot explain the deep loss, the complete letdown which would last until Monday morning. My sister and I would remark to each other every so often, in the middle of doing the washing or in the middle of a walk, "Cheups! Dallas could disappoint people, eh?" This would be followed by a pregnant silence and another "Cheups." The next Sunday, up until game time we'd be saying, "I can't watch that game, I just can't." But the call of the steel gray and the American star on the helmet was too much and Dallas! Dallas was good! You have to admit.

To be honest, if I really look back, it was the clandestine *True Confession* magazines from America which I read at thirteen that led to my love for the Dallas Cowboys. There was always a guy named Bif or Ted or Lance who was on the college football team and every girl wanted to wear his sweater. Never mind we didn't have sweaters or need them in the tropics, this only made them romantic items. We didn't have cars either in whose steamy back seats a girl became 'that kinda girl' or a wife.

So anyway because it was so boring in Canada on Sundays and because it was winter, morning, noon and night, I learned to like football.

And basketball. Mind, I always liked netball which was what they made girls play at Rima High School in San Fernando. And tennis, dying, dy...ing for Arthur Ashe to whip Jimmy Connors which he finally did at Wimbledon, which all north American sportscasters call wimpleton, which really gets me, like every broadcaster in north America says nukular instead nuclear and they're supposed to be so advanced. Me and my sister couldn't bear to watch it, the tennis game that is, because we had already said too often,

"This Arthur Ashe can disappoint people, boy!"

Nevertheless we gave in. We were walking along Dufferin,

that was when we used to live on Dupont, we were walking along Dufferin at Wallace and we suddenly made a run for Dupont after several long "cheups" and pauses and after hearing an Italian boy say something about the match to another Italian boy. We couldn't let Arthur go through that match alone. It was a battle of the races. Some people would be looking and cheering for Jimmy Conners. As we ran home it became more and more important that we watch the match to give Arthur moral support. Somehow, if we sat and watched the match, it would help Arthur to win. And if we didn't and he lost, it would have been our fault. So we sat in pain, watching and urging Arthur on, on the television. It was tense but Arthur played like a dream, like a thinker. Connors was gallerying, throwing tantrums like a white boy; but Arthur was cool. Connors would use his powerful forehand trying to drive Arthur to the baseline, Arthur would send him back a soft drop shot that he couldn't make. Connors would send hard, trying to get Arthur to return hard, but Arthur would just come in soft. Arthur beat his ass ba...ad. I swear to God if we didn't sit and watch that match we would not have forgiven ourselves. This was like the second Joe Louis and Max Schmelling fight. Nineteen thirty-six all over again.

And boxing, I liked that too, and track. Never liked hockey, except when the Soviets came to play. And golf, would you believe. That's to tell you how far I'd go to escape the dreariness of Sundays in the winter. I'd even watch an old, lazy, white man's sport.

Last Sunday, here, was a little sad . . . and tense. Only, on Sunday, the war hadn't started yet. There was a visit to Mt. Morris from which you can see, as from most places on this island, the sea. Talk, a little hopeful but bewildered, that surrounded by water like this, one could never be prepared for war even if one could see it coming over the long view of the horizon.

The war was inside the house now. The light from the flares ignores the lushness of this island turning it into an endless desert.

I used to love the Dallas Cowboys like you wouldn't believe. How I come to love the Dallas Cowboys—well I've explained, but I left something out. See, I wasn't your cheerleader type; I wasn't no Dallas Cowgirl. I knew the game, knew all their moves and Dallas had some moves that no other football club would do. They would do an end around, which most other teams would think belonged in a high school or college game. So it would shock them that here was Dallas, America's team, doing a high school move.

I learned about American high school and college lore watching American football. In my own high school, where football was soccer, we didn't play it because I went to a girls' school. We played whatever we did play rough mind you, but it wasn't soccer. Football was played by Pres' College and (St.) Benedict's. Boys' high schools. Benedict's always won but Pres' was the star boys. This was mainly because they were high yellow boys. Red skin, fair skin and from good families. Every high school girl was after them, god knows to do what with, because there was no place to do it that I could find. Benedict's was black boys, dark-skinned and tough, tall and lanky or short and thick like a wall. Convent girls and Rima girls vied for Pres' boys, Benedict's was a second choice. Benedict's boys were a little aloof though; they were the first ones to be turned on by the Black Power movement. They stopped wearing their uniform right, they were the first to grow afros and get suspended or expelled from school for it. They were the first to have a student strike and a protest march around the school. Then they became popular, or clandestine anyway. Pres' star boys looked pale against them and everybody now started to look for the darkest Pres' boy to walk with, because the boys in Pres' who weren't red skin began to join Black Power too. My friend Sylvia was the first to go afro in my school, and it was as if she had committed a crime, or as if she was a 'bad' girl or something.

That year, the Black Power year, I didn't get to go to see Pres' and Benedict's play in Guaracara Park. But I heard it turned into a Black Power demonstration. Well truthfully, I never got to go but once that I could remember, my family being so strict; and anyway, I was always at a loss to know what to do with a boy after, which was supposed to be the highlight of the evening and anyway, I never had a boyfriend really. The other thing was, I really couldn't get into jumping around in the stands as a girl, not looking at the game and yelling when everybody else yelled "Goal!" All of us who would leave without a boy would walk behind our next best friend who had one, looking at her boyfriend and snickering. The girls who had boyfriends on the teams that played were way above us.

But this was soccer, which we called football, so I didn't know American football.

I really didn't like soccer until television came in, in Trinidad, and not until years after that when we got a TV and we could watch Tottenham Hot Spurs at Trent and you could really see the game and the moves. And we watched the World Cup and found Brazil was who we could cheer for, because Brazil was Black; and then there was Eusebio of Portugal who was Black too. Now that's when the game got good. Pele and Eusebio made us cheer for both teams at the same time if they were playing each other because Black people had to shine anyhow they come. Never mind the Spurs, we wanted England to lose because they didn't have any Black players. That was an insult.

"What happen? They don't like Black people or what? They don't give Black people any chance at all?"

If the game was between two white teams, we'd root for the team with the darkest hair. So Italy and Mexico were our teams. If it was British teams, the most rough and tumble looking would be our favorites. So when TV came in, then is when I got into soccer.

Soccer didn't have any cheerleaders, but American football did. I was embarrassed when I saw them. They looked ridiculous and vulnerable at the same time. I suppose they were supposed to look vulnerable; but it looked like weak shit to me. Since I was a kid I had a disdain for that kind of girl or woman. I never liked not knowing exactly about a thing and I had always felt uncomfortable wearing a mini skirt or can can, when they were in fashion.

So I learned about American football. This standing around like a fool while men talked about football was not for me. Sometimes after Saturday night, and usually during the playoffs, someone, maybe Joe, would have a brunch and part

of the program was that we'd watch the game. That usually
meant that the men would watch the game and the women
would rap with each other (nothing wrong with that mind you),
walk around, hassle or humor the men about watching the
game or observe the new 'chick' belonging to whichever reign-
ing cock on the walk. Well see, I never came with nobody except that one time that I was almost married. But that's another
story, thank God. I'd get a place at the TV and not without
feeling that I was ingratiating myself and that I wasn't quite
welcome. Well, I'd make some comments about what call the
referee made on such and such a play and nobody would take
me on. Then I'd get a rise out of them if I said that their backs
moved before the snap of the ball. Well, at first they humored
me. Mind you the worst of them left the room, objecting to
watching football with a woman present. Then they realized
that I know my game, you see. I'd bet them money too, just to
prove how serious I was. I outmachoed the machoest. I yelled
and pointed and called them suckers and then I'd laugh and
tease them. Well, most of them were Trinidadian, so they rose
to the bait. You could always catch a Trinidadian man in an
argument defending the most unlikely prospect and the most
ridiculous outcome.

Before you knew it, everytime I lost a game, to be sure that
phone would ring and one of the guys would be taunting me
saying, "You see how to play football? Dallas is dead, bet you
ten bucks." I'd take the bet because the Dallas Cowboys were
magicians. They could take sixty seconds left in a game and
turn it into two touchdowns and a field goal. Robert New-
house, before he got injured, could plough through a Steelers
defense like an ant through a hibiscus hedge. See, I wasn't no
cheerleader. I knew my game. Roger liked the Steelers cause
they had Franco Harris; but to me Franco was kinda clumsy. I
know he ran so many yards and everything, but when he started to get old I figure he shoulda left, because he started to look
bad to me. Other people wouldn't say that, but I didn't like the
look of him. He looked too much like a white boy to me, which
is why I hated quarterbacks. They were always white, except
for James Harris who was with L.A. and then what's his name
with the Bears. Roger Staubach I had to tolerate and anyway,

he was clean. I mean he could throw a pass. He could go up the field in thirty seconds. Of course, one of *us,* Drew or Butch, had to be there to catch it. But Roger was clean. Never mind he was born-again and probably a member of the Klan, after all we're talking about Texas, where they still fly the Confederate flag and all.

Another thing about the Cowboys, all my football buddies used to say that they were the most fascist team. Well I agreed you know because football, or most any American sport, has that quality to it. I said that was exactly why I liked Dallas because in this gladiatorial game called football they were the most scientific, the most emotionless and therefore exactly what this game was about. I called my buddies a bunch of wimps. "How you could like football and then get squeamish? You got to figure out what it is you like, see!" Anybody can watch a game and say, "Oh I hate that. It's so violent." But they still live with it and in it. That person's just an intellectual. When I finally got to see the Dallas Cowboys in person, no set of intellectuals could have explained it and neither could anybody who didn't understand the game.

To cut a long story short, because I probably don't have time for a long story, even though I loved the Dallas Cowboys, I had to leave the country. So I had to wean myself off of football because where I was going there was no American football. There may be cricket but certainly no football. It wasn't easy. You get used to a way of life, even though you don't know it. And you take everything it has in it, even if you think you can sift out the good from the bad. You get cynical and hard-arsed about the bad, in truth. So you find a way to look at it. So cynical and hard-arsed that when you see good, it embarrasses you.

The jets breaking the sound barrier keep rushing over the house. I've never ever heard a noise like that. Oh, my God! It's a wonder I can remember anything. Remembering keeps the panic down. Remember your name, remember last week, . . . There's a feeling somewhere in my body that's so tender that I'm melting away, disintegrating with it. I'm actually going to die!

Someone in the corridor with me says, "It's the ones you

175

don't hear. . . ." Yesterday, we thought we heard MIG's overhead . . . Wishing . . . We know that no one will come to help us. No one can.

I was going to another kinda place, much quieter. A cricket match now and then, maybe. . . . One Sunday, in March this year, I went to one. It was a quiet Sunday, the way Sundays are quiet in the Caribbean and I slept through half of the match. It was West Indies versus the Leeward Islands. Cricket is the only game that you can sleep through and it wouldn't matter. They say it started in the Caribbean as a slave master's game. Of course, they had all the time in the world. Matches can last up to five days. They break for tea and long lunches and they wear white, to show that it's not a dirty, common game. Even the spectators wear white.

You can tell that it was a slave masters' game if you notice where most cricket pitches are placed. You just look and you'll find them all laid out, green and close cropped grass, at some remote end of what used to be a plantation, or still might be for that matter. Remote enough so that the players would have some peace from the hurly-burly of slave life, but close enough in case of an emergency whipping or carnage. If you pass by a cricket pitch in the Caribbean, not the modern stadiums they built but the ones that have been there forever, there's a hush over them, a kind of green silence, an imperious quiet. You will notice that children never play on them. They play somewhere on the beach or in the bush. See, there's no place to hide on them, which is why slave owners liked them, I suppose. While they had their dalliances there, they could be sure to see a coming riot.

Which, oddly enough is why I left, here first, then there. I could no more help leaving Toronto than I could help going there in the first place or coming here eventually. I came to join the revolution; to stop going in circles, to add my puny little woman self to an upheaval. You get tired of being a slave; you get tired of being sold here and there; you assault the cricket pitch, even if it is broad daylight and the slave owner can see you coming; you scuttle pell-mell into death; you only have to be lucky once; get him behind the neck; and if it doesn't succeed, . . . well, you're one of millions and millions. Though lying in a corridor in the end, or for those lying dead, it doesn't feel that way, you're trembling, you lose sight.

So no Cowboys, no apartment buildings, no TV to talk about, not so much time to kill on a Sunday. Today, if it turns into day, it's not Sunday. What day is it? The red smoke dawn of the flares has given way to a daybreak as merciless as last night. Each day lengthens into a year. Another afternoon, God fled a blinding shine sky; wasps, helicopter gun ships stung the beach, seconds from the harbor. Four days ago the island was invaded by America. The Americans don't like cricket; but deep inside of those of us hiding from them in this little corridor and those in the hills and cemeteries, we know they've come to play ball. Dead eye ship, helicopter gun ships, bombers, M16's, troops. I've seen my share of TV war — hogan's heroes, the green berets and bridge on the river quai. Well none of that ever prepares you.

Because when they're not playing, the Cowboys can be deadly.

I've had four days to think about this. War is murder. When you're actually the one about to get killed, not just your physical self but what you wanted badly, well then it's close. I find myself having to attend to small things that I didn't notice before. First of all my hands and my body feel like they don't belong to me. I think that they're only extra baggage because there's nowhere to put them or to hide them. The truth is I begin to hate my own physical body, because I believe it has betrayed me by merely existing. It's like not having a shelf to put it on or a cupboard to lock it in; it's useless to me and it strikes me how inefficient it is. Because the ideal form in which to pass a war is as a spirit, a jumbie. My body is history, fossil, passé.

And my thoughts. I begin to think, why didn't I think of this? or that? I think, why isn't it yesterday? or last year? or year after next? Even a depressing day, any other day, a day when my menses pained me occurs to me like a hot desire. I try to evolve to a higher form. I want to think out of this place where I'm crouched with four other people; but my thoughts are totally useless and I know it, because I think that too.

And the noise of the war. That horrible, horrible noise like the earth cracked open by a huge metallic butchering instrument. That noise rankles, bursts in my ear and after a while it drones in my ear and that droning says that I'm not dead yet. I don't know when I'll get hit; the whole house could be blown away and this corridor which I chose, if I really think about it, and all the safety which I imbued it with. I would stand in the middle of the street and wave to the bombers in the sky to come and finish me off.

If I don't die today, the one thing that will probably dog me for the rest of my life is that I'm not dead. Why am I not dead now . . . now . . . now . . .

I began well. I tried to make it decent, to die clean and dignified; but I don't want to die and my greed to live is embarrassing. I feel like a glutton about how much my body wants to hang on and at the same time it does not want to be here, in this corridor, in this world where I'm about to die. And so, in the middle of the noise, through the gun fire, the bombs and the anti-aircraft guns, I'm falling asleep. Can you imagine! I'm falling asleep. Each time I hear the bombers approaching, I yawn and my body begins to fall asleep.

Like now. Someone else in the corridor is watching me trying to sleep in the middle of disaster. If we survive, she will remember that I tried to sleep. I will remember that she watched me, tears in her eyes, leaving her. We hum and flinch to each crackkk, each bomb . . . We're dancing the breakdown. But if I fall asleep, I know that I won't wake up, or I'll wake up mad.

For four days now, a war in the middle of October, on this small unlikely island. Four days. I crouch in a corridor; I drink bottles of rum and never get drunk. I stay awake, in case. I listen for the noise of the war because it is my signal, like the snap of the ball, that I'm not dead.

But the signal is not from my team. I'm playing the Dallas Cowboys.

The day I finally creep to the door, the day I look outside to see who is trying to kill me, to tell them that I surrender, I see the Dallas Cowboys coming down my hot tropical street, among the bougainvillea and the mimosa, crouching, pointing their M16 weapons, laden with grenade-launchers. The hibiscus and I dangle high and red in defeat; everything is silent and gone. Better dead. Their faces are painted and there's that smell, like fresh blood and human grease, on them. And I hate them.

178

Mz. Kitty Leaves the Longbranch to Win the Battle at the O.K. Corral

(This story is for Nancy Mitchell, who actually DID!)

ANNE CAMERON

...and whatsoever Adam called every living creature,
that was the name thereof...   GENESIS 2:19

The first time Liz Brady heard her English teacher read out the line "What's in a name, a rose by any other name would smell as sweet," something inside her relaxed. Why, of course! Even if you called it a cabbage, a toad, or a waste-paper receptacle, it would be a rose and smell as nice, have thorns to rip your skin and come in any number of varieties and color combinations. People would still plant them along fences and in front of picture windows. Even if you called them stinking bait cans you'd want them rambling up a trellis alongside the back steps so you could sit of an evening in the dappled shade and listen to the contented hum of the bumbly-bees or the zinging zip of the burnished bronze or ruby throated hummingbirds. And not just roses; angels would still be angels, even if you called them chicken pox. They would still fly around heaven and play harps and watch over you at night and be there to whisper in your ear if you were in danger of being tempted. You could change the name of Haslam Pond, you could call it anything you wanted to call it, the silliest name you could come

179

up with, and it would still be what it was, and the dragonflies would still zip back and forth, stitching each minute into the fabric of the day, each day into the tapestry of time. Frogs would plop into the water, ripples would tremble wider, wider, until they were lost from sight out near the deep part where the big kids dove from the rock in the summertime. Whether you called them night hawks, or skeeter hawks, or mosquito hawks, or soapsuds they would still swoop and dive against the pastel evening sky, and their call would still make something in your throat tighten up until it felt almost like getting ready to cry, only nicer, and happy.

That one line solved a lot of problems for Liz Brady, and helped form her entire personality. She never did understand the big deal people made out of names. When Rupert Van Horne publicly stated he hoped his pregnant wife would give birth to a boy "to carry on the family name," Liz looked at him with open puzzlement and didn't say a word. Rupert, of course, misunderstood both the look and the silence and interpreted them as being some kind of radical feminist statement. "Of course," he hurried to add, blundering in ever deeper, managing without half trying to trap his own foot in his own mouth. "Of course, if it's a girl she'll be welcome; after all, more and more girls are choosing to keep their own names when they get married."

Liz continued to stare. The poor kid wasn't even out yet, and Rupert had her married off, he'd be a grandfather in five minutes at this rate. "Oh, now, Liz," Rupert acted and sounded as if Liz had said something incendiary. "You know what I mean."

"Rupert," Liz confided gently, "half the time I don't even understand what you say, how could I even begin to understand what you MEAN?"

"Ha Ha," said Rupert, preferring to pretend it was all a big joke. Better to pretend to joke than to run the risk; you never knew with Liz Brady. She might look at you with wide brown eyes and then burst into laughter, or she might lift you one alongside the ear and send you arse over appetite.

Liz did not, as did her many brothers and sisters, drop out of high school and take a job. She stuck it out, the first of the family to stay long enough to graduate. So, of course, everyone got into the act. Never mind the notes and letters mimeographed on pink, green, yellow, or buff paper explaining that the school hall was small, space at a premium, and it was suggested only the parents of graduates attend the big Do. They all scrubbed themselves shiny clean, pulled on their best outfits, shined their boots and shoes, and trooped off, to see Liz get her paper. No more was it in her hand than they were on their feet cheering and clapping, whistling as loudly as if they were at a soccer game with the home team sliding the tie-breaker past the goalie seconds before the whistle blew. "As if," sniffed the assistant vice-principal, "any of them had cared a whit for education at any other time of their lives."

She toyed with the idea of university and rejected it. There wasn't anything she wanted to do or be badly enough to spend all that money, and she had the idea if you didn't really Want something you'd go weird sitting around in school day after day listening to adenoidal explanations of things you hadn't really wanted to know about anyway. So she went to work on her Uncle Gus's fishboat, cooking and deckhanding, making good money during fishing season, and sitting around on pogey when the season was over and the fleet on the beach. She learned to drink draft beer, play pool, and sock her money away when it was coming in so she'd have some when there was only pogey between her and the cold winds of winter.

Then the bottom fell out of fishing and Liz sighed with relief because she had never really Dreamed about fishing, it was just a job, which she lost when Uncle Gus lost his boat to the bank. The government responded to the economic disaster which resulted, in the opinion of the coast people, from the government's own stupid policies. Seventy-thousand-dollar-a-year bureaucrats arrived to study the situation, and they met with sixty-thousand-dollar-a-year experts in marine resources, and they all sat around in board rooms and studied charts and statistics, graphs and analysis, and never so much looked at the ocean or the spawning streams, or the shameful logging practices which had turned the spawning streams into disaster zones.

The logging companies denied any responsibility and the

bigger the company the louder the denial until the corporations were screaming and yelling, hiring academics to proclaim and yell along with and for them.

Now any bushbunny or ridgerunner knows that it takes four to six years for the roots of a downed tree to start to rot, and that once the roots start to go there's nothing left to hold the earth in place. Enough wells have caved in, and enough outhouses suddenly dropped into their own hole for even the most slackjawed and vacant-eyed to make the connection between felling a tree and having the earth cave. But when a steep slope in the Queen Charlotte Islands, logged bare and left naked under the constant rain and mist suddenly shifted and a slide a mile across at the face went downhill, blocking and erasing forever a spawning stream, an academic with a degree in forestry said publicly the clearcut logging and subsequent erosion had nothing at all to do with the mudslide. "It's rain," he said seriously "causes mud slides." Which, all in all, ought to have been expected in a place known as a rain forest. Six other slides in six other places that year caused six other spawning streams to vanish, and it was the same all up and down the coast, and had been for years. But cast not too many aspersions on the forestry expert; there was once the President of an enormous navel-gazing country who believed acid rain was caused by trees, and water pollution caused by duck droppings.

"What you going to do, Uncle Gus," Liz asked.

"Me?" he laughed, "hell fire and damnation, girl, I'm gonna get pissyeyed drunk. Then I'm gonna go tell the man at the bank that if his parents ever decide to get married I'd like to donate a couple'a bucks to the party. And then," he almost managed to grin, "I guess I'll put in for pogey and when that's finished, I guess get myself into that there whoofare line."

Liz talked to Raspberry about it and he agreed with Gus. Raspberry's real name was, what else, LaFramboise, and if he had a first name, nobody seemed to know what it was. He cursed in two languages and vowed to god he'd kill someone sooner or later, but other than that everything he had to say fit hand in glove with what Uncle Gus had said. "Fuck 'em all."

"What you gonna do?"

"Me," Raspberry put Copenhagen snuff under his bottom

lip, sucked on it idly. "Ah hell, I don't know. Prawns, maybe, if the pulp mill dioxins have left any of 'em fit to eat. If not, well, I guess I could run dope the way they used to run booze. Be better'n'doin' charter for those goddam gringo tourists."

Liz was on Unemployment Insurance for five months, then got a job driving a five ton stake truck, delivering alder firewood, sixty dollars a measured cord. She didn't have to fell the trees, she didn't have to buck off the branches, she didn't have to cut it into stove-length rounds, she didn't have to split those rounds into pieces, all she had to do was load and unload the truck. All she had to do was back up the truck to a mountain of stovewood, heave it one piece at a time up onto the back of the truck, climb up onto the truck bed and stack the wood, load the truck from front to back, secure the stake sides, be sure her red plastic was flapping so the cops wouldn't have anything to bitch about, drive the load to the address, and then unload it.

Unloading was easy. All she had to do was find out where the householder wanted the wood, then start dropping off the wood, until all the heavy pieces of alder she'd put into the truck were heaped on the ground beside the truck.

Load after load, day after day, five, sometimes six days a week, and the pay stank like old camel shit. Sixty dollars a cord and out of it came the wood lot permit, gas for the truck, gas and chain oil for the saws, new tires and repairs to the truck when needed, new chain and repairs to the saws when needed, the wages of the dumb assholes sweating their guts out in blistering sun or bone chilling rain, and her own wages. Liz figured that, all in all, the gas and oil companies profited more from her callouses and her aching back than she did.

"I figure," the exhausted little man sighed, sharpening his chain saw with practiced strokes, "the fuckin' stuff costs us forty dollars a cord before we start payin' wages."

"You'd be better off on welfare," Liz suggested carefully.

"Hell, honey," he laughed, "I AM on welfare. And the fuckers subtract what I make doin' this from the monthly check. So," he shrugged and spat something more than tobacco juice into the fine sawdust, "so, official-like, my wife and me's split up. That way she gets better whoofare."

"Holy shit," Liz breathed.

"Oh well," he packed away his saw file, "adds some spice to it all. Been together eighteen years and here I am, sneaking away before dawn, just like when we was goin' together. That way, her'n'the kids is better off, and you can bet I can fuckin-well prove to the income tax that I don't make enough at this bullshit job for them to get too excited." He rose, slowly, crinked his back to get the ache out of it. "Read in the paper where the Prime Minister just spent hisself a hundred and fifty thousand goddam tax dollars to get his official residence redec-orated. Hundred and fifty thousand goddam dollars! To redec-orate. Hell, my entire life ain't worth a hundred and fifty thou-sand dollars. Ain't a house in the whole town worth that. You can just bet it'll be a cold day'n hell before I pay any more in-come tax, I tell you," he promised.

Liz nodded, pulled on her heavy leather gloves, and began heaving pieces of wood into the truck. She figured she was making about a dollar an hour less than the legislated mini-mum wage. The only good thing about it all was she had lis-tened to every word of advice from Uncle Gus, Raspberry and Howie the faller. The job was under the table, free and clear, and she didn't declare it.

Hung by the petard of widely advertised election promises, the federals were forced to stop talking and, finally, do some-thing. Their solution was re-education for the unemployed. Liz didn't really want to go to College for a year or so to become a hair dresser and prepare herself to go on welfare with all the other unemployed hair dressers. Nor did she want to go to Col-lege to become a practical nurse, to join all the unemployed practical nurses.

She didn't really want to go back to school at all. All she really wanted to do was get a job that paid a living wage with-out killing or crippling a person. But Trades Training For Women paid you at least as much as she was getting doing fire-wood, and maybe she'd get something out of it. Maybe an ap-prenticeship and a chance to work toward journeyman's papers. Although how a woman could become a journeyMan puzzled her, and she wasn't sure what good it would do to become a tradesman in a place where fifteen thousand master journeymen were already unemployed. But what the hell, the firewood season was winding down and her back ached like fire.

There has always been doubt on the coast about whether or not the governments, whether municipal, provincial, or federal, know what in hell it is they want or what in hell it is they are doing. But in this case, every level of government obviously knew what they did NOT want. They did not want any hard-headed ham-fisted red-necked instructors asking what in hell good it would do to teach the wife how to be a pipefitter, chrissakes, I been fittin' pipe for sixteen years'n' I got my ticket and I'm still outta work. They did not want any gravel-voiced old bozo squinty-eyeing them and asking what use could come of teaching a twenty-four year old five foot two and a half inches tall one hundred and twelve pound person how to be a diesel mechanic when eight per cent of the qualified diesel mechanics in the province were standing in line for a chance to be re-trained so they could step into the electronic age. They did not want any snoose-lipped second generation Swede who had gone from grade eight to the bunkhouse, from whistle punk to second loader asking what christly good it was going to do to teach women how to drive a truck when there wasn't a logging operation in the whole province with a full crew working full time. Above all, they did not want some smartass advisor like Uncle Gus telling the women to forget about fishing or marine mechanics and get into electronic technology. So they bypassed those steely-eyed losers and turned instead to a group of people who would never be a threat to any part of the firmly entrenched system.

Few, if any, had their tickets. Fewer still had actually worked at what they were going to teach, and those who had worked, hadn't worked full time or seriously, and certainly not soberly. But they could all talk like hell and before you even had a chance to ask them, would jump up, smiling widely, to tell you, whether it interested you or not, that they, in fact, thought, and practice, were feminist men. Nobody stopped to consider that the term Feminist Man makes just about as much sense as the term Peaceful Weapon or the term Military Intelligence, nobody stopped to consider that the idea of hiring counterculture people to supervise, organize and teach trades

185

training courses makes as much sense as expecting the academics to understand education from the point of view of the long-suffering kids.

These were gentle, sensitive, non-threatening men with highly developed communication and comprehension skills. Most of them had skipped over the fortyninth at about the time Viet Nam was dying on the color TV in the living rooms of the industrialized world. That noble and worthy act of conscience was, for many, the last move in any direction that got made for years. They brought with them some of the most highly advanced educations ever seen on the coast and took those educations into the toolies where they grew beards, ate granola, contemplated their karma, refused to use birth control because it was not bio-degradable, refused to send their kids to any kind of school, and designed and built houses with materials they scrounged and salvaged from the beaches, examples of play school art and tree house construction patterned on the principles of cosmic carpentry, which hold that what comes around goes around and what is held in place with a mortar of honey and bulgar wheat will never succumb to gravity. Electronic engineers smoked dope, kept goats, and had open-ended meaningful relationships with as many others as they could find time and energy to accommodate. Some sat for hours chanting Om mane padme hum and others stood twitching and humming hari hari until even the goats began to complain. They might all have still been up in the ferns, salal, and weeds except for two overwhelming influences; the word of Werner hit the west coast and feminism made it from the radical ranks to the india cotton crowd.

The word of Werner was heard and suddenly, incredibly, overwhelmingly, they all had elitist peer group approval to shave their beards, throw off their Pied Piper rags and tatters, pull on polyester suits and become exactly the kind of people their New York, Los Angeles and Detroit parents had wanted them to be. They sold their pickup trucks, phoned daddy and mommy, floated what were called loans but known to be gifts of money, and bought silver Malibus, then headed out into the world, only some twenty years late, to sell real estate to each other, re-enter the system with a mature view towards altering it in more humanistic patterns, and they ran headlong into the changes which had taken place while the gentle sensitive non-threatening guitar playing men had been out in the ozone.

They ran into women who were no longer ready, willing, able, and eager to leap into long cotton skirts and wander barefoot and passive, having endless numbers of inevitably snot-nosed and runnyeared kids, most of whom seemed to be named Comfrey, Raven, Sturgeon, or Evening Star. Nor were the women any longer willing to accept it was their purpose in life to do all the work while the men sat around discussing meaningful things like How I Coped With Primal. Instead of digging, hoeing, raking, planting, watering, weeding, harvesting and cooking the produce of the gardens while clearing land, milking all those goddam goats, fixing the roof, digging the wells and outhouses and organizing playschool, primary school and correspondence courses, the women were looking to their own ideas. Instead of listening to the men's analysis of birth control and abortion, the women were belatedly realizing who it was who had and cared for and worried over and brought up the toddling examples of virility and ego. Better late than never they said, and handed the kids over to the men for a change.

Stuck with the kids, up to their ears in goat shit, and facing the horror of possibly having to make some meals themselves, the men looked around wildly for an escape. And found it where they had always found it. In the system they had pretended to reject. They ran home to Big Daddy and he, in the form of government, rewarded them by making them the instructors in the Introduction to Trades Training for Women program.

None of the patrists cared that in a region where women have always somehow managed to find a way to learn how to drive logging trucks and city busses, deck-hand and own fishboats, apply their own shakes and shingles to their own roofs, chop and stack wood, and generally do whatever needs done, there might be some women who could teach trades. The patrists managed to overlook entirely any number of women carpenters and welders. They looked on the hippy men the way the father of the Prodigal Son looked on him, and if they didn't quite kill the fatted calf, they did add to the ranks of fat cats.

187

The gentle sensitive non-threatening men learned the few words of formula-speak required and made their moves. Gotta go to work, honey, they said, handing back the kids they had never wanted to have to actually look after. The counter-culture women gaped. What was this? Work? He is actually going to go to work? All their mother's conditioning snapped into place, they left the consciousness raising groups, and began to lay out the work clothes, pack the lunches, set the alarm clock, get up first, start the woodstove, make the coffee, waken the working man, feed him his breakfast, stuff him into his clothes, wind up his key, and head him off in the right direction.

And Liz Brady ran head long into them when she started back to school. Liz did not need to learn how to handle a chain saw or even a skill saw, there was nothing could go wrong with her car that she couldn't fix with her copy of the Greasy Thumb manual, she did not yearn to be a plumber and play around cleaning shit-encrusted pieces of plastic toys out of the gooseneck, but times were tough and they were willing to pay her to go to school.

She had expected almost anything. She had not expected what she ran into when she ran into the gentle sensitive non-threatening pacifist anarchist former longhairs. Most of what they said made no sense to her. Half of what they said contradicted the other half of what they said. They talked of the need for environmental awareness while insulating their vans with styrofoam, they talked of non-oppressive non-colonialist non-imperialist principles while vacationing in countries where people were so poor they sold their children to an industry geared and focused entirely on male tourists, they talked of not being part of the consumer society while buying the most expensive and trendy camping gear and photography equipment, and thought nothing at all of the end result of any personal action. The conversation of the women she understood.

"After all," one said, "if I have to have some kind of shit job, it might as well pay twelve bucks an hour as pay three-fifty an hour."

"After waitressing," another agreed, "anything will seem easy."

"After marriage and three kids," a third laughed, "even

waitressing seemed easy!"

"Yeah," agreed the gentle, sensitive, non-threatening instructor, "you could take the mechanics course and then you'd be sure of an oil change every day. Ha ha."

"Oh, god," the women groaned, "here come the barefoot-and-pregnant jokes."

"Get to play around with a dipstick whenever you wanted, ha ha," he laughed.

"Give it a rest, will you?" they asked.

"Or maybe you could take up electrician, get to pull a wire all day," he teased, and when nobody laughed, smiled, or grinned, he shook his head the way you do at a child. "The trouble with you women," he said, "is you don't have any kind of a sense of humor at all."

"Sure we do," Liz countered, "we're laughin' at you all the time." And the women guffawed, hooo-rahed, laughed, and chortled. Liz earned herself an enemy.

Gentle, sensitive, non-threatening counter-culture men do not like to be taken less than seriously or to be treated lightly. They expect nothing but the fullest and most gentle of consideration. They insist at all times on being treated as something or someone extremely precious and wise. It's their reward for pretending to be gentle, sensitive, and non-threatening. Otherwise they might just as well drink beer, eat pickled eggs, and fart all night like the others.

But, of course, it all had to come down in the guise of jokes. Anything else would expose how thin the veneer of supposed non-sexist awareness really was. Tradition, rumor, and mythos insist women have no sense of humor, and everyone has heard all that so often even some women believe it and laugh without humor just to avoid being told how humorless they are. Jokes about rape. Jokes about incest. Jokes about the guy who beat his wife over the head with a fifteen pound rooster, then charged her twenty dollars so he could buy a new one because the rooster had died and it was her fault for being so hard-headed ha ha ha. Jokes about how a woman is like a rug and needs to be beaten every day to keep her in shape ha ha ha. Jokes about how a woman is like a violin and has to be played every day to keep her in tune ha ha.

Liz Brady refused to laugh. She'd been hearing jokes all her life, some better, some worse, and had long ago given up laughing at what she did not find funny. She wasn't the brightest woman in the world but she knew if someone keeps on telling jokes to someone who isn't laughing, then there is more than humor coming down, and she thought about that. She thought of her immigrant grandfather, with nothing more in common with the men he worked with than his biological plumbing arrangement, but those men accepted him in ways they would never accept Liz. She could talk their language, read it and write it, had known them all from birth, but even if she bothered to learn how to pee standing up there would be a barrier. And those jokes. Woman driver jokes, woman doctor jokes, did you hear about the woman who got her Delfen mixed up with her Crest toothpaste and when she woke up she had forty percent less cavity, ha ha.

She knew if she went to Uncle Gus he would tap-dance all over the instructor's face, but what would that do, and anyway, if it came to punchout time Liz figured she could do the job herself. And even Uncle Gus, whom she knew loved her, made jokes about hookers and whores, about how if sex is a pain in the ass you're doing it in the wrong way, ha ha. Even Uncle Gus thought it was a compliment to tell her she had a mind as good as a man's.

Liz thought about names, and the power of names, she thought about naming and the power of naming, she even spent a bit of time thinking about the Trojan horse and how they had thought it one thing and it turned out to be another, and how a joke was supposed to be harmless but could wear a hole in your soul that let your courage leak out and evaporate.

"Hey, Liz," the instructor called across the room, already grinning and laughing, "what's the difference between a fertilizer salesman and a woman?"

Liz knew he aimed it at her because she never laughed, and she knew from the looks on the faces of the other women that they knew as well as she did what was going on. What was really going on.

"Ah, for cryin' out loud," she exploded, "you still on that put-down kick of yours? Why don't you just come right out and admit you hate my guts instead of hiding behind this string of insults you call jokes?"

"What's the matter?" he pretended to tease good naturedly. "Can't take a harmless little joke? What kind of person are you to get mad at a harmless little joke?" He looked around at all the women who refused to smile at him, refused to laugh at his jokes any more. "The answer," he said loudly, "is that the salesmen SELLS his shit, the woman hands it out for free." And then he was laughing again.

Liz took a deep breath and very carefully put down the hammer she was holding. Now, now, she warned herself, if you split the fucker's head open you'll go to jail the same as if you'd assaulted a human being. Don't kill him. Don't argue. Get the power. Do the naming. In the naming-of is power and control over, remember that.

And then Liz Brady had her finest hour and it only took a minute. She grinned from ear to ear, forced her voice to a companionable and friendly tone, even managed to paint the edges of her voice with appreciation and laughter.

"Hey," she managed not to choke on her words, "that's not bad." He stared. The woman who never laughed was grinning. "I've got one for you," she said easily. "Can you tell me two things every married woman does with her asshole every morning?" He gaped, unable to believe he was hearing misogyny from the humorless woman. "Why," Liz started laughing even before she managed to form the words, and even those women who had not already either heard or figured out the joke began to chortle, then laugh loudly and helplessly. "Why, she packs his lunchbucket and kisses him goodbye."

Grey Is the Color of Hope
(an excerpt)

IRINA RATUSHINSKAYA

Finally, my last search before entry into the camp zone. All my "civvies" are confiscated with the exception of tights and woolen kerchief. The junior official carrying out the search turns out to be quite a nice woman. Her name is Lyuba. She points out to me that the kerchief, strictly speaking, ought to be confiscated because it is checkered and not plain. However, she will let it through so that I can unravel it and knit myself some socks. Colored socks are not forbidden, so nobody will take them away from me. She issues my zek* wardrobe—two chintz dresses. I am allowed to keep my jacket and boots because they conform to regulation design. After a moment's hesitation, Lyuba returns the track-suit pants she had confiscated five minutes earlier: "Here, keep them, just don't let anyone see you've got them." She smiles at me, flashing a formidable array of metal crowns. "Well, let's go then, all the others are waiting for you, won't eat till you show up."

Her speech is a strange mixture of the formal "you" and familiar "thou" forms of address. The reason for this, I learn later, is that the "politicals" are known to be high sticklers, and take exception to camp personnel addressing them in the famil-

---

*Zek: derived from the abbreviation z/k, *zaklyuchenny,* prisoner.

iar form. Still, human nature is human nature, and even in the camp, ordinary conversations take place from time to time between prisoners and personnel: in such cases, if the conversation is an amicable one, the "thou" form may pass unchallenged. For the present, I make a mental note of Lyuba's strange grammar and follow her to a gate set in a high fence. So here it is, the political zone, a camp within a camp. Whom shall I meet there?

Cursing under her breath, Lyuba wrestles with a bunch of keys and a huge padlock. The gate shudders, then finally gives with a screech of hinges. Barbed wire. a path leading to a small wooden structure which bears no resemblance to an "institutional" building. Rather, it is reminiscent of a dilapidated little summer holiday cabin. Nothing unofficial, though, about the watchtower on the other side of the barbed wire and the submachine gun in the hands of the guard manning it. A few birch trees grow around the little hut, a few blades of grass poke up here and there. That's all. I shall spend the next six years and five months on this small patch, surrounded by barbed wire.

A thin grey-haired woman comes down the path toward me. There is something instantly winning about her, from the first glance and forever. How could they have put her on trial and looked her in the face? How did that make them feel?

"Hello, there. Let me take your things."

We look at each other, almost without smiling. Then that "almost" melts, melts, melts . . . and disappears. It's a tough test, the first scrutiny of a zek.

She carries my meager bundle to the little house, even though she is twice my age. This is how guests are welcomed here, and today I am a guest. Lyuba does not accompany us, but goes back out. There are no guards around—now that is a feeling to be experienced! Guards are out there, beyond the barbed wire, but here there is just us—in our own home. With conscientious concentration, I close the door of my new home behind me: I've lost the habit of closing doors . . .

The first person I see is a dark-haired, intense, painfully thin young woman: this is Tanya Osipova. She has just come off a four-month hunger strike.

Next is petite, smiling Raya Rudenko. You can see faces

193

like hers in any Ukrainian village. Your hands simply itch to wind a traditional scarf, ends tucked in, around her head to complete the picture.

Then there is Natasha Lazareva, wafer-thin and almost transparent, an unruly shock of hair falling over her forehead.

The one who came to greet me—the woman with the amazing face—is Tatyana Mikhailovna Velikanova. I had heard about all of them on Western radio broadcasts, and now here I am, among them. My name means nothing to them—this is not their first year behind barbed wire, nor was I mentioned all that much on the radio. The length of my sentence tells them immediately that I was tried in the Ukraine. I confirm their conclusion and outline the details of my case. This is useful information, but, even without that, they will have my measure before too long. We will be together for many years, and in that time, get to know all that there is to know about one another—maybe even too much. In the meantime, I tell them as much as I can about what is new "out there," even though my latest news is already seven months old. They, in turn, acquaint me with the history of our Small Zone: from now on, this is my heritage, too.

I am introduced to a very important personage—the Zone's cat, Nyurka; she is a fully fledged member of the family, has lived here longer than most, and shares our rations. In principle, prisoners are not allowed to keep cats or pets of any kind. Unfortunately the camp rats, blissfully unaware of this prohibition, had decided to make our Small Zone their headquarters, and became so rapacious and fearless that they drove not just the prisoners but also the guards to distraction. Just try rummaging through a prisoner's locker if there is a huge rat sitting inside! All very well if it only just leaps out and makes a run for it to the accompaniment of your startled yells, but what if it bites you? For this reason, when the women in our Zone obtained a kitten from the criminal zone, the guards pretended not to notice. Nyurka quickly grew into a large cat, sober of mien and the scourge of all rats, let alone mice. She brought the rodent population to book very quickly, and her progeny was always much sought after by camp personnel: excellent heredity plus Nyurka's training produced superb ratters. I shake Nyurka's polite paw with due deference. Her eyes are bright yellow and traditionally enigmatic. We try to determine Nyurka's pedigree, even though a greater mixture would be hard to find. "Mordovian Sentinel," suggests Natasha, and "Mordovian Sentinel" she is henceforth.

More discussion, laughter, a happy confusion of words and thoughts . . .

And I really do feel happy: this is my home. They are all impossibly thin, my new friends, dressed in a motley collection of rags and tatters, yet how they hold themselves! They have all known each other for a long time, but invariably observe the courteous "you" form in speech. Living in close quarters makes it essential to maintain some degree of psychological distance, and one way to achieve this is to use the formal rather than the familiar form of address. Scrupulous observance of norms of courtesy prevents the flaring up of irritation over trifles, inhibits the tendency to pry, helps to avoid that multitude of faux pas that make life in the criminal camps such hell.

"Prison is less to be feared than people," said elderly "Auntie" Vera to me during transportation.

Here, in our Zone, the inmates are not to be feared, though, simply because they are human beings in the full sense of the word. We may be crammed into a small house, we may be dressed in rags, they can carry out searches and lightning raids in our quarters, but we retain our human dignity. We will not get down on all fours to them, try though they may to make us. We will not carry out demeaning or senseless commands, because we have not surrendered our freedom. Yes, we are behind barbed wire, they have stripped us of everything they could, they have torn us away from our friends and families, but unless we acknowledge this as their right, we remain free. For this reason, we study every camp rule very carefully. We have to get up at six o'clock in the morning? Well, why not? Work? Certainly, unless we are ill or on hunger strike. We do not object to work: making protective gloves for workers is a clean and worthwhile task. Meet the output quotas? That will depend on what condition we are in, and that, in turn, depends on how you treat us: if we have the strength, you'll get your quotas in full; if not—blame yourselves . . . wear zek clothing?

There is no alternative, short of going naked. But if you expect us to clear the no-man's-land strip — forget it! We will have no part in the building or maintenance of camps and prisons, either directly or indirectly. Prison upkeep is your job, not ours. You forbid us to give things to each other? That is none of your business, screws and KGB scum; we shall give or lend each other whatever we will, the last thread off our backs, if need be, without your sanction. As for springing to attention at the entry of any member of the camp management — well, we don't acknowledge your authority, nor do we have the slightest interest in your penal pecking order — we don't belong to your ranks. Furthermore, elementary good manners decree that it is men who should rise to their feet when a woman enters the room, not vice versa. You have different standards of behavior? Yes, we've noticed that, it would be hard not to. But we'll stick to our own, with or without your consent. Of course, we know that we shall be penalized for this. However, we shall retain our sense of human dignity, and not turn into trained circus animals.

When a dog is trained to jump over a stick, the stick is raised a little higher every time. When a dog licks a hand, persons like you command it to lick your boot . . . But we are not dogs, and we will not jump at your command. Remember that. Exert yourselves to address us formally, or we will not respond, even if you shout until your lungs burst; we will simply not hear you. Stop pestering us to attend your political sessions, your lectures and similar propaganda; we shall walk out of the room without listening.

The result? Young Officer Shishokin had to admit, crestfallen: "It's easier to deal with two hundred ordinary criminals than with you in the Small Zone."

Yet why should that be so? We are invariably polite — to you, and among ourselves. There are no fights or thefts in our Small Zone, no escape attempts. We do our work conscientiously, all the gloves we turn out are without defects . . . In other words, we live like decent human beings and give our guards no headaches.

"It's because," admits Shishokin candidly, "when we are in the criminal zone, we feel the power of our position."

How true, how very true. *This* is what they value above all else — power. Let the inmates of the criminal zone brawl, swear, rape, sabotage working tools and machinery on the sly, sink to the lowest depths of depravity. Nevertheless he, Shishokin, is their master, and when he enters a room, they will stand to attention. As for us, we don't care about his good will, even though he has the power to deprive us of the right to use the camp kiosk for a month, or to have us thrown into the punishment isolation cell, the so-called SHIZO.* Our attitude gives Shishokin an inferiority complex — and not just him. Still, there is nothing we can do about that. We are not psychiatrists, and the chances are that he has been suffering from this complex for some time. Why else would someone become, quite voluntarily, a prison keeper unless he felt the need to bolster up his confidence at the expense of people who have been stripped of their rights? Well, you'll get no chance to boost your ego in dealings with us. Why, none of you even dare to look us straight in the eye.

I absorbed these basic tenets of Zone life as my due heritage, and they suited me down to the ground. In fact, I had observed these norms even earlier, in the frightening solitude of the KGB investigation prison, partly through instinct and partly through common sense.

Just because I am imprisoned it does not mean that I shall let anyone deny me the freedom to behave like a normal human being. High-sounding words? Yet they are worthless unless backed up by deeds. Had we in the Small Zone valued our skins above all else, we would not have ended up as political prisoners; we would have stayed put in whatever place decreed by our residence permits, licked boots as ordered, and called ourselves "free" . . . But now I am no longer alone, I am amongst my own kind. What luck!

The Zone does, however, pose a problem I have not encountered before: the wearing of a cloth identity tag on my chest. I had seen such tags en route to the camp, but on others. What are they? At first glance, something that hardly seems worth a fuss. A black cloth triangle, inscribed with your sur-

---

*SHIZO: derived from *shtrafnoy izolyator* — literally, punishment isolator.

name, initials and work brigade number. But what brigade? As far as I know, I am not a member of any brigades or organizations (International PEN Club aside). Joining organizations and brigades is something free people do voluntarily, and nobody here has asked my consent; merely, the camp administration assigns all prisoners to brigades, each of which has a number . . . The identity tag must be sewn on to one's clothing and be worn at all times. The official reason is that the tags make it easier to determine who is who. What utter nonsense! There are only five of us in the Small Zone. At times, both in the past and in the future, the population of the Small Zone exceeded ten people — but not by much . . . And anyway, everyone in Barashevo (our camp took its name from the nearest settlement) could recognize us at a glance from any angle. We do not make up a work brigade, nor do we need these ridiculous fictions. Therefore, why should we wear identity tags? Ah — it's regulations, is it? Now, what should I do? Should I sew on the tag, or not?

The question of wearing the identity tag or not is raised by the others on my second day in the Small Zone. As a measure of precaution, we go outside to talk. The house is bugged, so any conversations not intended for the ears of the authorities take place out in the yard. If anything confidential must be said inside, it is written down on a piece of paper which is later burned. But at present the weather is holding out, the discussion is likely to be a long one, so we spread our jackets on the ground and sit outside. Nobody tries to influence my decision either way: I am simply warned that as tomorrow is Monday, the supervisor of our fictional work brigade, Senior Lieutenant Podust, will be coming around to order me to don the identity tag. Therefore, it is best that I give the matter some thought now, and determine my course of action in order to avoid regrets later. I can see that the inmates of the Small Zone have rejected identity tags as a senseless and humiliating demand. But we are not a real brigade, and I am in no way bound to observe this Zone tradition: it is purely a matter for my own conscience. Not one of my new friends would expect me to emulate her behavior — we are free individuals, after all. The voice of my conscience has already given me a clear response, but nobody is pressing me for an instant declaration of intent.

Tatyana Mikhailovna explains that I, like everyone else on strict regime, am entitled to three meetings a year with relatives. One is a "long" meeting, lasting from one to three days at the discretion of the camp authorities. Two other meetings, at least six months apart, last two hours. These "short" meetings take place across a table (you cannot even exchange a kiss) and a representative of the camp administration sits between you, with the power to terminate the meeting immediately should the conversation touch upon any forbidden subject. The long meeting could be granted virtually straight away. What a blissful thought: alone with Igor in the small meeting room, if only for twenty-four hours. And, oh, how I need such a meeting: there is a full collection of new poems in my head, I must get them out of here . . . And the Zone needs it, too, for it is past time for more information to go to the outside world. After all, so much has happened since the last lot: things like Tatyana Osipova's four-month hunger strike, just about everyone has been in the SHIZO, there was a strike . . . But Tatyana Mikhailovna makes no mention of these events; the time has not yet come to discuss such matters with me. She stresses that the administration can deprive me of any or all these meetings for "violation of camp regulations." As yet, I have a clean record and, should Igor arrive today, the camp authorities would be obliged by law to let us meet. Still that is an impossibility, there is no way he could get here in under a week. First, he must receive my letter, informing him of my whereabouts, then the journey itself would take time . . .

But the question of the identity tag must be resolved tomorrow, and if I refuse to wear it, that will be construed as a violation. And that could mean a cancelled meeting. Before my time, the inmates of the Small Zone did not have to wear identity tags for some time; everyone realized the absurdity of it. Then the authorities began a gradual tightening up of the screws. Last autumn, Lieutenant Podust was assigned to the Zone, and she has a real fixation about identity tags. Indeed, the more ridiculous the regulation, the more it is to her taste. So, for the past six months she has been waging war with the

Zone: cancelling meetings with relatives, depriving the women of use of the camp kiosk, threatening confinement to SHIZO . . . Therefore, my possible meeting with Igor is under a very real threat. Nor are the subsequent ones likely to be granted, either; the authorities are bound to find plenty of reasons to cancel them in the course of a year. The choice facing me is clear cut: either I wear the tag and have a meeting with Igor — possibly the only one for the next seven years — or I refuse, and take the consequences. In any case, the outlook for the future is bleak — SHIZO is SHIZO. What SHIZO is really like I have yet to experience, but I already know that it means cold, hunger, filth and inaction. SHIZO is total deprivation. Yet at present I am not particularly worried about the future; the meeting with Igor is another matter . . .

My dearest love, will you find it in your heart to forgive me for placing our possible meeting under threat? You know that I cannot do otherwise, that I dare not jump even once over this prison rod at their command. What would you do in my place? Did we not once promise each other that in the case of arrest we would not let them use either of us as a tool to blackmail the other? So I say firmly: "No, I won't wear the identity tag."

Oh, how hard it is, at times, to do what one must! And, paradoxically, how easy it is, too: would I have been happier if I had donned the identity tag, pleased Podust, had a meeting and retained access to the kiosk, and then, burning with shame, watched Tatyana Mikhailovna going off for a spell in SHIZO because she wears no identity tag, and I do? . . . Beyond a shadow of a doubt, that tag would have been a burning coal against my breast.

Tanya Osipova and Tatyana Mikhailovna beam delightedly at my words. "That's the spirit," approves Tanya, while Tatyana Mikhalovna makes certain: "Irochka, are you sure you have thought everything through carefully?"

My dears, I have, and Igor will understand, no matter what happens. So let's all rot in the SHIZO together, if need be. That's what camp is for — a test of strength. Nyurka the cat prowls over and settles herself in Tanya Osipova's lap. Nyurka doesn't wear an identity tag either. She purrs contentedly and rolls over on to her back. The spring sun is making itself felt.

Raya Rudenko is poking around in the ground, sowing seeds: flowers (which the law permits) and vegetables (which it doesn't). We urban dwellers are not entrusted with such a vital task; it will be our job to water the crop later. Right now, Raya asks Natasha Lazareva and me to make some small wooden stakes to which future clumps of flowers will be tied. She needs several dozen of them. None of us are allowed to have tools of any kind apart from those essential for our sewing work. So there is neither a knife nor a hatchet to hand. Still, there is a hammer in the sewing room. What relation it has to sewing God knows, but one should never question one's luck. We dig around in the ground and find some longish, sharp pieces of flint—the soil around here is very stony. There are several boards in the woodshed, and we split them into pieces using a bit of flint as a wedge. Our success rate at producing suitable stakes is not high, but the unsuitable pieces can be used for kindling later. We laugh helplessly—talk about Stone Age technology!

Natasha is from Leningrad. She is serving a sentence for producing a *samizdat* journal, *Maria,* which was devoted to feminist issues. The problems raised in this journal, such as the double workload of Soviet women—eight hours at work followed by five to six hours queuing for food, the horrors of communal kitchens, doing the entire family wash in a hand basin—were to appear in the official Soviet press also, but much later, in 1986. In 1982, when Natasha was arrested, talking about such matters was classed as "anti-Soviet agitation and propaganda."

Natasha has tormented eyes and a merry mouth. We exchange jokes as we sit there, skinning our hands against the rough boards. Tomorrow, Natasha is being hospitalized: the camp food has wrought havoc with her intestines. Alas, she was not to be given any treatment after admission into the infirmary, but discharged for socializing with the maintenance staff. Right up to the beginning of 1984 the camp authorities accused her of malingering, and had her confined, time and again, to SHIZO. It took a number of our collective hunger strikes to finally secure medical treatment for her in 1984. She was diagnosed as suffering from neglected ulcerative colitis, an ailment impossible to cure in camp conditions . . . But for the moment, we are all enjoying a peaceful, happy day. One of the few that is left to us.

The evening meal is brought around. That means it must be five o'clock. The meal consists of very salty water in which bits of fish — scales, guts and all — and a couple of small potatoes float dismally. Raya sets to work: carefully, she removes the scraps of fish and cleans them (better late than never). The pathetic handful of edible fish is chopped up together with the potatoes, a bit of garlic is added for flavor and the whole is topped with a frugal dash of sunflower seed oil; by law, we are supposed to get 15 grams of this oil per head daily. As for butter — well, we can forget about that for years to come. Presto, Small Zone Salad is served. A light meal, by any standards.

"A real lady never eats heavy food after six o'clock," we decide, amid laughter. As there is nothing else, there is not much left to do but laugh.

Tanya Osipova switches on our ancient black and white television set. It is constantly breaking down. We patch it up, it works for a few days, then another valve goes. At one stage, the camp management decided to connect this set to a master switch in the guardroom, and thus control what we could or could not watch. But Tanya Osipova and I quickly learned how to jump-start it by crossing a couple of wires, and the guards pretended not to notice. Not everyone, after all, was like Lieutenant Podust and, truth to tell, they did not really care whether we watched television or not, so long as it was switched off after lights out. As far as the administration was concerned, steps had been taken to control our viewing, and that was all that was necessary for their report to tell to their overlords.

Today, however, nobody tries to interfere and we watch a play by Rostand: good old *Cyrano de Bergerac*. Tanya sheds tears as Cyrano dies. That's our Tanya; she'll cry over a book or a film, and then stick out four days, alone and unsupported in a solitary punishment cell, refusing food and water to get our confiscated Bible back. It worked, too. The administration caved in and our Bible was returned: they knew that the fifth day of a "dry" hunger strike — that is, when no fluids at all are ingested — is tantamount to a death warrant, and they did not want to risk the undesirable publicity that would ensue once the outside world got to hear that a political prisoner died because of a confiscated Bible. Admittedly, on that particular occasion, Tanya did get some quite unexpected support: there were prisoners from the criminal zone in neighboring cells, and they all conducted a twenty-four-hour hunger strike of solidarity. In fact, they intended to strike for a longer period, but Tanya herself dissuaded them — it is easier for the administration to implement reprisals against ordinary criminals than against the "politicals"; their situations would have been too disparate.

Tatyana Mikhailovna and I wander outside to look at the night sky. Nyurka follows us. They say that cats do not distinguish colors, and I wonder whether red Betelgeuse and yellow Capella look the same to her. We discuss the likelihood of this, then the talk veers to the human biological field, to Tatyana Mikhailovna's inexplicable aversion to cartoon films, to those we have left behind "out there" . . . It's harder for them than for us, right now. We have spent a quiet, pleasant day, whereas they will be tearing themselves apart with worry about us. By the time you write a letter, by the time it passes through censorship and reaches its destination, everything could have changed radically. They could be thinking that we are as well as can be expected, and in the meantime, we would all have been consigned to SHIZO. As a matter of fact, the censors will not let any mention of SHIZO go through; "Nothing about punishments" is the standing order. Absolute shrinking violets, our KGB: they are ready to torment us from morning till night, but they are too shy to let the world know about it. And we have to maintain silence, too, or our letters will be confiscated. But we'll get the better of you yet, boys — we shall do our utmost to spread the word about everything that goes on here. You can deprive us of our meetings with our loved ones, confiscate our correspondence, but the information will still go out and reach its target. How shall we manage that? Ah, these are our zek secrets. I would gladly share them with all decent, honest people, but — who knows? — this book may fall into KGB hands . . . As they say, the less you know, the sounder you sleep.

The Year I Was Ten

BONNIE MORRIS

This is a true story. It could have happened to any kid in my situation.

In 1971, when I was ten, my family moved from the radical hippie chic of southern California to a small tobacco town in North Carolina. My younger brother and I viewed this move with contempt and fear. We knew that our parents' unusual habits and avocations might very well appear marginal in the churning counterculture of Los Angeles, but how would we be received in the South? We were renegades, eggheads, long-hairs, outside agitators, practitioners of yoga. My father smoked that funny stuff. We owned a VW van. My brother and I, in order to nurture a respect for Eastern mysticism, had to put our lost baby teeth in the statue of Buddha on the mantel, rather than under our pillows. (The Buddha rewarded us as generously as any Tooth Fairy, I might add.) I was comfortable with my family's style, but couldn't help wondering if we would receive any portion of that famed Southern hospitality.

We spent that first summer in Carolina adjusting—an arduous process. My shaggy-headed brother was beaten up by neighborhood kids who accused him of being a girl. My mother was thrown out of the "Piggily Wiggily" (a grocery store chain) for wearing a halter-top which showed her navel to the shop-

ping public. I attended day camp (where the head counselor offered to kiss me) and visited a go-cart and soapbox-derby competition (which turned out to be rigged by a local dignitary's
brother-in-law).

In August, my mother forced my brother and me into the
VW van and drove us to the local public school to enroll us for
fall. The school was empty, cavernous, and smelly. We met with
the rotund and sneering principal, Mr. V, who announced that
he didn't cotton to none of that wild, California foolishness in
them wild, California schools (I supposed this to be a passing
reference to the student movements at Berkeley, but as a ten-
year-old I hardly felt responsible for revolutionary developments
in higher education, and frantically reviewed my brief grammar
school experience for indications of wildness). The principal was
confounded when I informed him that I had already read, in
fourth grade, the standard curriculum texts for fifth grade in his
fine school. In a spiteful gesture, and over the protests of my
mother (who had left her halter top at home on this day), Mr. V
assigned me to the lowest level fifth grade class.

On the first day of school in fall 1971, I found that my
classroom was in a warped old bungalow shack, evidently left
over from plantation days. This room was detached from the
rest of the sagging school, which allowed our teacher the leeway
to shriek at us angrily without fear of interruption. In tones of
boredom and scorn, Mrs. F informed remedial fifth that we
were a dumb group barely capable of wiping our own rear ends.
Her scatalogical references heightened as she added that we kids
would be responsible for bringing john-paper for the shack's
commode (I had no idea what she was talking about; in L.A. it
was a toilet). I sat in amazed terror as Mrs. F threatened and
berated us—the boy sitting next to me wet his pants.

In the evening my parents asked us how the first day of
school went. "I'm taller than my teacher," announced my
brother, who was wearing a plastic glove printed in religious admonitions—evidently a back-to-school gift in his classroom. My
parents refused to believe he was bigger than his teacher (he was
seven) and admonished him for lying. It wasn't until Parents'
Night that they met his teacher and discovered that she was a
midget.

•

What our elementary school lacked in funds it more than made up for in "spirit" — namely, a blatant disregard of the separation of church and state. Every day at noon, Mrs. F shouted at us to pray aloud. We then marched to the lunchroom, where grits, pork biscuit, collards, "slaw" and beans were served. There was no recess period or free time — only a brief P.E. lesson for twenty minutes each day, wherein one class at a time marched onto the tiny macadam "yard" to play a disciplined team game chosen by the teacher. Broken limbs were common, as students used this time to take out pent-up aggressions on one another's bodies.

I lasted for three weeks in Mrs. F's class — during which time I completed all of the work assigned for the next three months. After reviewing my thick notebooks, Mrs. F snorted and sent me to a spooky attic room in another plantation outbuilding, where, with no introduction or explanation of the process, I was given a battery of I.Q. tests. (I well recall the first question: "Define mutilation.") Three days later Mrs. F interrupted my biography research on Ponce de Leon to say "Git your books, you're going into the E.T. class."

Everyone gasped "Durn" aloud. E.T., at this school, stood for "exceptionally talented." In each grade there was one classroom for those presumed to be gifted, and I rushed to the shack's commode to brush my wispy braids in order to make a good impression. Mrs. F marched me over to the school building proper and dumped me into the sterile chamber occupied by twenty-five miserable precocious misfits.

As I soon found out, fifth grade E.T. offered none of the artistic stimuli, alternative curriculum, or creative challenges one might naively assume to be part of an accelerated program. We were merely worked to death: forced to complete four times as much boring, conventional, and reactionary state-approved stuff as our non-E.T. counterparts. There was no art, music, or extra-curricular aspect to this package. We had French once a week — a laughable hour of listening to recordings of middle-aged men singing about the joys of owning a bike and young girls obsequiously thanking their fathers for gifts of math textbooks. We had the standard, forced P.E. lesson every day, and every day it was German dodge ball, without exception — more broken arms ensued. The incredible amounts of homework reduced me to a near-nervous breakdown as I struggled to write nine reports assigned over the weekend. Over this ship of conscripts reigned the eerily smiling Mrs. S, a character far more disturbing than Mrs. F. Indeed, Mrs. F had confided to my mother that Mrs. S was "enough to scare the teats offen a witch." Still, I counted myself more fortunate than my brother, whose teacher regularly "paddled" the second grade, and whose curriculum included casual lectures on sin by visiting Baptist preachers.

But it was evident that Mrs. S disliked me. An early feminist, I refused to wear party dresses on field trips. I openly defended Chinese culture in our geography lesson, complaining that our textbook had no information on the artistic or spiritual contributions of Chinese history (Mrs. S barked at me "You wanna tell us about all them BABIES your COMMUNISTS killed, Bonnie?"). Finally, my father had written a letter, favoring the legalization of marijuana, to the local newspaper which everyone read. Mrs. S was pale with shock and took me into the hall to lecture me on the evils of weed, which, truthfully, I had not associated with my father until then (he told us it was "corn" in the garden). The stage was set; Mrs. S knew what I was. But it was not until the spring that I rebelled.

I had grown increasingly disgusted with our lunchroom rules. We were forced to sit family-style around a long table, each class isolated from the next, with the teacher at the head of the table dispensing etiquette. Mrs. S improved on this already indigestive system by forcing a different kid each week to be table monitor. The table monitor's job was to write down the names of anyone who misbehaved, ate sloppily, etc. With Big Brother watching, one's debatable pleasure in the lumpy grits and greasy pork fat was lessened still further.

One day after lunch, during the ritual shaming of each student in our class whose name appeared on the table monitor's list, I was called onto the carpet for allegedly eating a bean with my fingers. After telling me what she thought of such behavior, Mrs. S ordered me to write "I will learn better table manners" 100 times. I considered refusing, but satisfied myself by writing the whole assignment with crossed fingers (thus invalidating any sincerity).

During a rare moment of unsupervised socializing the next day, I gathered my classmates around me and spoke out against the tattletale system. I had thought long and hard about this and had my parents' support: I would not accept the job of table monitor when my number came up. I urged everyone else to follow my lead in noncompliance. In this way we could swiftly dismantle the table monitor system, which everyone hated. My classmates were impressed and vowed to support me. Then one kid, a handsome smartass who was table monitor for that week, announced that he would take down the name of Mrs. S herself at lunch and see how she liked it. Everyone raved about this bold new plan, which I somehow felt morally undermined our larger efforts. But my feeble protests went unheard. A doomed woman, I marched to lunch.

After eating that noon, we were marched back to class and sank back into our seats with nervous anticipation. Mrs. S asked Michael for the ritual reporting of names.

"There was only one name, uh—and it was yours," he muttered defiantly. The class paled in discomfort as Mrs. S icily enquired what she had *done* at lunch. Mad with power, Michael recited, "You played with your bread, you didn't use your napkin, you picked up your food with your hand and put it back down, you wiped your nose with your hand,"—an admirable combination of the various sins we had all been cited for. Mrs. S listened with deafening patience and then crashed her fist onto her desk, singing out sweetly "Well, MICHAEL, that is very RUDE of yew," and then push came to shove in the E.T. class.

I rose and stated my platform: I would never be a table monitor. I objected in principle to the practice of training kids to spy on one another and turn one another in. The world had many such problems and as kids we had the potential to rise above espionage. I urged a system of cooperation, friendship, and lunchtime privacy. I claimed that the entire class stood behind me. Mrs. S immediately snarled, "Class, why don't *you* like me?" and I witnessed the sickening capitulation of my classmates as, one by one, confronted by their enormously grim teacher, each kid denied association with me and claimed to love Mrs. S. "I don't know what Bonnie's talking about, I like you fine," they bleated, glaring at me.

Mrs. S had heard enough. She told us that we were the least ma-toor class she had ever had and that reporting on each other was going to be a part of college, did we understand? She cited the University of North Carolina honor code, which required students to report acts of cheating, plagiarism, and suchlike. I felt certain that table manners were not part of the above litany, but vowed then and there to avoid UNC.

After the entire class had been verbally beaten into submission, Mrs. S sent Michael and me to the principal's office for a little talk. The principal shook his fist in Michael's face and threatened to beat his butt. He reminded me that he was under no obligation to put up with that wild California stuff I used to get away with in them wild schools out there. We heard that we owed respect and obedience to all teachers and all persons older than ourselves and had no right to question any of their obviously wise and prudent governing of our ill-mannered and un-ma-toor lives. He swiveled in his chair, the wart on his forehead throbbing. After more threats, we were dismissed.

Mrs. S called in my mother and told her that none of the other children liked me and that troublemakers were always unpopular. She declared that I was full of "bull" and that her daddy would have taken off his belt and whupped her if she had dared say or do the things I attempted. My mother suggested the class homework load was absurd. Mrs. S said there were things we had to do whether we liked them or not and that I was, again, "full of it." "We'll just have to agree to disagree," declared Mom.

Ten days later I was preparing to give a science report on the role of the gonads in reproduction. I asked Mrs. S if there was any way I could avoid reading the paper out loud to my classmates, as I was sure they would snicker at the word "penis." Mrs. S looked at me and said "Well now, Bonnie, you don't want to do much for me, do you? Do you want to go to college? Do you think you'd get accepted at UNC? I don't think they'd take you." She said some other things, too.

•

Fifth grade ended. We roared gratefully into summer. However, lurking at the back of my mind was the forthcoming trial of sixth grade E.T. with Mrs. Y. Logic dictated that sixth grade would be even harder than fifth, and Mrs. Y was rumored to be even more eccentric than Mrs. S. I spent most of the summer of 1972 entertaining these dark thoughts in the orthodontist's chamber, where I had my new braces affixed to my teeth. Consequently, I showed up on the first day of sixth grade with a neck brace wrapped around my head—orthodontist's orders—and Mrs. Y's first words to me were, "Are you normal?"

To my distress, sixth grade E.T. met in the same smelly plantation shack where I had once studied early American explorers with Mrs. F. Apparently, after last spring's debacle, the principal had decided it was more prudent to isolate the precocious from the rest of the school than to isolate the remedial class. Now rearranged, the shack had its own non-paved play yard so that we were also isolated from the basketball court and equipment shed.

Mrs. Y, having heard about our little group from Mrs. S, put her cards on the table on the first day of school. She announced that she did not believe in women's liberation and that there were certain things boys were capable of doing and certain things girls might do. As we "exceptionally talented" girls digested this, Mrs. Y added that we were all far too young to have boy-girl "friendships" and thus would be segregated as much as possible. No longer did we sit at the lunchroom table as an entire class; the boys had their own bench far across the room. Naturally, this exacerbated rather than alleviated any tension between the sexes, and, giddy with male superiority, the boys began to bash us during P.E. lesson and turn us in for the slightest academic infractions.

Hygiene was another of Mrs. Y's political obsessions. We came to dread her frequent lectures on what happened to bad children who bit their nails (germs lurked beneath). Bad boys with long hair would develop fungus molds on their foreheads. Parasites were all around us on walls and ceilings, and the foolish student who touched surfaces and then put his/her finger in mouth was only asking for a disease. Mrs. Y actually went so far as to establish a reward system for the healthiest.

Our greatest terror in sixth E.T. was the "country booklet." This was Mrs. Y's one original contribution to the mega-rote E.T. curriculum. Each student in her class had to produce a twenty-five-page research paper on a particular country. Not surprisingly, the countries were selected and assigned by Mrs. Y with a hearty contempt for Asia, Africa, the Middle East and anything Communist-affiliated. Once again, my bid for cultural examination of China was rebuffed with a lecture. All of us trembled at the seemingly insurmountable task of producing an extensive research paper of graduate seminar length while simultaneously churning out the other sixth grade E.T. homework and reports. We were eleven but walked bowed down as if ninety.

A few weeks into the school term, I became numbingly aware that an entire year of academic prison was barely underway. I had no idea how I would survive the stifling, repetitive routine of sixth grade. Each day was longer than the next. In our cramped bungalow, I watched the clock as its hands slouched toward ten-thirty each day, at which time we were allowed to stand up and move around for ten minutes. My brave attempt at political anonymity in this class failed me as Mrs. Y, in a phony civics lesson, made each student stand up and announce who their parents were voting for in the November election. I was the only student whose parents were not campaigning for the re-election of Richard Nixon. Everyone stared as I miserably confided that my parents intended to vote for George McGovern. Mrs. Y lectured me on the evils of the Democratic party platform and the weakness of McGovern and the beauty of the war in Vietnam. From then on, every kid wore a Nixon button to class, and so did Mrs. Y.

I was dimly aware that long days, meaningless work, and lunatic teachers were standard fare in grammar school, but in California the "E.T." classes had been somewhat of a route *out* of such purgatory. My mother assured me these were my golden years of childhood as I stood painfully swabbing my newly-tightened braces. Then, one crisp fall day, I arrived home to be told that my brother and I were changing schools. Apparently, we had been placed on the waiting list of a private progressive school months before. Now we were officially enrolled and in two days would enter a new world of art, music, drama, creative writing, dance, gardening, Asian and Hispanic history, and individualized coursework guided by Quaker teachers who all planned to vote for McGovern. My brother and I sat in open-mouth suspicion as our parents described this cornucopia of unharassed and pleasurable learning. Could such a place exist?

The next day I slept blissfully late and returned to Mrs. Y's class during what I well knew was the most boring part of the day to collect my books with a sensational flourish. In a loud, nervous voice I announced that I was leaving sixth grade E.T. to attend the Carolina Friends School. Mrs. Y informed me that it was a wild school full of undisciplined longhairs where no one ever learned anything; she had once gone there to visit and had been hit in the head by a book thrown across the room. My now former classmates stared at me in noncomprehending envy. They would go on, some of them, to Duke and to MIT, to UNC and its honor code; some of them would go on to high school pregnancy, early marriage, abusive spouses, accidental death. One or two became criminally insane. On that day I had no sense of the Southern gothic legacy of poverty and discipline that was my classmates' lot, no regard for how humbly they endured the curse of intellectual ability. I remember only my rapt departure from the shack, standing on the steps letting the autumn wind scatter, all over the country, the first pages of my never-finished Country Booklet.

How Grandmother Spider Brought the Light

PAULA GUNN ALLEN

Oomaa-oo, as they say when telling a story at our Pueblo. Of course, this isn't a Pueblo story, but I'm a Pueblo woman, after all. The people were in the dark and they were tired of not knowing when to go to sleep and when to get up. They didn't have Oshrats to pray to in the mornings when they went to the water to greet Mother water and immerse themselves in her. True, there was a place of greater heat during some hours, and the air around them was more gray than dark, but they didn't have much light to work and play by.

They were also yearning for a cozy fire to sit next to when they told stories after the little ones went to sleep, after the daily hanging out was done. Besides, they knew that fire was very powerful, and they wanted the joy and power that came to people who had fire to grace their lives.

They really liked hanging out with one another, and the only reason they didn't do as much of it as they liked is that when the darkness got a little darker some of them insisted it was time to go to sleep. They believed that if they had fire and some regular daylight they'd be able to spend even more time telling stories and gossiping and being together. Maybe they would even have new ceremonies to hold and go to.

So anyway, the people learned about some other people in a

distant country who had fire light. They heard that those people got to hang out all day and all night telling stories, singing, dancing, and generally carousing till all hours.

Well, they thought about all this for a long time. They thought about what they needed and wanted. They thought about those rumors and they even sent some men out to see if they were true. They listened to each other's ideas about what they might do if they had some fire light, and dreamed up all sorts of interesting activities. Even those who liked to sleep early got caught up in the goings on. They began to think that maybe they could sleep more in light time, when there was true light, so they could also enjoy the fire when it was very dark.

There were a few, of course, who had some reservations about the whole affair, but aside from mumbling a bit, mostly among themselves about possible dangers and hazards from such a volatile and untested force, especially when it was in the untrained hand of the would-be merry makers, they kept their reservations to themselves. And this, of course, is how reservations first got started.

After a proper length of time planning and dreaming, discussing and surmising, mumbling and wondering had gone by, the people settled into the serious business of strategy. "How will we get some fire light," they asked. "The people over in that other country who have some won't give us some. We tried."

H'mmm, they sighed. They stopped discussing for a long pause.

"I know," one of the people finally said. He was a tall skinny man who decorated himself magnificently with feathers. He was especially proud of his luxurious thick hair that he wore all brushed up in a spiky punk style. He kept it in place with a nice sticky clay that came from the nearby clay bed. His name was Buzzard.

Buzzard uncoiled his lanky form and stood. "Maybe someone will take a little jaunt over there long after it gets dark over there, maybe just before light, and try and snag some," he intoned sonorously.

"Yeah, you need practice snagging," someone hooted. The others laughed.

After the general merriment at Buzzard's expense subsided,

it was agreed that Buzzard would go. When the first rays of light were just emerging over the saddleback rise near the village, Buzzard came limping in. He was definitely the worse for wear, his fine feathers matted and blackened. He sported a bald spot right at his crown. The hair there never did grow back. "I blew it," he said resignedly. "Maybe someone else should try."

Well, a couple of others went, but with the same negative result.

Everyone was feeling pretty glum about how matters stood. They were trying to reconcile themselves to doing without the exciting fire light—which meant adjusting their plans, dreams and hopes to fit their accustomed circumstances. Most were disappointed, except for the few who were relieved. They went whistling and giggling about their tasks, relieved that nothing fearful and different was going to unsettle their equilibrium just yet.

But Spider got to thinking. She was always doing that. She couldn't help it, of course, anymore than Buzzard could help swooping, strutting and snagging. She spun out her thought and wove implications, extrapolations, and a few elegant daydreams into a satisfying pattern. Her Dreaming done, she joined the folks sitting dejectedly around the empty place where they could almost *see* the fire light snapping cheerily on the sticks and branches they had carefully laid out in such anticipation just a few days before.

"Well," Spider began softly. "Maybe someone might try to get some fire light," she said to no one in particular. she sat down carefully so as not to jar her fragile joints unduly. "It's true I'm old and slow," she continued. She paused again for a silence, breathing it in and out comfortingly.

No one looked at her. As was their way, they just kept on sitting as they had been, doing whatever they had been doing even if that was just brooding or wishing over their regrets. But of course, they were all attending carefully to what she said.

"It's true I'm a very small person and not very strong," she said at last, to no one in particular. "But I think I could give it a try. My old body would appreciate some fire light at night sometimes. And I wouldn't mind having a little brightness to

215

tend." They sat companionably in silence after that. Some wandering off, some coming over to join the group from time to time.

So Spider set out, much earlier than Buzzard and the others had because she was much slower. Along her way she stopped off at the clay bed and dug up some smooth, damp clay. She took some time to shape it into a tiny pot with a lid that she kept separate so they wouldn't stick together while they were drying. Her Dreaming had told her that the fire light would dry them more quickly and more finely than Heat Giver in the sky could. She had seen some fine potteries in her Dream, and she was looking forward to making and firing them.

The last one of her folks watched her make her slow way across the rise beyond the saddleback on her way to the Fire people's land. Her tiny figure soon disappeared in the deep grayness that met the top of the rise and clung to it like a u'tynaatz, a woman's short, light cloak.

As the next day was well advanced, the people saw her returning. She had a round lamp on her back and looked a bit misshapen in the gray distance. Their hearts fell to the ground in dismay when they saw this. "Oh, no," they said. "It's one thing for Buzzard to get a new hair style, but if something so horrible has happened to Spider!"

They were too heartsick to finish the thought, but waited as calmly as they might, busying themselves with whatever came to hand as was their way when worried or anxious.

At long last Spider was close by, grinning a satisfied grin. "Well," she said, "looks like I got it." She reached up and took the clay pot from her back, revealing a change such as they had feared. For on her back pulsed a bright red-orange design that hadn't been there the day before. But it was a very handsome and wise design, one she had dreamed of herself, and it exactly matched the one her pot lid sported, and she seemed happy to wear it.

She set the tiny pot down in front of her, sighing a small sigh of satisfaction as she removed the lid to reveal the bright glowing ember she had carefully carried so far. "Look," she said. "Fire light."

And there was a hot time in the old town that night.

Solitary Pleasure

KITTY TSUI

The room was large. It reminded her of meeting halls in church basements. In the center of the room tables had been drawn up to form a large rectangle. Behind it lines of chairs had been arranged. The room was crowded with people. How unusual for a mid-day meeting, she thought. The only empty chairs were close to the door so she didn't have to make any decisions about where to sit based on who had the friendliest face. Half of one wall was all windows and bright noon light flooded into the room. It's terribly bright in here, she thought. Good. I can keep my sunglasses on without appearing too strange.

She looked around her. There were young people, old people and every age in between. Women in dresses and heels, women in jeans and Birkenstocks. There were people in torn tee shirts, Ben Johnsons, designer sunglasses. Men in dirty work pants, in need of a shave and men in three-piece suits. Everybody seemed to be chainsmoking with one hand and drinking coffee with the other.

A nervous-looking woman with hennaed hair and a polyester print dress at the head table cleared her throat. It was one o'clock on the nose. "Hi, I'm Elizabeth. I'm an alcoholic." The meeting had begun.

217

Six in the morning and still dark outside. She was wide awake. And for what? There was no one in bed next to her. No one to snuggle up next to. No long legs to rub up against. No sleepy face to kiss awake. She was alone. Hadn't had a lover for a long time. For what? The last one she'd been with had been cheating on her for six months. Six months. Not one night, one time. Six months. She couldn't believe it. But it was true. And that was that. She vowed never to let herself be in love again. For what? All you ever got was hurt. And she was no masochist. Hell, she had herself. And that was plenty.

She yawned and glanced up at the clock. Six-ten. That all? Should be at least seven. She guessed that another long day lay ahead. She stretched out her arms and noted, not without a tinge of pride, that she could still discern the horseshoe of her triceps. Not bad for an athlete turned vegetable, she thought. She'd competed in track and field in college. Six months into a new job after graduation she'd been hit by a car. She spent five months in a hospital, three weeks in traction. That had been some time ago but her back still bothered her terribly. After the prescriptions for pain pills had run out she took to drink. Not hard drink or heavy drinking. Just beer. What was a beer once in a while? Nothing beat a cold beer.

Nothing beat a cold beer except perhaps a good fuck. That was the only thing she missed about not having a lover. Still she had been with herself for a long time. She knew best what she liked and how she liked it.

She took off her nightshirt and threw it to the end of the bed. Morning light was filtering into the room through the rice paper shades. She looked at her body with a critical eye. Small breasts, long arms and legs still with the markings of last summer's tan lines, prominent stomach and no waist. The perils of drinking beer, she thought. What the heck. I'm the only one who sees. Or cares, for that matter.

She ran her hands slowly over her body. Her skin was smooth. Smooth as silk all of her lovers had complimented. She felt goosebumps as her hands cupped her breasts. The nipples hardened. She turned over onto her stomach and found her clitoris with her fingers. She pushed her pelvis down onto her hands but could not find or feel any excitement. Frustrated, she entered into her fantasies. A beautiful woman with long black hair on her back, legs spread wide. Sandwiched between two women, two pairs of hands, probing, seeking out warmth, wetness. A three-way kiss. Soft lips, urgent tongues. Someone moaning softly, calling out her name.

Frustrated, she sat up in bed abruptly. Nothing was happening. The fantasies were orgasmic in her head but her body was not responding in the least.

It was not yet seven. Now she was really wide awake. And frustrated to boot. She thought about her options. Get up, make the bed, take a bath, eat breakfast. Turn on the TV and watch Joanie Greggains do her daily aerobic routine, read last week's stack of newspapers, think up some new fantasies and try it one more time. Then there was that leftover beer in the fridge. Two bottles from the night before. No harm in just finishing it off. So what if it was only seven in the morning. There was no one there except for her and she sure wasn't going to tell.

Eight-thirty she was at the store. Eggs, juice, bread, a jar of honey. What else could she get? What else did she need? Ajax, sponges. Maybe she could wash the car later. Did they have car wash here? She had to load up on something. She couldn't just go to the corner store and buy a six pack by itself. It was eight-thirty for crying out loud. In the morning.

It was a weekday. But that didn't mean anything in particular. Since the accident she had been living quite adequately on Disability. Couldn't afford anything grand, no luxuries. But she got by okay. Could buy whatever kind of beer she fancied, domestic or foreign. Whatever the whim, she catered to it. She got by okay, could easily sacrifice a meal, a movie, a magazine for a beer.

Why drink? Why not? It passed the time in a pleasant enough way and helped her forget her pain. The pain in her back, the anguish of going from jock to vegetable, the loneliness of not having a lover or a friend, the frustration of not being able to work. Right after graduation she had joined forces with a good friend who was a carpenter studying frantically for her contractor's license. One night high on reefer and beer she had laughed about having spent thousands of dollars and four years of her life studying dead languages. Her father had been a linguist, had paid for her education at an expensive university to follow in his footsteps.

Her only joy at school had been on the track. Her studies bored her and she began to resent having made the promise at all. She had stuck to her books, barely made the grades, but she stuck by her promise and sought release in her athletics, something she loved and at which she excelled.

Right after college she had rebelled. She became a carpenter, working with her friend, a handsome six foot woman who had passed the contractor's exam on her first attempt. The only woman taking the test in a room filled with hundreds of men.

She loved working outdoors. Working with tools and with her hands. The rhythm of hammering, the sound of saws and drills. Sweating under the hot sun, laboring on a redwood deck. Seeing a structure appear in a previously bare space. She even enjoyed lugging four-by-fours up countless flights of stairs and knocking through sheetrock and stucco. She enjoyed driving a full load to the dump and driving home with a beer between her legs.

She had no time or reason to train now. But her body stayed tight and tanned. She loved it. And she loved her work.

Nowadays it was a different story. The months in the hospital and the long convalescence had taken their toll on her body and her spirits. Her beloved grandmother was dead and now her only family was her father. He had been so disapproving of her becoming what he called a manual laborer that he had cut off their relationship. Even implying that her getting hit by a car had been her fault for not having complied with his wishes by following in his footsteps. Her fault? She'd just been jaywalking. What kind of crime was that? Friends had been supportive at first but she'd been so angry she'd lashed out at everyone. Being a total bitch all the time to all her friends had succeeded in alienating her from everyone she knew. She'd been so angry. Why did it happen to her? Why was she flat on her back and in pain? Why?

Nowadays she barely looked at or cared about her body. In fact she hated it because it was a constant source of pain for her. She stayed alone most of the time, making minimal contact with a few acquaintances. She let her subscriptions to sports magazines lapse, retaining only Rolling Stone. She read little, mostly mysteries. In truth what she did most of the time was watch TV and drink beer. She felt depressed and sorry for herself, angry at her body and at its betrayal.

It was afternoon that same weekday when she awoke from her stupor. The TV was on and the house smelled like burnt toast. She staggered downstairs and discovered charred, black remains in the toaster. Her mouth was dry and her head felt like a bowling ball. Her muscles were stiff and her back was killing her. She put water on for coffee and noticed her hands were shaking uncontrollably. She put both hands straight out in front of her. The fingers looked like Mexican jumping beans with a life of their own. She couldn't believe her eyes. What the heck was going on here? She hadn't been getting enough sleep and she really needed some coffee. That was all there was to it. She'd make some strong coffee and get to bed early. She'd run herself a hot bath, soak and try to relax. Then she'd be fine. Jumping beans be damned.

After the bath she felt a little calmer. She scrambled two eggs and ate them with toast. Afternoon. Now what should she do with herself? Perhaps she could call someone and go for a walk in the woods. She flipped through the pages of her phonebook. Most of the people she knew were at work. Some were friends whom she'd lost contact with and others were acquaintances whom she didn't even want to be bothered with. But it was a beautiful day outside. She thought about taking a walk by herself but decided against it. These were dangerous times for a woman alone anywhere, she thought, and I refuse to be a casualty.

She went upstairs and switched on the TV, a habit she had picked up at the hospital. Having a remote control was one of the handiest things in life. She skipped through the channels. All soaps except for Bugs Bunny and a wildlife program. Nothing she was the least bit interested in. She muted out the sound, left the picture on for company, and pulled out a stack of the previous week's newspapers. She preferred to read old news, it didn't affect her as much. After all, the dead were dead, the fire had been arrested and the storm had blown over. When the stack of papers had been gone over she decided to reward herself with the last two bottles of beer.

Halfway through the evening news she realized with a start that she felt totally sober. How could that be? She'd drunk two beers in quick succession and expected at the very least a small buzz. What the heck was going on? The only thing she did feel was very bloated. Another peril of beer drinking. She was cold sober. The only solution was to go to the store and get another six pack.

Six beers later the only thing she felt was sick. She couldn't understand why she couldn't get high. She felt like she'd been drowning in a bathtub and to save herself she'd drunk the contents of the tub. She fought the nausea that threatened to engulf her and went gingerly down the stairs to put on water for tea. Perhaps a cup of mint tea would help. It didn't because she couldn't swallow another drop of anything. She tried to force herself to pee in the hope that it would alleviate the bloated feeling but it only aggravated her nausea. She dragged herself back to bed and finally passed out to the sound of the TV.

She woke up shivering, chilled to the bone. Her nightshirt was wet. The TV cast a ghostly white light into the room and she had a big headache. All of a sudden a fierce gust of wind blew in through the open window and sent goosebumps scurrying over her body. She had a sudden, strange feeling that she was not alone. She rubbed her eyes and looked slowly around the room. It was empty except for furniture, plants and her. She was suddenly afraid that she had fallen asleep with the front door open and that a stranger had walked in and was at this moment in her house, going through her things. Or worse, on his way up the stairs. Panic gripped her. A hundred possibilities raced through her mind. Call 911 about a burglary in progress; wake up "husband Jim" in a loud voice; grab Webster's New World Dictionary for protection; break a beer bottle like in the movies and confront the foe head on. She couldn't decide what to do. Call 911 now, wait, what? Calm down, she told herself, it's probably nothing, she was just feeling paranoid. There was no man downstairs. No demons or ghosts. Just her imagination on the loose again.

She turned off the TV and settled back into bed. The night was still. Except for the occasional siren that tore through the air. She lay listening to the minutes tick by. Sleep would not take her and there was no more beer in the fridge.

She was dozing when she suddenly awoke with a start. She felt someone else in the room with her. How could that be? She had checked the lock on the front door and no one could come in through the windows without breaking the glass. Had she slept through the sound of glass shattering?

She lay still in the darkness, gathering strength, her wits and the will to move. A rush of cold air swept over her face. She froze, remembering from somewhere about ghosts in the wind. For a second she wanted to bury her head under the covers and just pass out until morning. But then she wasn't sure if one was safe in the light of day either. If ghosts did exist, surely they could roam about at will, day or night. She shivered and started to move out of the bed. Her arm would not move. Nor would her legs. Panic seized her. She started to scream but no sound came out of her mouth. She was lying down on her left side, facing away from the door and totally paralyzed. She felt something come perilously close to her. The hairs on the nape of her neck stood on end. She tried desperately to free herself from an iron grasp and couldn't. Suddenly she felt a presence next to her in the bed. Strong arms wrapped around her from behind. A leg lay heavy on her thigh. Oh God, help me, help me, she sobbed wordlessly. When she began shaking uncontrollably she forced herself to move. She groped wildly for the arms, the legs that had invaded her bed. She turned over. She was alone. How could that be? Did she have a waking nightmare? Had her past experimentation with drugs suddenly plunged her into a paranoid, catatonic state? What? But when her own heavy breathing quieted down, she realized that she'd been alone with herself. The arms that had wrapped around her had been her own. She had been hugging herself. She fell asleep into a night full of dreams.

Swimming in a body of murky water. Using a lot of energy, strength draining out of me. Labored breathing. Body heavy, going nowhere. The water gets thick and clings to me like mud. I am sinking in quicksand. I am sinking and start to tread water wildly. My frantic movements are in vain and I sink into darkness, the quicksand pulling me into its center.

I am on a crowded street. Many people around me moving fast, all going in different directions. People push against me and step on my feet with no apologies. My feet are sore and hurting. I look down at them and discover, to my horror, that I am wearing an old pair of bedroom slippers with holes in them. My first thought is that of shame and embarrassment. Where to go? How to hide? I try to run. In my haste I trip and discover I am wearing only socks. A mismatched pair. And with holes in them. A strangely familiar voice from the crowd calls my name. I turn and see my grandmother in the mass of people. She has a disapproving look on her face. I try to get up. Can't. The crowd swallows my grandmother.

When morning came she awoke with an amazingly clear head from a day and a night filled with drink and dreams. She'd really been bored with herself. TV was no substitute for friends and activity and drinking was no longer filling the gaps in her life. Besides, she was sick of the headaches, the bloated stomach, the lapses in memory. There was nothing going on in her life. Small wonder she didn't want to talk to anyone. What was there to say about what she had been doing? Nothing. She hadn't done anything, hadn't gone anywhere, hadn't seen anyone. No work. No play. No friends. No feelings. No sex. Nothing. Just beer and TV. And depression and headaches and feeling generally sick of herself. And she was sick of it all.

She resolved to try to make a change in her habits, her life. On top of the list was to stop drinking. No more beer. Outdoor activity would help. That was second on the list. Then came the TV. No more sitting mindlessly in front of the tube. Just the evening news and movies. Selective viewing. Making the list was easy. The hard part was how and where to begin.

Lately she'd seen a lot of commercials on TV about the perils of alcohol. There was one in particular she'd never forget. A close-up of two hands holding up beers in a drinker's salute, about to clink glasses. In slow motion the glasses come together, smash against each other and shatter. The sound was that of an automobile accident, the screeching of tires, glass shattering. Every time the commercial came on she would mute out the sound. But even without it she could still read the caption: drinking can kill a friendship. There were also numerous ads for treatment programs and support groups and hot lines on TV and in the paper. She couldn't afford to enroll in a program and she sure didn't need to sit around and talk about it. Besides, groups like Alcoholics Anonymous were for real alcoholics, skid row types, not people like her. She wasn't really an alcoholic or a problem drinker. She just needed to be able to function without a six pack. She could easily do it on her own. She knew she could.

She wasn't sure what kind of outdoor activity to pursue. With her bad back running, lifting weights and cycling were out of the question. So were aerobic classes which she hated anyway. She thought about swimming but the few times she had been to a pool the chlorine had irritated her eyes badly. Besides, swimmers looked so silly in their rubber swimming caps and goggles. She couldn't think of what else she could try. Yoga was not exactly an outdoor sport. She had tried it a few times on the advice of her doctor but found it too slow and boring. When she was supposed to be meditating her mind was racing. Perhaps she could get some kind of a big dog and go for long walks. On second thought she wasn't really that fond of dogs and getting one just for protection wasn't a good reason to get one at all.

Back to square one. What to do? There was a public pool close to where she lived. Perhaps she could give swimming another go. She called up and inquired about the hours. Seven to nine, twelve to one-thirty, five to seven. She wanted to go at the least crowded time so five to seven was definitely out. Twelve to one-thirty was a possibility but she guessed that working people swam during their lunch hour. That left the two early morning hours. She'd never enjoyed getting up early except to train and she certainly wasn't in training now. She dug out an old swimsuit and grudgingly set the alarm for seven.

That night she had a hard time sleeping. Her back ached and all she could think about was having a drink. How many days had it been? One, two? She couldn't be sure. All days seemed the same to her, one day segueing into the next. Then she recalled the waking nightmare, the dreams. It had only been last night. This was her first day dry. And all she could think about was having a drink. Popping open a can. Taking a big swallow. Feeling the coldness going down her throat. She really enjoyed the taste of beer. Could drink it anytime. Anywhere. Day or night. She suddenly paused in her train of thought and forced herself to quit. She had to stop thinking about drinking. She had to stop drinking.

When the alarm went off she had second thoughts. What if her swimsuit fit her funny? What if she couldn't maintain a pace fast enough for the swimmer following her? What if she couldn't remember the correct form? What if she got cramped and started to sink? She realized she could stay in bed all day accumulating dozens of what ifs. And they wouldn't be worth a damn. She forced herself out of bed and into the car.

It was not quite eight. The natatorium was not as empty as she had hoped. Still, she had a lane to herself for which she was thankful. The air smelled of chlorine and the water was cold. Her nipples hardened instantly. Not usually an unpleasant sensation but today she wasn't so sure. She pushed herself off from the side abruptly, before other doubts had the chance to propel her out of the pool.

Water hit her face, went up her nose and stung her open eyes. She took in a mouthfull and started coughing violently. Great beginning, she thought, but continued her strokes. At least she was moving through the water. Besides, no one paid any attention to her. She went eight laps and stopped. She was out of breath and her eyes felt like they'd been marinating in vinegar. Eight laps were better than none. She got out, dressed hurriedly and drove home.

The day went well. She did laundry and made two phone calls. One to a friend who wasn't in and the other to make an appointment for a massage. A year-old birthday present she had never taken advantage of. Fortunately there was food in the house so there was no excuse to go to the store. The day ended well. She was in bed by eight and had a brief but satisfying session with herself.

The week passed smoothly. She swam every morning and was able to increase a few laps each day. She went to the library and checked out some Agatha Christie novels; all of which she had read before, had raced through in various stages of intoxication. She even got to the store a few times and made it through without incident. The TV stayed dead. It was a good week. She rewarded herself with a pair of goggles and a new suit that had been marked down.

She woke up each morning with anticipation, eager to add more laps. Memories of the track came back to her and she remembered how she loved running faster, farther, feeling strong, clipping off the seconds.

The days went well. She was amazed that she didn't crave a drink. In fact she felt great. Clearheaded. Strong. She felt a freedom she'd never experienced before. She didn't have to feel guilty going into a store to buy beer early in the day; didn't have to justify, rationalize or find excuses for a beer. Her swimming was going good. Her strokes were more coordinated with her breathing and getting stronger every day. She was up to fifty laps.

One afternoon in the middle of doing dishes she thought about having a drink. It had been almost two weeks. She felt great. What harm could there be in having just one drink? She left the pots to soak in the sink and hurried out to the car. As she turned on the ignition she heard someone calling out her name. The voice was harsh and belonged, without a doubt, to her grandmother. She looked around her in horror. The street was empty. Her grandmother was dead. She took some deep breaths to calm herself. It was okay, just her imagination on the loose again.

She drove to the store and bought a six pack. She had planned to get just a couple but it was cheaper to buy six. She could save the rest for another day.

Six beers later she was drunk. Upstairs the TV was on and in the kitchen the radio was going full blast. The phone kept ringing but she couldn't talk to anyone. She hadn't eaten anything but decided it was easier to go get more beer than it was to fix dinner.

The next morning she couldn't get up to go swim. She couldn't get out of bed until late in the afternoon when she had to throw up. She was horrified to see beer bottles strewn about the kitchen. Nine empty bottles and one half full. The smell of beer made her start retching. The heater had been left on full blast. It was ninety degrees in the house. Small wonder she felt

227

nauseated and dizzy. Perhaps she needed to throw up again. She hated throwing up. It was the worst. Afterwards she barely had the strength to drag herself back to bed.

When she finally woke up she felt like hell. The light in the room hurt her eyes. She squeezed them shut and pulled the covers up over her face. Her mouth was dry, her head throbbed painfully. That was it, she decided. That was the last straw. Or rather, the last bottle.

The last straw. The last bottle. She knew that she would not be able to change anything else in her life until she made the resolution to stop drinking.

She dropped into the water like a hawk on its prey. She was suited and goggled, a tight fitting white swimcap on her head. The water was clear and blue. Shafts of sunlight hit the surface and sent hundreds of amoeba-like figures dancing at the bottom of the pool. She focused on her strokes, her breathing and counting the laps. She sped through the water, breathing every second stroke, her limbs working in unison, propelling her effortlessly through the wet world. Her back felt good; there was no pain in the water. She grew more confident in the cool, sensuous world as she logged up the laps and needed less and less rest intervals. She loved the solitude of swimming. It was just her gliding through the water, exploding out all the breath from her lungs and taking in fresh air. It was just her gliding through the water. Sure. Sleek. Strong.

The days went well. She swam every morning before breakfast. Her back felt good. The TV stayed off. She was able to curb her drinking. Feeling as good as she did, she could not afford to go back downhill. She started reconnecting with friends and even made a date for dinner and a movie. She slept well and had auspicious dreams. She felt generally good and wanted desperately to keep it that way.

She knew she felt good. She knew she would continue swimming. She knew she had friends and she had herself. But she knew she would need help on days when she didn't feel so good. On days when it wouldn't be easy. She went through the yellow pages and found a listing for an A.A. fellowship in her area.

It was one-ten on the nose.

228

"Anyone here for the first, second or third time?" the woman with the hennaed hair asked.

She looked around the crowded room. Not one person raised their hands. She knew she was one to whom the question applied. But she wasn't an alcoholic. She was just visiting.

"Anyone here in their first thirty days of sobriety?"

She looked around the crowded room. Two people had raised their hands. She breathed a sigh of relief. The two spoke. Then there was silence in the room. She shifted in her seat. It was getting warm. Why didn't somebody open a window or something. She clenched her fists, her breath coming in spurts. I'm not really an alcoholic, she kept repeating to herself. I'm just here to check this place out. One twenty-five. She was sweating. She could smell herself. Her lips were dry. She really needed a drink bad. She really wanted to get up, go out the door and get a drink. Slowly she raised her hand.

"Hi, I'm Frances. I'm an alcoholic."

Nothing Safe
in Crabtree Meadow

SANDY BOUCHER

When I wake, it is so cold that my cheeks are numb; all around me the night is thickly black under a starless sky. The sound comes again — metal on rock. One of our cook pans is being moved at the fire pit. A marmot, I think, and lie listening. Squirrels and chipmunks aren't big enough to move a pan like that.

Silence.

Then another noise. I listen with strained attention, trying to identify it. *Either* it is the sound of my son Rob unzipping his sleeping bag, *or* — and my scalp tingles — or it is the sound of claws dragging across canvas.

Stealthily, a little at a time, I turn over on the ground inside my sleeping bag until I lie facing Rob. Now in his eighteenth year he is already broad-shouldered and sturdily muscled. His big body lies turned away from me. Fast asleep.

There is another scratching noise, loud in the night.

I turn over again, slowly, as quietly as possible, and when I am lying on my right side I unzip the top of my mummy bag and reach a careful hand out into the cold to close it around the flashlight. I direct it at our packs, propped against the log near our feet, and flick the switch.

Looking straight at me in the circle of light are two yellow

230

eyes in a dark furry head. The animal is hunched over from behind the log, his massive forelegs wrapped around my pack.

The light does not frighten him. He goes on ripping at the
side pocket of the pack, pulling things out the hole he's made.

My body is paralyzed for a few moments, while my mind
leaps back to a conversation with some campers in Junction
Meadow. "Make noise," they had advised, "yell. Jump up and
down. Beat on pans. Only don't mess with a female bear who
has cubs." How can I know the sex of this beast who is pulling a
tube of peanut butter from the pocket of the pack, staring me in
the eyes all the while?

I desperately want this not to be happening. Oh how I wish
this were not happening.

Keeping the flashlight on him, I sit up, unzipping my bag
farther, and I start to yell — a karate yell, from the diaphragm,
deafening, terrifying. But all that comes out of my tight throat
is Eeeeeeeeeep, eeeeeeeep, eeeeeeeep.

The creature goes on looting my pack. I keep moving backwards as I try to yell, until I'm practically sitting on top of Rob
in his sleeping bag. He grumbles and rolls away.

Yellow claws pull a chocolate bar from the frayed hole in the
canvas. The small shiny eyes watch me, the enormous furry
shoulders hunch tighter around the pack.

I struggle upright out of my warm covering and dance in
my thermal underwear on top of my sleeping bag, shouting
Hup, hup, hup!

What the hell's wrong with my hardy teenage son? Why
doesn't he get up to help me?

I leap and stamp and throw one arm out like a pump handle, my yell getting louder now.

The little eyes watch me warily as the claws pull a bag of
trail food from the hole and stuff it in the mouth, spilling
peanuts and sunflower seeds down the front of the pack as the
plastic splits.

I jump in the cold air, knees jerking up and down, shouting
Yow, yow, yow! I'm afraid to turn away from the bear to find
out what Rob is doing.

Out comes a tampax. The animal shoves it in his mouth,
bites into it, and one half is left dangling like a cigar butt

down his chin.

God *damn* it! Here I am, dancing like a madwoman and screeching not eight feet from him and he just goes on with his midnight snack. "Throw something," they had said in Junction Meadow.

All I have is the flashlight. I pull back my arm, aim, let fly.

It sails toward him and bounces off his head just above his eyes, spiralling up, its beam of light looping crazily in the darkness.

The bear stops all motion, stunned. And in that instant I know I have made a terrible mistake, for something was illuminated by the spinning flashlight beam, something small and furry moving up behind the log. I just glimpsed it. Now I look around for a place to run to. The bear's great body rears up clumsily off the pack, hesitates, and I get ready to go. Anywhere! Up the nearest tree—no. She can scramble up after me. Out through the underbrush in the dark—but surely she can move in it faster than I. The creek is too far down the slope. There *is* no place to go.

The moment seems endless as she teeters there on her hind legs, her cub shuffling about in the weeds behind her. I understand fully what I've done, now. The knowledge paralyzes me.

And then with astonishing speed she has scrambled over the log and comes thrashing toward me. I turn to run just as she lunges forward on her hind legs. The raging weight of her drags me down, claws tear at my back. I scream and struggle against thick rough fur. She mauls me in the dirt, holds me in a crushing murderous embrace, as the pain rips down my side from my shoulder. Her rank odor curls my nostrils. I see the black sky above her black head, my mind filled with her roaring.

It has been a quiet morning. Earlier the garbage men thumped their way through the basement and out again as their truck grumbled in the street. But I was already awake. I don't sleep as I did before, all night long.

Rob brought me some tea and toast. He stroked my face. He knelt before me and asked me how I am, does my shoulder hurt? Can he do anything to make me more comfortable? His dark red curls fall down over his forehead, his eyes are a mottled greenish brown in his sunburned face. I smile at him, wishing he were not so anxious.

On our first night here at home, I asked him to explain. Patiently he told me each of the thoughts that passed through his mind as he lay there almost asleep, each one giving him an excuse not to act or confusing him, until the final moment when he saw the light wobble crazily in the darkness and thought it was a space ship landing, or someone with a flashlight stumbling down upon us. He is good-natured and big for his eighteen years; he has enormous feet, thick wrists, and a weird science fiction-filled imagination. My beloved son. Perhaps there would have been nothing he could have done that night. My anger at him passed quickly. Still, he says he feels guilty, and I can see in the tentative way he looks at me that he suffers.

He brings me books and magazines; he describes the movies I could watch on TV. Today there will be *Flying Down to Rio* with Fred Astaire and Ginger Rogers, or maybe I'd like to flip the channel to . . . a star-filled afternoon. How about it, mom?

It seemed we were caught in a dream as Rob cut away the shreds of my thermal underwear top and bound a T-shirt around my shoulder. Dawn light was arriving. Trees, branches began to appear out of the darkness. I sat propped against the log. I remember how heavy my head felt, hanging down, as I stared at the blood spreading on the white cotton of the T-shirt bandage.

Then there was the ordeal of getting my trousers on, and my boots, for I would not let Rob go off by himself to get help. I would not be left alone in Crabtree Meadow, wounded and vulnerable. There was a ranger station just at the other end of the meadow; it was there Rob would take me. He got a belt, put it around my neck and rested my arm in it like a sling. Then he wrapped a jacket around my shoulders and lifted me to my feet. I tottered sideways, grabbing at him with my good arm, as the pain engulfed me in a dizzying wave. He wanted to carry me. But I told him I would walk. Just to feel the ground under my feet, to move one leg forward, then the other, kept me connected to consciousness.

When we got to the ranger station, we found it locked and

deserted. I remember the padlock hanging on the door, with its little key-shaped mouth.

I sat on the stoop, and it was then I noticed that my whole side from shoulder to knee had turned scarlet. I'm finished, I thought, all my body fluids are leaving me, I'll be dry inside soon, white and weightless. My brain will stop. My heart will go slower and slower until there is no more blood to pump.

A ragged whimpering sound came to me. I looked up to where Rob leaned against the door of the hut, bent forward and shaking. Tears ran down over his dirty hands, making pale crooked tracks in the dust on his skin.

The magazines are piled on the floor next to my chair. I'm not interested in reading. If they'd let me, I'd go back to my job tomorrow. But instead I must stay in this room and receive the guilty ministrations of Rob and the visits of Mrs. Linenthal who comes down from 2B to see me. I'm not even sure Mrs. Linenthal likes me; certainly I've never fulfilled her expectations for someone my age. I am a small woman, and even now in my fifties I am feisty and quick. I don't mean that I seem younger than my age. No, older even, if you look at my face. But I am the person I've become.

Rob says, "I think mom's tired now. She wants to rest." And he leads Mrs. Linenthal out of my room, leaving me alone again.

I know I'm difficult for them to understand. They expect me to need their comfort. But, as I said, I am the person I've become in all these years of living, and what engages me now is the mystery of my actions that night. How, when it seemed I would surely be killed, was I able to get my right arm free, bring up my fist, and hit blindly at the one sensitive and unprotected spot on the animal's body, the nose. And hurt or startled, she staggered away from me and ran into the underbrush, her cub waddling after her.

The campers who arrived in Crabtree Meadow that morning were two young men and a woman, all about Rob's age. They were carrying enormous packs, and they had tanned legs under loose hiking shorts. While the two men worked with Rob

234

to cut poles and drape a poncho over them to make a stretcher, the woman knelt before me. "Let me give you some water," she said. And she unscrewed the canteen for me and was going to hold it to my mouth until I took it from her with my good hand. When I tilted my head back to drink, I saw a blue jay sitting on a low limb of a tree. The jay cocked its head, regarded me for a few moments, and then began to squawk. I stared helplessly up at it while it screeched insults at me, chiding and complaining. And I thought, I'm done for.

They loaded me carefully on the stretcher, and while one young man ran off to try to locate the ranger, the woman and Rob and the other man carried me out of the meadow on the trail going west. I shut my eyes against the sky's brightness. My body rolled in the poncho, limbs jiggling, until I felt the nausea pressing up out of my stomach. The men's and the woman's voices came — short utterances as they struggled to keep me level on a steep incline, as they waded through a stream. "Careful now." "Protect her shoulder." "Watch out!" Their grunts and strenuous breathing surrounded me.

My stomach roiled as I breathed the stink of bear musk clinging to my skin.

Rob and I were hiking through Sequoia National Forest toward Mt. Whitney in hot dry August.

That evening we had made it to Crabtree Meadow, where we were the only people. The sun was behind the mountain, and a swatch of apricot-colored cloud hung above the ridge in a clear blue sky. All was silent, except for the rush of Whitney Creek below us.

After eating, we propped our packs against a log, spread out the sleeping bags, not bothering with a tent. Normally we would have hung our food supplies high up on a tree limb, but in our eight days of hiking we had seen no sign of bear, and this night we let fatigue overcome our better judgment.

Exhausted and peaceful, we lay in our warm sleeping bags and talked about the last few days, which had been tough ones.

Two nights before, only eighteen miles from Whitney, we had been stopped by a forest fire across the Wallace Creek Trail. Closing my eyes I could see it, burning quietly in the windless night, eating away at the trees and underbrush on the ridge above Junction Meadow where we had been camped. Orange flames crawled the tree trunks, bushes ignited, sizzled, flared up, branches fell, spraying sparks. It burned with a curious sound like paper crumpling.

To get around the fire, we had to go eight miles out of our way up the Tyndall Creek Trail. That day we came up 2,800 feet in eight miles, on short switchbacks up a steep mountainside, with no shade. It was the hardest climb we'd done.

But hiking the next day was glorious. The trees on the slopes up to Bighorn Plateau were yellow pines or sugar pines — dead but still standing, without bark, in twisted spiralled shapes, their wood the color of poured honey.

And then the plateau itself, where we had experienced that great lift to the spirits, the elation of the high country. Eleven thousand feet high and perfectly bare, Bighorn Plateau offered a view of almost 360 degrees. We took off our packs and walked across the wide dome to its center. Furry orange marmots came out of their holes to peer at us, sneak up to examine our packs. We sat on the rocks taking swigs of warmish water from the canteen, looking around us to blue distant peaks. West to the ranges we had come from, north toward Forrester's Pass, and southeast in the direction of Mt. Whitney.

It was delicious to let these pictures move through my mind, as I lay in my mummy bag, the muscles of my legs slowly relaxing, the sound of the creek lulling me. We were safe in Crabtree Meadow, and until morning there was nothing that had to be done.

"I think we'll make it up Mt. Whitney tomorrow, after all," came Rob's drowsy voice from his sleeping bag.

Those words were like a float bobbing on the surface of an ocean into which I sank, farther and farther down, until they with everything else had disappeared and I lay in exhausted, dreamless sleep.

When I woke, it was so cold that my cheeks were numb; all around me the night was thickly black under a starless sky. The sound came again — metal on rock. One of our cook pans was being moved at the fire pit.

And I lay still and thought, this is a dream, the dream is

always like this.

Another noise. I listened with strained attention, trying to identify it. Either it was the sound of Rob unzipping his sleeping bag, or—and my scalp tingled—or it was the sound of claws dragging across canvas.

The dream is always like this, right up to that denser bulk of darkness lumbering toward me, engulfing me, pulling me down farther into chaos than I can stand to go, the ground made wet beneath me, my mind falling out the back of my head. Rob cannot enter between us now as I wonder if in the muscles of that animal there is the memory of my body caught against it, whether my odor lingers in her nostrils or has made its trace in her brain. Did she, cleaning herself the next day, lick my blood from between her claws along with the twigs and moss and dried pine needles lodged there?

I wake, my injured back throbbing, to stare up into the darkness of my room, wait for morning light, for the day's requirements to assemble me once again out of the night's vast disorder into my familiar, finite self.

Snowwalker

JOYCE RENWICK

Agnes closed the door quietly behind her and stepped off the porch into a drift of knee-deep snow. The evergreens bordering the driveway were bent under their winter's accumulation, and wet snow fell into her boots as she left the driveway and trudged over the white pasture, leaving a herringbone pattern behind her. She thought of a night like this one when Edward had lain beside her as they slept at the foot of the bed in front of the open window—the shade raised, the snow falling silently outside, the room heavy with moisture.

Edward had held her so close she thought he would suffocate her as they slept. In the small of the morning he pulled her tighter to him whenever she moved to breathe deeply or break free. He didn't love her, she suspected, yet he wanted her warmth, her body close to his, and he had tangled her in the sheets with desperate hugs.

"Don't do that," she had said to him, "it's too much for me," knowing he would hold her close, make her stir, make her breathing fitful and warm against his chest, and then say, "Go to sleep, Aggie. Go to sleep." But that night in front of the open window the falling snow had a strange effect on him, seeming to peel away his leathery indifference and make him very human. Later, of course, he became increasingly preoccupied.

He let her go as he had let go of everything, absentmindedly; his love for something else simply had superseded his love for her. In the years since his death she often dreamed of him suspended in a cloudless sky, holding something — she could not tell what or who — close to himself like a lover.

When Agnes reached the deserted road she turned right and headed toward the river. A light snow was falling. She closed her eyes. On the lonely road she was as unconcerned with navigation as if she were on a large deep river after all the boats had been called in and the storm was over. The sound of the wind mimicked the flap of a breeze through half-lowered sails. When she opened her eyes she noted the snow had changed texture, a fine-grained snow was falling, and on the unbroken surface of the road's shoulder beside her thin, mica-like flakes glistened like small golden disks.

After an early dinner of boiled beef and potatoes, her son Bert had eased her into the sparsely-furnished living room that smelled of dust. As soon as he left, Agnes rummaged in the log-bin by the fireplace and found a dog-eared *Readers Digest* in with the disgarded newspapers and rotting wood. She carried the magazine to the sofa, turned on the lamp, adjusted her glasses, and in the chilly room read about allergies, Eskimo snowwalkers, and Mohini, the white tiger at the National Zoo. The allergy article irritated her, scornful as she was of people who choose to be allergic to life. She thought the white tiger might be interesting to see, but she was intrigued by the snowwalkers. When she finished reading she put the magazine face down on the coffeetable.

Bert wandered back into the room and dropped into the lumpy brown chair opposite her. He was in his early thirties, and with his dark wavy hair and blue eyes looked a lot like his dead father.

"Bert?"

"Yeah?"

"Oh, nothing." Agnes looked past him to the straggly wandering jew that was hanging in the window. Beyond it, a few scattered flakes were falling.

"It needs water," she said.

239

"What?"

"The plant." Agnes pulled herself out of the hole between the sofa cushions. She yanked down her navy blue dress then moved around the coffeetable, careful to avoid the ashtray of shredded cigarette butts that sat precariously near the table's edge. "I'll help Sally clean up."

Bert glanced at the dying fire. "Rest. Sally has it under control."

"I have been resting."

Bert sat back in his chair, yawned, and stretched his arms out in front of him.

Agnes shook her head and sat back down on the sofa. She looked at his hands and noted again the black grease under his nails. "Even mechanics can have clean hands," she said. "Why don't you use that Boraxo? Your father used to wash his hands clear up to his elbows with it. Doesn't Sally object?"

"She has never objected to me or my hands."

"Then maybe you two should get married."

Bert looked at her sharply. "We'll make our own decisions." He turned and stared at the fire.

She watched him for a minute then picked up the magazine she had left on the table. "Have you seen this?" Agnes held it up to him. "There's a story in here about a white tiger." She turned the magazine pages slowly, looking for the article. "It's here somewhere." She wet her fingertip and turned another page. "I wonder if your sister's seen it."

"The tiger or the article?" Bert stood up, the familiar tic jumping in the side of his face.

"Well, I mean, Ellie's . . ."

"Would you get off that? Ellie doesn't know everything." He yanked back the fire screen.

"I just thought you'd be interested," Agnes said looking down at the magazine in her hands.

"Okay. I liked animals when I was a kid. That was a long time ago. God damn it, you've pointed out every animal story to me since I was four years old."

"They're still magical to me," she said quietly.

"Well, then maybe you ought to grow up."

Agnes put the magazine face down on her lap. She thought

of those years in Canada, the evenings reading stories to Bert and Ellie, the mornings standing rigid at the frosted window watching Edward wave goodbye with a smile. In the three years since he'd died she had lived with her children a season at a time—three months at Bert's Wisconsin farmhouse, three months at Ellie's in Virginia, and back to Bert's again. Agnes had begun to feel her real home was the bus station, she had spent so much time there since she sold her house.

She turned to the window beside her and pulled back the limp curtain. When did Bert become so inflexible, she wondered? Didn't he remember how they used to sing together in the mornings? Didn't he remember the Sambo story he insisted she read over and over each night until he fell asleep? She watched the powdery snowfall outside the window. She thought she saw something move swiftly across the yard.

"It's March, Bert, this might be the last snow," she said turning back to him. "Do you want to take a walk?" When she looked out the window again whatever it was, was gone.

Bert went to the logbin. After selecting a sturdy piece of hardwood he tossed the log into the fire. "It's too cold," he said. "I've been out all day." He reached for the iron poker.

"Bert, I'm sorry," Agnes said. "I mean about the getting married. I'm afraid for you. I don't want you to be lonely."

"I'm not lonely." He jabbed the fire with the iron poker until the room filled with the odor of woodsmoke and ashes, and sparks exploded in the air around his head. "It's just you women that don't have enough to do that are lonely. You had a marriage certificate in a gold frame above your bed for years, Mother," he said, "and it was just a license to sleep together with your backs turned."

A blue flame leaped up at the back of the fire. Agnes watched his plaid flannel back as he poked the logs around on the grate. "Oh," she said under her breath.

"Don't you understand," Bert said turning to her, "that's made me cautious."

"Yes," she said. She stared out the window at the light snowfall. "I understand."

Bert turned back to the fire.

Agnes watched her son's muscular back for a moment then

241

quietly walked out of the room. She pulled her overcoat down from a peg by the side door and leaned down to retrieve her boots from a pile by the entryway. She jumped back as the yellow-eyed cat, sleeping on a nest of hats and scarves, woke wide-eyed and hissing.

In the cold wind Agnes smelled the sticky tar-like odor of the creaking pines on either side of the road and another odor she couldn't name. Frozen ruts under a light dusting of new snow made walking slippery and difficult for her, and her face was beginning to sting. She turned her back to the wind and looked behind her for the depressions in the road where some of the white had been blown away and a hint of the black macadam appeared beneath. The snowfall was getting heavier. She struggled into the drifted shoulder, her hands dug deep into the pockets of her overcoat.

Agnes heard the sound of a motor and looked up. A dark car was barrelling down the icy road toward her, its snowchains flailing and clanging against the wheelwells. When the car was only a few yards away she stumbled back into a roadside drift. The car went into a spin in front of her, its brakes squealing. It slid diagonally across the road, then came to a stop with a thud, its nose buried in the snowbank of the opposite shoulder. From where she had fallen, Agnes watched the motionless car. The snow fell around it. After a minute or two it pulled out of the drift with a furious spinning of wheels. It backed up, its wheels whirring and slipping, until it came to a sliding stop beside her. Agnes stiffly got to her feet.

The car window rolled down and the hatless heads of two teenage boys appeared through the thickening veil of falling snow.

"Why don't you watch where you're going lady?" one of the boys shouted at her. The car sped off, its snowchains clanging.

Agnes brushed the snow off her coat and watched the car fishtail away over the icy road. She stood there, shaking, until the small red lights disappeared into the haze.

What's wrong with them, she thought. She rubbed her bare hands together and squinted through the steady snowfall.

The flakes, now larger and more insistent, landed and remained on her bare head. She brushed them off her eyebrows with numb fingers and turned to find the road empty behind her. Maybe Bert was talking to Sally again about her undrinkable coffee over the soapy water and the clatter of dishes in the grey clapboard house. She started walking again.

Agnes had found that if she made the morning coffee very strong, and sang to herself in a voice that had grown embarrassingly harsh, through sheer power of her will she was able to steel herself for another day. The decision was one she made anew each morning as she spooned the coffee into the pot. In her visits to her children's houses she never had time to establish friendships, or even to know each morning with certainty where she had put her shoes. She vowed to her children that it didn't matter. But often as she rode the bus between Wisconsin and Virginia, the upholstery soiled and stiff behind her, she wished the bus would go careening off the road into a ditch. Then she would force her head back against the padded headrest, close her eyes and dream her recurrent day dreams of Edward or the other thing that appeared in a form she did not understand.

Her body ached with the effort of walking in the increasing wind and her legs were as heavy as the large, rotting wood at the bottom of Bert's logbin. She paused to rub her stinging ears with numb fingertips. As she walked she let her mind drift.

In a young woman's lust for conception—her body roaring before her mind—Agnes remembered naming the infant she was sure she had conceived the night before the open window. But in a few weeks the idea had been washed away in the red river of her blood.

Edward was not sympathetic when she told him shyly of this lust for children, and her disappointment.

"Don't expect anything from me, Aggie," he told her. "I know how things are. I'm a glacier."

"Yes, I know," she said, looking into his pale eyes in an attempt to find a thread of understanding there, a minute indication that he might in some small way bend to her will. "But a glacier melted, moving," she said, "is a river." Later Bert was born out of an ordinary need—then came the ever-crying Ellie.

Agnes passed a stand of pines that whistled and shuddered

in the wind. Behind it was a somber, deserted pasture. White drifts were piled high against a faded red barn and snow eddies rose from the sloping roof which was fringed with huge icicles which seemed ready to fall like clear daggers into the soft snow beneath. Seeing the drifts and icicles, Agnes thought of a place on Lake Erie where they had once lived as caretakers after the Second World War. In the black mornings Edward got up at five to plow the parking lots, and by the time everyone else was rising at seven and eight his face would be as purple as a grape in the cold wind off the lakes. In the late afternoons he would knock the six foot icicles off the eaves with a long pole. As she passed an icicle fell silently from the barn roof. Agnes pulled her head down into her collar and peered into the snowy haze on the road in front of her.

The cold didn't bother Edward, but Agnes knew he had never gotten the sand out of his vital parts from that wartime beach landing. He told her the heat of that day changed to fog, then cold, but he never revealed the mystery, what it was that left him ever after in a fog of disconnection, the ice solid around him and unyielding. She was too old to be surprised by this any longer, and she had been able at times to escape its sting. But she wanted for once to fight a battle that was her own. She had written too many polite, safe little letters, subdued too many passions to take this time of her life in comfort. She walked into the howling wind with her head down, her chin tucked into her damp coat.

Agnes swallowed another sharp blast of cold. The storm, now more vigorous and biting, slowed her progress to the river. The sun had long ago set in the grey sky and she was impatient, knowing her destination was only about half a mile ahead. She wanted to see the trees along the river, the oaks and elms she remembered from the summer before when she had spent the season with Bert, and he and Sally had taken her there for a picnic.

That day Bert had told her the story of a woman who walked out into the snow the previous winter, folded her clothes carefully on the riverbank, and then waded into the frigid water. Agnes wondered if the woman first sat down on the black rocks at the water's edge to decide whether she would yield to that greatest of temptations. Maybe she had spent months thinking of it in bus stations, or maybe she decided as she walked there. She would have had to break the ice first with the heel of her hand, her boot, or a stick or rock found in the snow. They had discovered the woman's boots, Bert said, her coat, and her blue dress in a neat pile on the shore. The searchers then followed her footprints in the snow to the river. But Agnes thought it would be easier and somehow more comforting to be clothed at the moment one sank beneath the icy surface. She could understand the woman's decision, but not her compulsive neatness.

As she walked on the snowy shoulder numbed by the bitterness of the wind, Agnes briefly thought of turning back, but comforted herself instead by thinking of warmer times. She thought of a morning at her daughter's house in Indian summer, the yellow tail end of Fall. A tulip tree had been gold outside the kitchen window and the house smelled of lemon furniture polish and toast. At the table Ellie bent her wiry head over a coffee mug.

"You can stand a spoon up in this stuff, Mother," Ellie said making a clucking sound. "I can't drink it."

Agnes looked out the window at the buttery ring of leaves at the base of the tulip tree.

"You know, Ellie," Agnes said, "I could never go to work each morning like you do, and never spend a life happily waving at the window, either, even though your father wanted me to."

"Mother." Ellie scraped the crumbs off the table into her cupped hand and dumped them on her plate.

"Remember how we used to dance in the kitchen after he went to work?"

"Mother, don't talk like that." Ellie pushed her coffee mug away from her and looked down at the table cloth for a minute. "I read this really interesting book on creative dreaming," she said.

Agnes stared out the window. Ellie was talking but she couldn't listen. She looked down at her empty plate and silently cursed Edward for leaving her stranded; her mind slipped so often into the past that she felt she must grasp it with two hands and hold it firmly in place in order to attune to even an ordinary breakfast table conversation.

"What, Ellie?"

"I was saying that instead of saying good morning to their children these Malaysians ask them what they dreamed the night before." Ellie folded her napkin and placed it in the holder. "If the child says he saw a fierce animal and woke up, his parents tell him to go back and dream again."

She still has the same face, Agnes thought. Her body's changed but Ellie still has the face of the little girl who cried all those alligator tears. Agnes took a long drink of her coffee.

"They teach their children to learn from their dreams, you know." Ellie stood, gathered the empty plates, and took them to the sink.

Agnes nodded. A familiar story. So many years telling my children bedtime stories, Agnes thought, and now my daughter tells me breakfast stories as if I were a child. She pushed her chair back from the table.

"No, Mother, don't get up. I can do it." Ellie was running the water, the steam rising up through her wild head of hair. "If the child is smart," she said, "the next morning he'll say he saw a tiger and when he faced it, it disappeared."

"You mean if he was brave," Agnes said. "Yes, Ellie." Agnes watched the leaves on the tree outside the window. "That's a good story."

"Mother, don't you believe it?"

"No, the only thing I believe in is a good strong cup of coffee."

"But Mother." Ellie came back to the table and sat down.

"I give you this," Agnes said looking at her daughter with a half smile, "at least you haven't put me on the bone pile."

Ellie looked down into her mug. "I won't put you into a home."

"Thank you, Ellie." Agnes poured herself another cup of coffee from the pot on the table. "But I might have some friends there and we could talk. Maybe embroider pillowcases."

"You've never embroidered a pillowcase in your life. You don't mean that." Ellie looked at the older woman for a minute, her eyes pale brown on a wide face. She pushed her mug toward Agnes.

"Is it too strong for you?" Agnes said. "I'll make another pot."

"No, it's all right — give me some warm on top."

Agnes poured the coffee and then turned again to the window. She noted the brown edges of the leaves lifting and falling as if something had just passed by. It was time for another bus ride to Bert's. Soon the leaves would be decaying in the Autumn rains.

"Ruth McGrory," Agnes said, "remember her?"

"No." Ellie changed her position in the wooden chair.

"I used to talk about her all the time. We used to play under those trees at the side of the house."

"Grandma's house?"

"It was my house."

"No, I don't remember." Ellie gazed out the window. "What's out there?"

"Well, she's not much older than I am."

"Who?"

"Ruth McGrory. She's in one of those homes."

Ellie stirred her coffee silently.

"I went to see her once. She was all tied up and sitting in piss."

"Mother."

"Okay, sitting in urine. Same thing."

Agnes looked at her daughter's dark hair as she bent over the coffee mug. She hoped when Ellie lifted her head she would suddenly see something in her daughter's face that would remind her of herself.

The newly risen moon was obscured behind a green haze that hung over the road. Agnes pushed her hands deep into her pockets as the moaning, snow-laden wind whipped past her. It was dark now and the road was empty in both directions. If the cat at Bert's door hadn't driven her away she would have picked up her gloves. Sally brought the cat with her when she moved in, but Bert was the one who fed it. Agnes knew Edward would not have understood any of this, especially a woman moving in with their son without marriage.

247

Agnes was tired. Her face and hands were tingling. She squinted through the increasingly bitter storm looking for the trees she knew should not be far away. Within the snowy haze lurked the eyes of several stars. She thought she saw someone ahead of her in the snow and she called out, but there was no answer.

She turned off the road and lowered her head against the wet blast from the river. This morning the coffee had not been strong enough.

"I went to the Animal Fair." She sang the child's song into the wind. She peered through the blinding snow and listened carefully. She heard her father laughing in the wind. Suddenly he picked her up and turned her in his arms. "We'll go to the circus, Aggie." She heard his voice at her ear. "We'll see the big cats and the pretty ladies." He's not there, no, she thought.

Agnes waded through a waist-high drift, her legs numb. She smelled something as aromatic as her mother's stew simmering at the back of the stove. As she walked she heard the mantel clock ticking at the back of her mind and then the sounding of its Westminster chimes, and she thought of summer evenings after dinner long ago. She and her brother would chip away at the sycamore trees at the side of the house, pulling off the grey patches of bark until the trees were peeled down to their waxy yellow souls.

She felt nearly frozen. She had not realized that the river was so far. Her lips were cracked and tight. A blast of frigid air brought the faint odor of smoke and ash. Agnes leaned down to scoop a handful of the grainy tasting snow to her lips. She gave a short cry and lost her balance as the surface caved in beneath her.

She tottered in a moment of fear and then fell into a large ditch partially covered with a piece of snowladen plywood. She bit her lip. Her glasses shattered against her face as she landed in a painful heap on top of something hard and cold.

Tasting blood in her mouth, she pulled herself to her feet and brushed off the snow. Beside her in the ditch were frozen sections of an exposed water main. The white surface was far above her. She tried to climb the steep sides of the hole but slipped back onto the snowy wet floor. She tried a second time and fell back against the frozen mud of the cavern's wall. After a few more attempts she sat down on a section of pipe and rubbed her sore angle which, even in the bitter cold, was beginning to swell.

In the thin moonlight that filtered down to her she thought it would not be difficult to face. It would be there. It would be at the river. She took off her boots and rubbed her ankles. After a few minutes her right ankle looked silver, then purple, in the moonlight. She took a handful of snow and packed it around the foot, shuddering as she did so. She looked around her.

The black wall of the ditch was partially frozen, partially muddy and slick from the previous day's thaw, and much of the hole was filled with patches of new snow, fallen branches and dark puddles thinly iced over. The surface loomed above her head.

"Help! Over here."

Her voice was lost in the howl of the wind. She tried again to scale the steep sides of the ditch by digging her fingernails into the cold mud and bringing her body up to them, but her arms were weak and on her painful ankle she could not get a firm foothold. She slipped, and slid back into the snowy cavern. Her ankle throbbed.

The howl of the wind frightened her now. It was the only sound she could hear and it became not a howl, but the open-mouthed screech of a tiger. She pulled her damp coat collar up around her neck as a ledge of soft snow fell down on top of her. She tried to put on her boots with shaking hands but was unable to force them over her swollen feet. She thought of Bert back at the house stoking the fire and of Ellie in her house in Virginia polishing the furniture with long rhythmic strokes.

As she sat on the frigid pipe and rested she could hear her own teeth chattering. A long time passed. Agnes was very cold. She was not sure exactly where she was, as place and time were beginning to be obscured for her in an oblivion of snow. She could see in the faint moonlight that her hands, red at first, were now white.

"Help!" Agnes called out in a voice she did not recognize. "Is anybody there?" Surely not Edward. It was a horror to him to reveal any secrets, although at the end he became unexpectedly joyful. "Give me the life," he'd say, his eyes fixed on some distant vision and Agnes dutifully would give him a drink. He didn't eat. He wanted to be spirit only, Agnes finally decided. And surely the lost child was not there, nor her mother, or father, or brother. They were there only, if at all, as ghosts, as haunting as footprints in the snow.

"Does anybody hear me?"

Her only answer was in the roar of the wind. The air was thick with damp. She was near the river. The arctic wind growing ever stronger blasted down into the ditch. She sat on the section of pipe and in exhaustion briefly fell asleep.

She woke with a start. There had been no sound or movement. Five large dots had been held in front of her without comment, long enough for her to perceive the pattern, and perhaps also, the meaning. But she didn't understand any more than her impression that there was no beatific smile on the face of this dream, no creamy white lotus held high above her head. Instead, she reacted with a kind of loathing; she could not interpret the signs and symbols in the unarticulated realm of dreams. She wondered how long she had been asleep. She gained no clues from the sky above the ditch, obscured as it was by heavy snowfall and the overhanging branches she noticed now for the first time.

As she looked up the moon reappeared as a faint illumination behind the rolling haze above her. She was not sure if time exists in dreams, it exists only when one must wake and account for the progress of the world while one has been gone from it. We come back reluctantly, she thought, and must grab onto our minds with two hands.

Agnes got up and walked in a small circle in the ditch, avoiding the pipe and the icy puddles, but her ankle was still painful, and she sat down again. She felt colder than she felt in her days as a young woman in Canada when it was a coldness of spirit that held her. She would not think of it again. She would think of the heavens stretched out like a curtain — the words came from somewhere in her past.

In the moonlight she picked the caked mud from her numb fingertips. She listened for the tiger. It would be as white as Mohini but not Mohini, a white tiger blending into the snow.

She had seen its footprints so this would be the place she would meet it. She knew it was prowling silently in the snow above her, stalking her in a gradually decreasing circle. It had been following her during the walk to the river. Its yellow eyes had been in the small lights in the distance, and sometimes it had padded behind her in the depressions where the black macadam showed through the snow. She had turned to see it several times but it had evaded her, moving to the left as she looked right, sometimes hiding in the tree of her thoughts high above her head.

She looked upward and saw the snow in mid-air above her, suspended like blossoms amid the bare trees that bordered the ditch. A dog barked off to the right, an alarmed piercing series of barks that carried through the thick dream of night above her. The dog could also smell the sweet, wild odor of the tiger.

Agnes heard the big cat padding above her. Small avalanches of wet snow fell down on her head. She held her breath. Then she heard nothing. After a few minutes of strained listening she rubbed her ankle, huddled down in her wet coat and rested her head on her arm.

When Agnes opened her eyes the tiger was in the ditch beside her. It was sleeping on its side, one muscular leg over her, pinning her down in a fearful embrace. The huge white head rested on a grey paw in front of them, and the great expanse of trunk and legs filled the den. Agnes sucked in her breath. From the damp chest fur of the white mass came the warm odor of ash and wet leaves. She stroked the tiger's chest with a delicate touch of her forefinger. She gasped. The fur was damp, the flesh solid behind it.

With all her strength Agnes lifted the heavy white limb off her shoulder and jumped up. She pressed herself flat against the muddy side of the cavern, her ankle screaming with the pain of her sudden movement. The sleeping animal's body expanded to fill the den.

In the moonlight the tiger's ear was a convoluted cave of pale red, its nose and paw pads glistening triangles of black. The rest of its body was a mound of grey and white shadow.

Agnes was trembling like the small leaves of a tree she had seen by the river. Her feet were bare. She forgot her throbbing ankle and the dried blood on her lips. Her mind leaped into confusion. She thought of a dozen lions yawning and sleeping in a small den, surrounding a quiet man whose name at the moment she could not recall. If the man's friends threw hunks of meat down to the lions in the dark of night to save him, would that be less of a miracle? Are lions more docile than tigers, she wondered, less fearsome than leopards, more inclined to spare a small man who believes in something?

Agnes stroked the rough wool of her overcoat. It was soaked through to the lining. She took if off and folded it neatly in a pile at her feet.

The white tiger lifted its large head, blinked, and then stared at Agnes, its vertical pupils black, shining, unseeing. As she watched dark stripes shot from the tiger's eyebrows, and its slanted, intelligent eyes focused and gleamed with bright inquiry. The tiger gazed at Agnes for a moment and then opened its black mouth in a yawn of white teeth that soon was transformed into a roar.

Slowly the tiger stood and stretched first forward and then back on its haunches. A second roar echoed in the small muddy den and in her fear Agnes had a sudden urge to release her bowels. Not even wild animals foul their own dens, she thought, they groom themselves and their young with barbed tongues and cover their wastes with the brown-edged leaves of Fall, or the dry ash of spent fires.

Mohini stared at Agnes, the tiger's ebony pupils large within the yellow irises. The tiger roared again, with a piercing sound that vibrated through Agnes and obliterated her thoughts. She moved further against the cold side of the ditch. Agnes wondered how in a dream or no dream she had happened upon Mohini's secret place.

The tiger raised an eyebrow and then swiped at her with a bared claw, knocking Agnes against the opposite wall of the ditch. She slid to the floor. Agnes felt as if all her bones had been flailed against the loose bag of her body. She pulled herself up on her swollen ankles, her numb feet, and lunged at the yellow-eyed mass. The tiger's head was cocked to one side, and it peered at her with one surly eye a slit over its open mouth. As she watched black stripes swirled up the tiger's chest, met at its jaws, and curled around its neck. Agnes took a deep breath.

The sound of the wind blasting into the hole became louder. "Aggie, Aggie." Somewhere in the treetop of her mind she heard her name being called. She lunged at the tiger and knotting her fingers into its sides she climbed onto its back. Black stripes zipped around the animal's broad trunk and locked her legs against its thick fur which was pale yellow in the changing light. She fell forward onto the tiger's head. The cloud of moisture from the creature's nostrils smelled of straw and rain.

Agnes rolled with the beast in a tangled embrace over the ice puddles and the black mud of the den's floor. She crashed again and again against the frozen water pipes as blood streamed from her eyes and face where the giant's claws had torn the flesh of her eyelids and cheek.

She pulled herself up on numb feet and then fell back against the wall as her breath came alternately in wheezes and sobs. The tiger stood facing her, its head down, a low vibrant growl coming from deep in its throat.

She knew she could not walk away from her fear as it stood all spark and moan before her. Her body gave off a sharp scent of despair.

Above her she heard the deep rumble of the ice breaking up on the river, the thunderous rumble of the thawing, moving ice floes growing louder as the boulders broke loose and crashed against the black rocks, scooping them up and hurling them ahead in a glacial roar downstream.

Agnes lunged at the tiger a third time. Her breath came in painful gasps as she fell upon its muddy, strawcolored coat. She could feel the tiger's muscles tighten beneath her.

She fought the tiger as fiercely as Jacob met his foe. She called up all her strength by calling off the gasses of defeat, drying the blood on her lips, denying the frostbite of her hands, the emptiness of her womb, the pain in her ankles, the numbness of her feet. She forgot the dreams of her childhood, the sadness of her young womanhood, the anger and fear of her mid-age, the despair of her most recent loneliness. She gathered all the courage she had forgotten she had been born with, the joy, the pleasure, the pain of small things done well and grand things

253

believed in. And when she had let go of it all, when she had seen the pettiness of even these concerns, when she had given it all away in order to muster the strength for this one grand battle, the white tiger roared, its hot fragrant breath upon her face, and disappeared.

Agnes kept very quiet and listened. She heard the wind whistling through the trees and the lonely howl of an animal far in the distance. Then she heard the sound of a motor being cut off and muffled talk.

"For God's sakes, Jimmie—" Agnes strained to listen.

"—the ditch has got to be here somewhere. The storm hit and the laborers just left."

"Damned stupid thing to do."

"Yeah. Well, you find it and I'll get the flashers up, and we're gone."

Agnes wiped the blood off her face with her sleeve. Maybe Bert told Sally she had gone off to bed. Maybe first they had searched the house for her. She took off her soiled, wet dress and folded it neatly on top of her coat and boots.

"I went to the Animal Fair," she sang the song into the waning blizzard above her. It came in a harsh whisper. "The birds and bees were there." Her voice was a rasp. She tried again. "The old raccoon—"

The muffled voices of the men faded and then came near as they combed the dark roadside. The snow fell steadily.

"Do you hear anything, Jimmie?"

"No, just the wind."

Agnes stopped singing. Above her were people allergic to life. She knew it now with certainty. She saw Edward with the blue behind him, heard the clink of dishes in a sink, dipped her hands into the warm suds of an understanding as someone coughed. The yellow eyes of a portable hazard sign blinked above her as a small avalanche of snow fell into the ditch.

She shook the snow from her head and steadied herself on legs that had lost their feeling. Mohini stared down at her with curiosity, tail hanging into the hole like a rope, yellow eyes glowing.

Agnes leaned down and picked up her dress from the top of the cold muddy pile of clothing at her feet. She stood, holding it in her hands.

The men's voices were fading. To catch them before they left, to let them know she was there, she would have to yell now as the curtains flapped at the open window of her mind high above her. She would have to yell above the yawn of the tiger, yell louder than she could yell above the swirling moonlit snow and the loose luffing sail of the wind. Some small fear made her want to shout, but then she remembered that snowwalkers are silent as they walk into the river of their dreams.

Nore and Zelda

JESS WELLS

Eleanora pressed her shoulders against the side of the barn, holding the thick braid of hair in one fist, the hedge shears in the other.

She squinted against the searing afternoon as she looked around the corner of the barn at the men filing past her uncle, their faces blurred and their gestures exaggerated by the heat baking off the yard. The farmhands shook the dust out of their hair and slapped at their pantlegs while Uncle Jack, hay still clinging to the back of his shirt, wiped the sweat from around his neck and handed the next man in line a packet of money, then reached into a box and pulled up a pint of whiskey. The workers folded the money solemnly into a pocket, grabbed the whiskey with anxious hands and made it the subject of jokes.

Eleanora leaned back against the barn. She clenched the braid tightly in her fist until it made her palm itch and sweat as if she held something alive, something demanding the freedom to slither under a rock. She was as dirty and covered with hay as the men; she wanted to wash the grit from her own face. She wouldn't join them though—she was family and she was a girl. But she wasn't family. Word of it had been hissed in her ear today, the sting of it smarting her burned and dirty face.

"You're just a field hand like the rest of us," the man had

said scornfully as he tipped back a jug and let torrents of water run over the sides of his mouth.

Eleanora turned back to watch the men jostling each other nervously, as they held the pints and tried not to scratch at the shafts of hay that had flown into their shirts and the waistbands of their pants. The haybaling was finished. Eleanora herself had been on the top of the wagon, as she always was, working as hard, as long, as well. In the fields the boys would joke with her but away from the wagons they'd suddenly feel distant, look puzzled, as if she and they were somehow different when they laid down their pitchforks. Eleanora, every night, would sit on the porch until they had finished washing, then go to the trough alone.

Today, though, even the porch didn't feel safe, she thought, as she looked down at the braid hanging in the dust. Earlier that day, she had come to the house to rinse some of the heat out of her bandana. Across the porch, two of the girls who did the baking were combing each other's hair, lost in some dream of soothing strokes and the shine of hair dried in the sun. Eleanora watched their little motions, the way they touched an ear, a cheek; Eleanora watched them quietly as if beneath nesting birds. The girls never looked up. What was their life like, Eleanora thought? She had braided her own tangled rope of hair herself and it had fallen across her shoulder more times today than she could tolerate. She had never been a girl like that, never been touched like that before. Eleanora had stood on the porch feeling dirty and torn, a scarecrow in comparison to the girls in their pressed frocks and smooth hair. The only dirt on either of them was a tiny smudge of molasses clinging to the wrist of the youngest as she slumped dreamily against the swing with her hand dangling over the armrest as if it had never had anything to do.

Eleanora wasn't a girl like that, and yet now, with the men streaming towards the trough to wash off the day's dust, she didn't feel like a field hand either. She had come back to the house when the men began their procession but seeing the porch swing where the girls had been, couldn't bring herself to enter. Wasn't she a member of the family? Adopted, but a member of the family. A girl at least?

As the men lined up for their money, Eleanora had run to the tool shed, slammed the door. Seeing the hedge clippers, she took them from the wall, glaring at them as if they could cut a pattern, a definition into her life. She hacked at the thick yellow braid with sawing, tearing motions, her tears and her hair falling onto the front of her shirt.

Now, with the ends of her ragged hair flapping in gusts of wind, Eleanora turned away from the line of men and walked the barnyard slowly, mesmerized, as if she had been enlivened for a moment, then left once again chilled and silent as after a storm.

She had not begun here, on the farm. Eleanora was born in Chicago in 1895 on a day of celebration, with noisy children banging tin and hollering under her mother's window. Eleanora, though, was quiet and still. Even at five and six years old, her life was silent, making little impression on her mind except the sound of the door closing in the morning when the light was pale on the wall beside the bed, opening in the late afternoon when the light was warm. She was certain she had spent time with her mother but somehow could never remember the woman's arm around her or the feeling of her cheek against her mother's breast and, though she often tried, she couldn't remember the woman's face in much detail.

Eleanora told herself this wasn't particularly upsetting. She understood the burden the woman (she always called her mother "the woman") had lived under. The only recollection she had of her mother was holding her hand as they stared at a stranger, "Aunt Mildred," in a buggy, the day Mildred McAleer drove to Chicago and took Eleanora to the farm, leaving no trace of her mother, no mention of the city.

Eleanora, the oldest girl and the only one adopted, grew up surrounded by children fed on solid answers. Wide-eyed, the other girls looked up and saw Mother. Eleanora looked up and saw questions. No one provided her with answers. She grew up with a fog around her, a thin mist that obscured her understanding of what she saw, kept her passive and silent. She sought explanations in the birds migrating from the trees by the creek, mornings that smelled of flour, the odd shape of flies dead in the cream at the top of the pitcher. She asked questions of the plow horses resting at the top of the hill on Sunday afternoons, wondered at the feel of the pump squeaking under her own, strong hands. Eleanora was raised by the hayfields, the gold lawns stretching to the trees, the pattern of wind across the field in S-shapes and double Z's. She watched, in the late spring, the wind punching at the stalks of hay like a boxer, hitting the field in five places at once.

She was the supreme haymaker. Eleanora lifted, tossed and spread the hay with a rhythm, swung a fork all day like a man, counted the conical heaps of hay in the field and came closest to the number of bales it would make. She paced through the field with this man she called Uncle Jack, her hands behind her, him clutching a pipe in his mouth, both of them watching for weeds, calculating in their mind how much, what price, sometimes pretending to decipher when they were simply reciting their work and their patience like a long, slow stanza. At the end of the season, like today, she stood on top of the hay wagon, catching on her fork great bundles tossed into the air.

Eleanora was a big girl by the time she was 14 and after puberty seemed to put on more muscle. She never thought about her size and no one else on the farm did either; Aunt Mildred had put her into knickers and white shirts almost from the day she had arrived because a quick perusal told her that there wasn't a girls' dress in the house to accommodate her. It seemed sensible, the woman had reasoned: they were miles away from anyone so the girl could change her clothes when company came or she went into town. Eleanora grew up with the sleeves of her white shirt rolled up around her biceps and her cotton britches cinched tight around her waist, quietly lost in the mass of children and work to be done.

Today, Eleanora wandered the barnyard with her shorn hair and a mind full of fog despite the sunshine and heat. She took her braid to the corner of the property, looked down at the dusty ends of it, the twigs it had gathered from the ground. Now she wouldn't have anything to brush, any reason to sit on the porch swing at all. she flung the braid as far as she could, watching it twist through the air and disappear into the bushes. Slowly, quietly, she walked to the trough to wash for dinner.

Aunt Mildred set down a plate of yams. What on earth had she done with her hair? Boys' clothing was fine for work, but now the girl wouldn't be presentable even for going to the store.

"It got in my way, Aunt Mildred," Eleanora said quietly, picking up her knife and fork. Mildred stared at the child, then passed the serving spoon to her husband as if asking for an opinion. Jack dug into the yams without comment and Mildred sighed: with four daughters and five sons of my own, she thought, this one will have to make her own way in the world. Mildred took off her apron and sat at the end of the table.

After dinner Eleanora walked the edges of the fields as she did nearly every night, sometimes with Uncle Jack, usually alone. Pacing over the wagon ruts with even, methodical steps, Eleanora walked to the far ends of the field where she could look back and see the house, small lamps burning in the rooms, sometimes hear the family closing doors, hauling buckets and tubs. Tonight she ran a hand through her ragged hair, feeling as if she could stand in the field for hours and not sense the dew that was dampening her jacket, not even understand that the sun going down meant night. There had to be a place away from the sleepy patterns she had lived in, simply planting, then waiting, then hoeing it under. There had to be a place where she could wake up from this pain. It was more acute when she stood in the dark, in the cool night air and saw it from a distance. No one had ever touched her like those girls touched each other. No one had ever stroked her or lightly tickled the back of her neck while putting a thong around the mass of her hair. She had never sat in the sun . . . to feel pretty. There had to be someplace she could do that.

Eleanora resolved to take the train eighty miles north, back to Chicago.

Uncle Jack was in the kitchen with an empty cup of coffee when she came in from the field.

"I want *my* money, too," Eleanora said quietly. Jack looked up from his cup.

"Your money?"

"If I'm a field hand, I should be paid like a field hand," she said.

Jack regarded her cautiously, then got up and went to the

260

pantry where he pulled a packet of money from a tin box.

"I'm assuming you don't want the whiskey."

"I'm going to Chicago, Uncle Jack."

Jack looked at the floor, pushed his hands into his pockets.

"You be sure to tell Mildred. It would hurt her pretty bad if you didn't say goodbye."

Mildred McAleer had blanched when she heard the girl's decision, then puzzled for hours over the idea of Eleanora among city people: what to do about her hair? People were more accepting in the country, where practical attire had its own value, but in the city there would be little leniency towards a broad-shouldered girl who lumbered around in britches. How could she teach the child to walk properly at this late date?

Mildred and the girls fussed over Eleanora for hours, measuring her, tailoring blouses, combing, assessing, debating this jacket and this second-hand petticoat, never really including Eleanora in the discussion, but being attentive like never before. Mildred's eyes had filled as she took Eleanora's hand and faltered over her words: get a buggy directly to the place recommended by the church auxiliary, the New Chicago Hotel for Ladies. Give them money for one week and look for a job first thing the next morning. Food was not good in the cities, Mildred said, and Eleanora would have to work hard to afford the vegetables she took for granted around the farm.

Eleanora listened, puzzling over the tears in the woman's eyes. When she was packed and started down the road to town where a wagon would take her to the train, Mildred and the girls watched as if marveling at the odd stripes of a retreating animal.

Eleanora arrived at the New Chicago Hotel for Ladies with a small bag of clothes and her first hat, carried in her hands like the heaviest burden she'd ever borne. Skirts of navy blue cotton slapped around her ankles and dragged on the side, showing the pointed toes of shoes that hurt her feet. Stepping out of the taxi, she gathered the skirt in her fist like so many unruly blades of hay, and stopped at the ten-foot windows of the Chicago Bazaar next door to the hotel. They were stuffed with brass picture frames, linaments, eyelash curlers, glass dolls with ten different dresses, lamps, licorice, soap and boxes of pills. The Bazaar was like a month of visits to the farm-store, Eleanora thought. Next door, sleds and carts and little wagons piled outside the shuttered doors proclaimed The Chicago Baby Buggy Company, and in No. 14, Henry Siede's Furs, the window was decorated with hats and shoulder shawls with the little animal's feet still on, ladies' coats fur-trimmed inside and out, pelts that in the setting sun shone like copper.

The New Chicago Hotel for Ladies wasn't as grand as the building for the furrier and the Chicago Bazaar. It didn't have fluted columns or flowered designs etched into the cement around the windows. It was a plain brick building with three stories of shuttered windows and two dormers poking out of the roof.

Women were lounging on sofas in the lobby when she entered. They stood in clusters and talked together as they climbed the stairs. Eleanora conducted her business in faltering sentences, never turning from the woman at the desk, feeling the back of her neck grow hot with fear of the women. Could they see she didn't belong in shoes like these? In skirts, even? Every whisper was a woman who knew she had worn pants all her life, every other sound someone laughing at her hair. When she got her room assignment, she dashed up the stairs two at a time and closed the door quickly. Why had she left the safety of the farm? There at least she had a purpose, she was the best. If she couldn't talk to the girls on the porch, why on earth had she come someplace where there were so many of them? She didn't belong with women, that was part of the problem. She hadn't the first idea what to say. Eleanora took off her skirt, threw it in the corner and climbed into bed.

The next morning, Eleanora woke with a start, anxiety driving her out of bed. Aunt Mildred had told her to get a job right away so Eleanora put on her best white blouse with lace and pulled the blue skirt from yesterday over her wide thighs.

Bounding down the stairs, she realized she was the only one up this early in the morning and, looking around for some sign of life, Eleanora saw a notice on the wall. "Help Wanted: Chicago Equity Corporation."

It took over an hour of walking and numerous requests for

directions before Eleanora got to the office. The Equity Corporation was in a huge brick building with vaulted windows and gilded bears guarding the doors. As Eleanora walked across the polished floors to the reception desk, she wondered what an equity corporation did and what her job might entail. A man in a blue uniform directed her to an office at the top of the stairs.

When she opened the door, though, she stopped, puzzled. There were four other women there, though the doors could only have opened minutes before. They sat stiffly on a large sofa, staring but not seeing an older woman in very proper dress sitting at a desk.

"May I have your name, please?" the woman asked.

"Eleanora McAleer."

"Take a seat. The typing test will be given in just a moment."

"Typing?"

"We have the finest new equipment here: no complaints from our typing pool. Now, just take a seat beside the other girls, there."

The women on the couch shifted without moving their eyes from the wall. The woman sitting closest to her looked at Eleanora from under the brim of a hat bright with ribbons. The other women were those small-waisted, tight-lipped girls, Eleanora thought, like the girls in town who seemed able to suck themselves into rigid little lines. She didn't know how to type; maybe the woman could offer something else.

"Excuse me, Ma'am."

"Take a seat. We'll get to you."

The woman with the ribboned hat turned and gave a little grin, motioned with her eyes to Eleanora's hair. Eleanora cleared her throat, put her hat on and tried to push her hair into it. The young woman crossed her legs, turned and put her elbow on the back of the seat, covering her mouth with her hand.

"Now hold your hands in your lap," she whispered to Eleanora, who stiffened, then did what she was told.

"Right. Cross your legs. No, no, at the knee."

The woman at the front desk looked up from her papers.

263

"Alright, we'll start on the left. You, dear."

"Yes ma'am," Eleanora said.

"Where were you last employed?"

The ribboned hat whispered, "New Orleans."

"Uh, New Orleans, ma'am."

"And how many words per minute do you type?"

"Type, ma'am?"

The whisper came, "25 per minute."

"Oh, well, 25 per minute."

"I see, and where can we reach you if necessary."

"Well, I just moved into . . ."

"I see, well . . . and you, Miss, where were you last employed?"

The ribboned hat turned towards the desk. "I was an executive secretary to the Treasurer of the Mobile Trust Insurance Corporation for four years, Ma'am. I take dictation, file, of course, type 35 words per minute, handle telegram requests and personal organization. I'd be happy to show you references, naturally."

Eleanora watched the woman as she talked. She had seemed easy and natural while she whispered into her hand, but when addressing the woman at the desk, had suddenly gone stiff and proper like the others. What most astounded Eleanora, though, was the way she was dressed. The other women were in pastels with lace here and there, little jackets over their arms, gloves with tiny pearls on the clasp. This woman wore black, a close-cut black skirt and a short jacket that stopped at the waist, a white blouse with small, severe tucks down the front. And a tie. A man's tie. Eleanora couldn't take her eyes off it.

"Excuse me, Miss," the woman at the desk interrupted, pointing her pencil at Eleanora. "This is a private interview."

Eleanora glowered. How could it be private when she was sitting right there? The other women stared straight ahead as if forbidden to hear. Bad enough she had to sit there in these stupid clothes amongst all this lace and high fashion but nobody was going to treat her like a child. She may not know about the city but she certainly knew when she was being insulted.

"I think it's more than my eyes that are in the wrong place, Ma'am."

"Fine," the interviewer said. "And you can go, too," she waved her pencil at the neck-tie.

The woman in the ribboned hat slammed the door behind them.

"I'm sorry," Eleanora said, when they reached the street. "You shouldn't have to leave just because I did."

"It's not your fault. She started with our side of the couch for a reason, you know."

"What reason?"

The woman didn't answer, but walked to the main intersection with Eleanora.

"I can't get trussed up like a monkey to make a living," Eleanora said quietly.

"It's just a game, don't you think?" the woman said. "Rich, conservative people like to hire rich, conservative people, so you pretend." The woman took off her hat and her black hair fell to her shoulders, curling just as it hit her collar bone. "I don't know very much about the city," Eleanora said, "but isn't that . . . a man's tie?"

"Yes. You like it? It's all the rage in New York and this one's really a man's. I got it from a friend of mine, this boy who looks as ridiculous in men's clothes as . . . well, anyway, I just love to sit in those stuffy offices thinking 'if they only knew where this tie has been,' " she laughed. "Anyway, good luck finding something." She touched Eleanora's arm and strode towards the intersection.

"Hey," Eleanora called. "Thanks for the help."

The woman waved a bare hand, put on her hat and turned the corner.

Eleanora wandered through the streets. The places hiring women were staffed by tight-waisted types and Eleanora couldn't bring herself to walk in the door anymore. When she found jobs she could do, she looked in at sweaty men with blackened forearms or with wood shavings clinging to their pants. She knew that the threshold of the door was her boundary.

Every day, the formlessness tightened around her until it forced Eleanora back into her room. She had less of a feeling of belonging than when she was on the farm. Her money was running out. Four days into her search, Eleanora lay in her white shirt and britches, sleeping in the late afternoon. A door across the hall slammed, waking her with a start.

" 'From the remotest time,' " a woman's voice pontificated, " 'man has tried to rule her who ought to be comrade and colleague.' No, Zelda I will not shut-up. You should read this. 'Every protest against this law was a women's rights movement and history contains many such protests.' "

Eleanora cracked open her door and peeked out at a woman with one finger in the air, her other hand cradling a book.

"Ack, I don't care Ellen," said a second woman whose back was to Eleanora's door. "Any book on the modern women's movement that doesn't include C.P Gilman is *not* a modern book."

"Zelda, there *are* important contributions made that don't come out of the mouth of your beloved." The woman looked up and saw Eleanora's eyes, grabbed the other woman by the arm.

"Good . . . afternoon," the reader said. The second woman spun around and Eleanora, though only half visible, tried to back into her room to hide her britches and white shirt, her collar open to her cleavage and her hair mussed from sleep.

She grabbed her skirt from the bed where she had thrown it earlier and struggled into it, opening the door for fear of missing the only contact she'd had in days. Looking up at the face of the second woman, dressed in black, she stepped into the skirt and tore the opening.

"It's you again," the woman in black said, taking off her hat and letting her hair fall to her shoulders. "My name is Zelda," she said, extending her hand. The reader looked at the glow on Zelda's face, looked at Eleanora, and closed her book.

"Eleanora McAleer."

"Ellen Olsen," the reader said. "Pleased to meet you. You just get in?"

"Monday."

"Oh, Ellen," Zelda moved to Eleanora's side. "We had quite the amusing little run-around with the employment office at Equity earlier this week. Come in, come in." Zelda grabbed the skirt that Eleanora was still struggling to clasp. "Don't worry about that. I'll fix it." Eleanora let the skirt drop, as Ellen leaned against the wall and folded her arms. "Please," Zelda said, "come in."

Ellen straightened her hair. "Oh yes, I'll fix it," she mimicked under her breath.

The three went into the room, Zelda throwing her hat on the bed and lighting a lamp. Ellen plopped herself on the bed and Eleanora moved cautiously to a chair on the far side. Zelda relayed the story of the Equity Corp. as she fussed in the room, opening a window, undoing her shoes, pulling up another chair and propping her feet on the bed. Zelda and Ellen grew silent. Eleanora felt as if she were being examined, her biceps, exposed by the rolled-up sleeves, her thighs, belly, forearms, legs, the ruddy color of her neck and chest.

"I hope you're not offended by the pants," she said, "it's just that on a farm . . ."

"You look great . . . very nice," Zelda said.

Ellen gave a sidelong glance at Zelda, then got up. "Well, I'm off. See you at dinner Zelda?"

"Yes, of course. We'll come and get you."

Ellen frowned at her friend, gave a little smile and a wave as she closed the door.

"Where are you from?" Zelda asked.

"Country. Near here. I was a haymaker. We had a lot of acreage."

"You look strong. I've always thought that was very . . . admirable." Looking at the woman's muscular forearms, Zelda's nostrils flared slightly, a little grin tugging at her face.

"Admirable," Eleanora laughed. "Well, it might be 'admirable' in the country but it isn't getting me anywhere here."

"Maybe you're just looking in the wrong places, Elen . . . could I call you Nore, or maybe Nora. Somehow Eleanora seems so lacey and old-fashioned."

Eleanora circled the room looking at posters and newspapers Zelda had pinned to the wall.

"You're a . . . suffragette?"

"And this," Zelda said, walking to her dresser and pointing to a framed poster, "is Charlotte Perkins Gilman, the finest theoretical thinker and writer of our time. Her book *Women and Economics,* have you read it?"

Ellen stuck her head in the door again. "Has she launched into you about CP, Eleanora? Don't listen to her. There's more than one mind in this movement. Come on you two, we'll be late for dinner and you know how the boys fuss if they have to go into the hall by themselves."

"Oh God, it is late," Zelda said, grabbing her bag. "Nore, will you have dinner with us? It's not expensive and maybe we can come up with some work for you: I'll bet the boys know a trick or two. Grab another skirt and we'll meet you downstairs."

Fifteen minutes later the women were rounding the corner of 10th St., Zelda in the middle chattering about occupations for their new friend. Two young men leaning on a wrought-iron fence across the street joined the human chain on either end.

"Here you are. I just can't stand it when you're late, Zel, and who is this?"

"Bertrum, meet Nore," Zelda said. "And this is Louis."

"Charmed," Bertrum said, doing a little curtsey.

"We're just trying to conjure up a good job for Nore," Zelda said.

Bertrum threw back his head. "Well, when you find the recipe for employing a misfit *do* let me know, won't you?"

"I thought you liked it at the dry goods store," Ellen said.

"The fashions are so boring lately," Bertrum said. "You women are looking so dowdy — nothing but black and white and little jackets."

"You long for the day of the whale-bone corset and ruffled neckline, Bertrum?"

"Oh yes, there were bright colors and ribbons and . . ."

"Well, then you wear them," Ellen said.

"My dearest," Bertrum said, walking backwards to face Ellen, taking her hand to his cheek. "Then you give me your permission?"

"Alright, alright you two," Zelda shushed them as the group passed the theater and joined the stream of young people headed for the narrow stairs to the Ladies and Gents Dining Rooms, the third floor of the Oyster Saloon at No. 28.

"What do you think, Louis?" Zelda asked when they sat

down with their plates of beef and potatoes.

"Well, Danille and Sons Haberdashery needs someone."

Ellen looked at him scornfully and Zelda snorted. "I don't really think she's the type to sell clothing, Louis."

"Well, what type is she?" Bertrum cooed.

"How about Sol. Feinber's Antiques?" Louis continued.

"You don't understand boys, this woman wants to *work*, not babysit the passerby," Zelda said.

"My, my," Bertrum rolled his eyes, "perhaps she should try the stockyards, then."

Ellen dropped her fork. "Absolutely not."

"I'm very good with livestock," Eleanora said, encouraged.

"Don't even think about it, Nore," Zelda said quietly. "Bertrum, you pig."

"Alright, I'm sorry," he said under his breath. "You don't want to do that, Nore. It's brutal."

The hall was a large open room, table after table filled with noisy diners. Nore noticed more than one group of women dressed in bright colors and low-cut dresses, women Aunt Mildred would consider of 'dubious morals.' The boys seemed either very threadbare or delicate, like this Bertrum and Louis. Maybe the food really *was* bad here in the city, though her plateful was certainly adequate. There only seemed to be one real gentleman in the entire crowd and he, stout in his double-breasted suit with round lapels, was striding in their direction.

"Well, Miss Zelda. Good evening dear," the gentleman said to the startled group. "Do we have a newcomer to our party?"

Zelda stiffened, then gestured formally. "This is Eleanora McAleer."

"Evening," the man nodded in her direction, then took Zelda's hand and drew it to his lips. "Scouting on train platforms are you, dear?" he murmured to her knuckles, kissing them lightly.

Zelda's face tightened, her eyes squinting in anger.

"Nore, this is . . . Mr. Henry Collier."

The gentleman saluted to Nore. He bowed to Ellen and kissed her hand slowly, with relish, then backed away and disappeared down the stairs.

"My," Bertrum said, circling his spoon in the air, "we are

certainly being bold tonight, aren't we?" He glanced sideways at Ellen, whose face was bright red as she sat clenching her purse and her coffee cup.

Home from dinner, Eleanora crossed the floor to her room in the dark and lit the lamp on the small table by the window. Zelda followed her, tossing her bag onto Nore's bed.

"I can't believe that woman," Zelda said, sitting beside her bag, her back to Nore. "Wearing that get-up in the dining hall."

Nore had gone behind her screen and had changed into her farm clothes. She threw her skirt on the floor, kicked the shoes into the corner, and stepped into the room in her chamois-colored pants and a clean white shirt.

"I'm sorry if this offends you but I can't wear that stuff anymore today," Nore said sheepishly. She sat nervously at the far end of the bed.

Zelda turned on the bed to face Nore, whose gleaming skin contrasted with the white shirt. In those clothes, she looked whole, Zelda thought, she looked graceful, as if suddenly the parts of her body knew how to move.

"You just have to be very careful, Nore. That woman tonight was taking a terrible risk."

Nore scowled, confused. Zelda looked at the door, thought about running to the safety of her own room, wondered why she was there.

"The man I introduced you to, Henry Collier . . ."

"The one who kissed your hand."

"Yes. Well, he is a woman."

"He was wearing . . ."

"A suit, that's right. And that's why we thought it terribly brazen of her. Everyone in the dining hall knows her, but as a woman. She wears that get-up to work, do you understand? She's a very bright woman and there just isn't much of a market for intelligent women, particularly ones who are fat, so . . ."

"I've never heard of such a thing . . ."

"Well, you mustn't breathe a word of it, not a single word," Zelda said, standing up and putting her hands on her hips. "You know how apprehensive you are about wearing your pants in your own room, imagine how much danger she's in."

Zelda gathered her things to leave and picked up the skirt to be mended.

Nore, Zelda and Ellen shared morning coffee in the hotel lobby, then rushed off in different directions, Ellen to her job as a telephone operator in a brass foundry, Eleanora and Zelda in search of jobs. Both the prospective employees came home, day after day, with nothing for their efforts but crumpled newspapers and dirty hemlines. Eleanora sat quietly staring at the fireplace, increasingly nervous about renting her room while the money dwindled from her bag. Zelda paced the floor.

After two weeks, over a glum cup of morning coffee, Ellen suddenly sat up as if poked.

"The Trinity Building, Zelda. They must have at least 15 companies crowded in that place and they're all doing very well—based on the traffic in the street anyway. Maybe there's something Nore can do there," Ellen said.

"And maybe the insurance companies need typists," Zelda said dubiously.

Thirty minutes later they got off the trolly in front of a five story building that housed The Pennsylvania Coal Company; E.B. Ely and Co., Shipper; the Kansas Colorado Gold Co.; Atlantic Mutual Insurance; W.B. Smaats, Attorney at Law and, monopolizing the top two floors, Hatch and Co., Lithographers. Zelda squeezed Eleanora's hand and they parted on the stairs.

Eleanora climbed the five flights to a Dutch door, the kind that opened on the top. The din of the print shop met her with a wall of sound. Men in black pants and white shirts stood in front of cabinets, pulling out a myriad of drawers and setting individual letters into trays in their hands. Presses whirled and clanked on either side of them and occasionally a young boy would wheel a rolling dolley loaded with crisp, white paper across the floor. The smell of gasoline and ink wafted over Eleanora's head.

A man approached the door, wiping his balding head. He set his ink-stained hand on the top of the half-door and leaned against the jam.

"What can I do for you, son?"

"Excuse me?" Eleanora asked, unable to hear.

"I said, what do you want, boy?"

Eleanora was dumbfounded, then looked at the door. Clearly, from his angle, he couldn't see the skirt she was wearing. Her face grew hot. She thought about standing on top of the haycart with her muscles flexed and warm.

"A job, sir."

"What?"

"A job!" she shouted.

"You a printer?"

"No sir, but I'm strong," she shouted.

"You honest? I can see you're strong."

"What, sir?" she shouted.

"Alright, we'll start you hauling paper, tomorrow."

"Excuse me?"

"Tomorrow! Damn if you're not the biggest kid I've seen through here in years. Seven a.m. We'll talk wage after you work," he shouted. "What's your name?"

"Nore."

"Norm?"

"Nore!"

"Alright, Norm, seven a.m. and I don't need to tell you that in this place, you be prepared to work!"

"Zelda! Zelda!" she screamed, tearing up the stairs two at a time, her skirts up to her knees. "I'm taking you to dinner."

Zelda threw open the door to her room.

"I got a job!"

Zelda shrieked and Ellen came out of her room, full of congratulations.

"Finally! Finally!" Nore said. The three stumbled into Zelda's room, and Eleanora paced as the others fell onto the bed.

"I really didn't know what I was going to do."

"Where? Doing what?" Ellen said, sitting up on her elbows.

"In a print shop. Hatch and Co. I waited for you, Zel, but I didn't know which office you went into and I was so excited I ran all the way back here. I couldn't remember which tram we took."

"A print shop?"

"Yeah. Tomorrow I haul paper. That's what they're going to start me on." Nore looked at the perplexed faces. "I guess they think I'm a boy."

"Nore," Ellen admonished quietly.

"Well, this man talked to me across a half-door so I guess he didn't know."

"Oh my God, Nore," Zelda said.

"It was noisy and when he asked my name he thought I said 'Norm.' You know, like Norman."

Ellen started laughing and fell back across the bed.

"I want this job, Zelda," Nore said.

"Well, you should keep the job, then," she said.

"Zelda," Ellen said, standing up to pace the floor beside Nore.

"Seriously," Zelda said to Ellen. "If they think she looks like a boy like this, wait 'til they see her in drag."

"It is very dangerous to impersonate a man," Ellen said with deliberation.

"Only if you're caught, Ellen," Zelda countered.

"Well," Ellen murmured, reconsidering. "I suppose she is a prime candidate, isn't she?"

Zelda rummaged in her drawers for a pair of scissors.

"Now wait a minute, Zelda, you can't just mold Nore into what you want her to be," Ellen protested. "When the chips are down *she's* the one who's got to carry it off."

"I want this job, Ellen," Nore said quietly, watching the women discussing her like the girls did with Aunt Mildred before she left the farm.

"Zelda, you can't make an innocent into your loving husband just because you want her!" Ellen said.

"Why not? Then we could double-date, eh, Ellen?"

Ellen put her hands on her hips, her face reddening. "Help yourself dear," Ellen slammed the door behind her.

"What is she talking about, Zelda?" Nore asked quietly.

Zelda held the scissors and looked at Nore. How could she not see whom she was surrounded by? Could Nore really be that innocent, that unknowing? Her body radiates vitality, it announces her, but her face seem oblivious, unaware of what lies inside or beyond. Could it be right to give her body the

273

challenge of passing when her mind was so clearly unprepared? How could Zelda tell her about lesbians, when Nore had no point of reference for anything but pitchforks and wagons? Zelda turned away, went to her dresser and set down the scissors.

Looking up at her posters of C.P. Gillman, Zelda felt very alone. Her excitement over Nore's job had gone and she felt attacked, invalidated by the woman's naivety about lesbianism, threatened by her possible reaction. Even the need to explain herself offended her. Especially when she felt a deepening attraction for this woman whose tanned skin at the neckline of her shirt called out to be touched.

"We're lesbians, Nore."

Zelda crossed the room, hoping to hide her own fear and vulnerability. She took Nore by the hand as she would a child and sat down on the bed to explain.

Later that evening, Nore sat on the edge of the bed, her hands folded between her knees, a deep crevice in her brow. Zelda was pacing the room. The explanation had not been difficult, since Nore was like a blank page that needed no correction, a clear space for Zelda's information. But Zelda felt agitated, hurt by the necessity to explain her life in such detail, frightened by the risk she was taking. Nore had said very little.

"I didn't ask you," Nore said, breaking the silence, "did you find work today?"

"No," Zelda said tersely. "I didn't."

"I don't understand it," Nore said, "with all your experience."

Zelda stopped in the middle of the room and threw up her hands.

"I was never anybody's secretary, Nore," she said, irritated. "You think I would get a job in their prissy little offices if I told the truth? I'm a fishmonger's daughter. I know fish, Nore, not typewriters. I know John Dory and lingcod and periwinkles." She leaned on her dresser.

"Skate. Catfish. Cabezon—I'll bet you've never heard of that one, have you? I've worked with knives since I was 10 years old and let me tell you, you get used to your hands being in guts all day. My mother and I had a stand on the dock where the customers on the pier bobbed up and down one way and the dock rolled in the waves another way, like kids on see-saws."

Zelda threw the curtains open with an upward sweep of her arms, then let them fall and turned back to Nore.

"You want to know why I don't care what the world thinks of me? Because every night walking home with my mother, the sidewalks would clear from the smell of us."

She sat on the bed.

"You give me a sharp knife and I can slice fish so pretty a rich girl would think it *swam* without bones. But where would that get me in this world, do you think? Being rich is a game, Nore, that's what I tried to tell you the first day we met. You can live whatever you can play.

"So I decided, alright, if being rich means pretending you're too fragile, too pure for things like fish then I'll play the game. I'll cross my legs and fold my hands across my little lace cuffs and tell them how refined I am. They'll make it a reality, Nore, because it's true, you can live anything you can play."

In the morning, Nore lay in bed wondering if she was the same woman. Zelda had trimmed her hair carefully, struggling to find a cut that would look mannish when slicked back with pomade during the day but womanly enough to not arouse suspicion in the boardinghouse. Zelda had clipped and stared, walked to the side and clipped a little more, moving back and forth in front of Nore, her skirts rustling close to Nore's face. Zelda had run her hands across Nore's temples, her fingers combing, then smoothing the hair onto her neck. Zelda had worked for nearly two hours while Nore sat speechless, watching the flicker of a candle burning on the dresser and the movements of Zelda's skirt. When she seemed to be finished, Zelda cupped Nore's face in her hands, tilted her chin upwards, then moved behind her and put her hand along the left side of Nore's face, held her protectively, set the scissors down, then, without a word, opened the door for Nore to leave.

Nore walked to the Trinity Building, comfortable in her favorite black pants and white shirt, uncomfortable in her hidden identity. After leaving the boardinghouse in a skirt, pants

275

underneath, Nore darted into an alley to slip off the skirt and stuff it into a paper bag. She stepped back into the street with hesitation, expecting the traffic to stop, crowds to jeer or push her off the sidewalk. Instead, people moved out of her way. Men walked with her stride, at her shoulder, as if she belonged in their group. Hawkers asked to shine her shoes and sell her newspapers. It was as if she were suddenly in a completely different city, a town of greater riches. Nore glanced to her side as she moved down the street. People who didn't try to sell her something ignored her completely, as if she had suddenly become invisible. They didn't look her over as they did when she walked in her skirts. Nore stuffed her hands deep into her pockets, the paper back stuck under her arm.

"Alright, Norm, this is Mickey," shouted Mr. Henry, the balding manager, as he brought the two together. "There's a shipment of paper coming in the elevator. Stack it on those roll-away pallets. See the. . . ."

"What?"

"I said see the man with the mustache, Norm?"

"Mustache . . ."

"John . . . the foreman. You got questions, ask him first, then me . . ."

Nore nodded and went with Mickey to the gated elevator.

"Must be the fresh air makes those country boys so hairless," someone shouted above the din. Nore stiffened and glanced at Mickey, who either didn't hear the remark or didn't care. When the paper arrived, he simply motioned to the other end of the box and the two began their day of work.

With the first motion of her muscles, Nore felt her spirits lightening. Just to be moving again, working, the feel of her body doing something with which it was familiar. And to be making some money, she thought. Who knew if the charade would fool anyone but maybe if she kept her head bent and worked she could make it through just one day to get paid.

"Alright," Mickey shouted, "wheel this load over to the biggest press, the one on the end over there. Another load's comin'."

Nore pushed on the stack with her shoulder, then maneuvered the roll-away down the center aisle between the cabinets and the presses.

"Thanks . . . I'm Jim," a burly white-haired man offered his hand.

"Nor . . . Norm."

"Pleasure."

"What?"

"Pleasure to meet you."

It was nearly dark when Nore left the Trinity Building and headed home tired and sweaty, but more at ease than she had felt since arriving in Chicago. Despite the strain of the masquerade, Nore was now living like the woman she had been in the country, a hard-working, strong-armed woman outside the world of the feminine, still invisible to men. She strolled home, too happy to sit in the tram and too unsure to be in close quarters with people. The manager had wanted Norman back in the morning, had slapped him on the back, promised him a future. Now all he had to do was find a suitable alley in which to transform into Eleanora again.

When Nore came home to the New Chicago Hotel for Ladies, a cluster of women were gathering in the lobby. She smiled at them, but the confused looks she got froze her heart and made her take immediate inventory. She had forgotten the pomade, her hair was still slicked back, her face was probably covered with dirt. Nore dashed up the flight of stairs to her room and closed the door tightly behind her, then stumbled to the bed. First one disguise, then another. She threw off her clothes and climbed under the covers.

"Nore!" Zelda whispered into the darkened room a few hours later. "Are you here?"

"Zelda?"

"When you didn't come to the dining hall I was afraid something had happened to you."

"I'm so tired. It worked, Zelda," she laughed as she sat up in bed in her undershirt, pulling the blankets up modestly. "They thought Norman was a really hard worker and they want him back in the morning."

"Oh, God."

"I don't know, Zelda, you think this will work?"

"Well, I brought you a little something to help," Zelda said.

"You sound tired, too. How did it go?"

"The only thing that kept me from screaming in the street was the thought of your hair, my dear."

"You should have seen the women in the lobby when I came home."

"That's why I got you this." Zelda put a hatbox on Nore's lap and went to the bureau to light the lamp.

"Zelda, you've hardly got money for food. You city people do things in the screwiest manner."

Nore opened the hat box and pulled out an oversized beret, so large and floppy it sat in folds in her lap. Zelda arranged it on Nore's head with a peak and a dip, like an elegant sculpture or a massive bird. It hid every strand of her hair and made Nore's eyes the focus of her face. Zelda brought her hands down slowly from Nore's head, dropped them into her own lap and stared at the woman's big open face, sleepy and soft.

"I was thinking about you today," Nore said softly. "I don't know what it all means, but I was thinking about you."

"Go to sleep, dear," Zelda turned off the light and shut the door softly behind her.

As the weeks went on, Zelda became more distracted, first nervously reciting lines and tactics for interviews, then slumping into her chair, despondent. She stopped pressing the ribbons for her hat, the wrinkles from her skirt, giving up on their ability to help her. This morning, Zelda had taken only enough time to clasp on a little bracelet and it hung around the cuff of her wrinkled shirt like a talisman.

Zelda's loose dress contrasted with the fury on her face. The second and third weeks of walking through the city she berated employers, the upper class, the chances for happiness in such a world. She was surly during interviews, shouted at trucks that crossed her path on the street. Zelda was becoming more difficult to give to as time went on, Nore thought. Zelda, drawn inside her fury like a crab, was a struggle to comfort and a struggle to ignore. She took dinner from Nore without comment, since her pride stopped her from being grateful and her gratitude made her ashamed of her silence.

Nore, at first confused by the occasional sharpness of

Zelda's replies, hung back. She had never tried to understand a woman as she was attempting to do with Zelda. She had never thought about Aunt Mildred's life; the girls were too young, too foreign. Zelda was a woman in dresses and pointed shoes like the girls on the porch, but a woman who could be understood, Nore thought. In between the hopeless clothing and the indignant face, Nore saw a woman who was fragile, and she thought there was beauty in such a vulnerable woman choosing to be a fighter. The woman wore her masks uneasily, as Nore did her britches and her blue shirt.

Nore watched Zelda holding the cup as if the warm tea promised comfort. The bracelet seemed shabby compared to Zelda's skin and the rounded bone of her delicate wrist. The little bracelet held none of the strength of the woman, the jewelry's steady patterns and aura of grace a mockery of the way Zelda set down the cup, touched her lips, brushed her hair from her cheek. Zelda was talking softly with Ellen, her voice straining to sound reasonable and measured, but it was that small wrist that Nore watched, as if it contained both the beauty and pain of the woman.

To Zelda, the problem was more than just a shortage of money. The lack of a job called into question her ability to play the game with those in power. Did people see through her disguise as she walked through the streets, clutching a newspaper and her small blue bag, she wondered? Perhaps she looked like a painted doll, as much a poor imitation as the mannequin in the furrier's window. She began glancing in others' direction when she walked, losing that self-assured forward gaze and the confident way she usually pressed herself through the crowd.

Zelda had been raised to carry herself well at all times. She had stood beside her mother and watched the woman use fish to tell the story her body wouldn't divulge. Her mother slipped lemon in with the lingcod for the chatty women in bonnets or the men to whom she told stories, gesturing with her knife, leaning far across the wide table's rim to deliver a punch line. When the dealing became hectic and price the only factor, Zelda's mother would fling the fish back and forth across the

table, victimizing them for a penny lost here, another bar-
gained there, the little fish bodies slapping against the sides of
the trough and flinging bits of scale onto Zelda's blouse. When
the crowd built around them, Zelda and her mother trimmed
and gutted with precision, standing back to back yet pulled into
themselves for protection.

In the summer when she was twelve, a man with a red nose
had stuck his face towards Zelda from the crowd as she furiously scraped and cut and wrapped.

"It's not that one, girl, I've bought the trout," he growled.
"And the lingcod. Be quick."

Zelda looked around her. There was no other fish to be
cleaned. Further down the trough was a lone trout, probably
set aside by her mother for the man from the university.

"That one," the man said shortly, pointing at the isolated
trout. "Quick. I haven't got all day, pretty girl."

Zelda looked up into the man's face, red and veined.

A knife cut the air between them, gouging into the wood
where it stayed, upright. Her mother leaned over, grabbed a
handful of fish guts until her hand was bloody and covered,
then threw the guts onto the table in front of the man and stuck
an accusing hand in his face.

"You *ever* try to confuse my girl . . .You get outta here. I
don't need your money that bad."

That wasn't true, Zelda knew. They needed every penny,
every sale. And now that his fish was gutted and wrapped it
would be harder to sell as fresh. She leaned against her mother
and felt the tightened muscles in the woman's legs. The man
backed up, offered his money with a grumble. Her mother took
it without taking her eyes from the man, then scooped up the
package and shoved it at him.

"You ever see that man again you stay away, Zelda," her
mother said, "you don't ever talk to him, you don't get near
him, you come straight to me and say so."

At the end of that long day, when their blue working coats
were covered with entrails and scales, and her mother was
carefully wiping her hands in a ritual of each finger, then nail,
the man with the cap drove up in the carriage. It was the driver
for a family Zelda had never seen but he came every week at

this time.

Her mother, her hair wisping after the free-wheeling trade, stiffened and smoothed her clothing. With a simple nod, the two walked to the end of the dock and Zelda's mother, with great ceremony, drew back the wooden doors of a cabinet that held a huge salted salmon. The fish was nearly as large as Zelda. Her mother had taken off the head a week ago for their own soup and the dark pink flesh was the brightest color on the dock. The driver nodded. Zelda's mother drew out a very large knife from the cupboard and, steadying herself as if chopping wood, she began sawing on the massive hulk. The driver stood motionless as she cut slice after slice and laid them gently on white paper.

Her mother was perspiring and disheveled when she returned with the tall stack of cutlets and wrapped them on the table. Zelda did not look up but felt keenly the woman's discomfort. The man in front of them wore linen, with brass buttons that shone. His hair was slicked back and untouched. Zelda, without looking, could see on her own dress every mended hem and spot of fishguts, could see on the woman above her every wrinkle and cut and strand of unruly hair. Her mother took his money and folded it quickly into her skirt but as he turned to go, she reached under the table to the little plate where she and Zelda saved bits of fish for their own dinner. She deftly wrapped them in white paper.

"And for you, sir, something for your own wife and children," her mother said in a smooth and refined tone that belied her dirty smock. "From Stanley," she said, then looking down at Zelda, "From Stanley and Co."

Zelda was horrified. That was their dinner. There was no fish left. They were not a fancy 'company' that could give presents or anglers on a big boat who threw fish in the air for seagulls to catch. Zelda knew they were only a plateful of scraps away from having no dinner. The man was surprised and the sudden light in his eyes made her mother straighten.

"Oh," the man breathed. "They rarely . . . get such things," he said. Instead of his usual stiff nod of the head, the driver offered his hand, then departed.

Zelda looked up at her mother, confused.

"Salmon tonight, Zelda," she said with a laugh, then strode over to the salting cupboard and drew out her knife.

After dinner with Nore and Ellen, Zelda went directly to bed. The next morning she walked on the streets with irritation, as if she were late, though she knew she had nowhere to go. She occasionally stood undecided, then changed directions. She growled at men who bumped into her, then drew into herself and was silent. Ellen had forced her to press her clothes and do her hair in a special way but her heart wasn't into the job search and she spun her hat in her hands, kicking stones with the toe of her boot.

Zelda went into a huge department store on the main thoroughfare and wandered through the aisles, running a finger along the glass cases, looking at the hats and baubles. Zelda felt as if it was the repository of all the things in the world she would never be able to buy. She pulled on the belts, held bottles of perfume as if they were weapons.

When she turned the corner past the scarves, Zelda stood in front of a "Help Wanted" sign on a glass case. She read it several times before waking up and seeing the lingerie section. Zelda peered at the neatly folded rows of panties, the white pantaloons and, hanging from their little straps, the rows of camisoles in pastel silks, ribbons, lace. The showpiece of the department, displayed at the corner junction of all the display cases, was the wooden bodice of a woman in a slip, the cream lace barely covering her large upright breasts. The mannequin was surrounded by flowers and huge peacock feathers, a jewelry box spilling its contents, a cup of fine china. Zelda stared at the warm color of the wooden figure, the fall of the silk. She felt herself warming inside. They wanted to *pay* someone to look at this all day, she thought, narrowing her eyes and grinning to herself.

"May I help you?" a woman said.

"Good afternoon," Zelda said, regaining her composure and drawing herself into a regal manner. She extended her hand. "I understand you are in need of assistance, Madam. You surely must be the manager."

"I am."

"I am Zelda Stanley."

"Fine. Fine. Do you have experience with ladies lingerie?"

"Oh, gracious yes," Zelda said, wanting to cackle and slap her leg. She talked about the job as if seducing it, drawing down her voice, rolling her words off her tongue. She talked with the woman at length but saw in front of her only the bodice, the lace, the breasts. Within the hour she was walking into the personnel office to sign the papers.

Listening in the dining hall to the news of Zelda's job, Ellen put her cheek in her palm and shook her head. The boys simply turned in their chairs and looked away.

"Bosoms," Bertrum whispered to Louis.

Nore sat very still, pleased that the search was over but curious over Ellen's knowing smile.

"Our dear Zelda," Ellen said, "fitting . . . ladies all day."

Zelda just sat with her head thrown back, her arms stretched against the table and laughed.

Ellen ate a last forkful of peas. "Alright girls, down your coffees, we have to go. C'mon Nore, you're going with us."

"Corrupting the innocent," Bertrum said, slapping the tabletop lightly. "Maybe she doesn't *want* to be a part of your espionage club."

"Be quiet, Bertrum."

The women coursed through the backstreets until they reached a small carriage house with a dark blue door and a brass knocker. The three were admitted to a square brick studio. Women pulled chairs from hidden corners and struggled to marshall the seats into straight lines. Other women were engrossed in a discussion in the corner. Ellen joined their group. Soon the studio was so full it was necessary for everyone to sit down to find room.

A woman in blue gabardine, book and papers in hand, stood in front of the thirty-five attentive women.

"She's reading Charlotte tonight," Zelda whispered, eyes flashing as if in some private triumph. Ellen rejoined the group, sitting at Zelda's right, accompanied by a large woman in a brown dress.

"As to Humanness," the woman in the front intoned in a high theatrical style. "Let us begin, inoffensively, with sheep."

"Oh Christ," the woman beside Ellen grumbled. Zelda shot her a glance.

"Nore," Zelda whispered, "this is Beth Collier."

Nore looked at the woman, recognized the gentleman from the dining room. Beth offered her hand, and Nore searched the woman's face for a sign, a mole, a color in her eyes that would tell her why she had begun dressing like a man, and more importantly, how she got away with it.

"Industry, at its base," the speaker intoned, "is a feminine function. Woman became the first inventor and laborer; being in truth the mother of all industry as well as all people."

"Yes yes," Beth leaned back and put her arm on the back of Ellen's chair "but what about action!"

"Could we have it quiet in the back please," the speaker said. The women in the back of the room, leaning against the wall or sitting less demurely than the lace-clad women in front, crossed their arms over their black jackets, their tailored blue smocks, and shifted in their seats.

"In the earlier part of the women's movement," she continued, "it was sharply opposed on the ground that women would become 'unsexed.' "

The women in back laughed heartily.

"Let us note in passing," the speaker said, "that they *have* become unsexed in one particularity—the peculiar reversal of sex characteristics which makes the human female adopt the essentially masculine attribute of special sex-decoration . . ."

Beth and Ellen exchanged glances, laughing.

". . . she blossoms forth as the peacock, in the evening wearing masculine feathers to further her feminine ends."

"Yeah!" the women in the back called out, applauding.

"Madame Chairwoman," Beth said, standing and leaning her weight on the chair in front of her, "where, may I ask, are the cookies?"

The woman in front snapped the book shut and touched the ruffle around her throat.

"Where *are* our little tiny purses, filled with our little tiny lives?" Beth said, her voice rising in tone and intensity. "We are becoming like the ladies clubs downtown—all chit and chat and *lemonade*. Our sisters in England stage . . ."

"The counterproductive activities of the English women make a mockery of responsibility for women . . ." the speaker said, setting her book down while women from the front of the room rushed into clusters at her side. The women in the back leaned forward from their casual stance, the meeting changing gears like a machine.

"Zelda," a voice beside Nore whispered. A gaunt young woman with long loose hair, a hat low over her forehead, leaned in front of Nore, then cast a glance her way.

"This is my friend Nore," Zelda whispered.

The woman nodded her acceptance. "We're planning something new. Ellen's representing you: we're meeting at the wharf after."

From the front of the room, the speaker raised her voice and stood on her tiptoes. "We *have* an action," she growled. "The Auto Tour through the State of Illinois will send speakers for street corners, continuing our drive to educate."

"In England, the women hunger-strike, here we ask permission from the town square," Beth shouted, striding into the aisle.

"It is our duty . . ." interjected one of the pastel-dressed women, "to support Americans choosing American tactics. Our representatives are . . ."

"A distinguished group alright," Zelda said, jumping to her feet and startling Nore, who had been frantically trying to follow the action. "All upper-class women and all *ladies.*"

"Which is not an insulting term!" the speaker hissed.

"And who will speak from the laboring woman's viewpoint?" Zelda shouted. "The Equality League of Self-Supporting Women . . ."

"Which is *not* a part of this meeting!"

". . . has done more to gather support for suffrage than a trainload of society ladies . . ."

"I move that we vote to support the Women's Autotour and begin a campaign to gather funds . . ." said a woman, who stepped from the side of the speaker.

". . . with a provision that the funds be available only when a member of the working class is included in the line-up of speakers," Zelda shouted.

285

"I second the amended motion," said a voice in the back of the room.

"All those in favor say Aye," called the speaker and the room roared its approval. "So be it."

"Meeting is adjourned," shouted Beth, slapping her palms together.

"This meeting . . ." the speaker said icily, watching the women already moving towards the door, "is hereby . . . adjourned."

Ellen and Beth quickly left through a side door and Zelda took Nore's arm to lead her out the front. When Ellen returned late that night, Zelda slipped from her room into the hallway to confer. Every evening, Ellen joined the two for dinner from a different direction, suddenly breaking away from a group of women just as they turned the corner and disappeared. Nore had never seen any of Ellen's group before, except for the woman with the hat.

Nore's arms grew thick and sinewy as the weeks progressed. The work and the sweat on her forehead made her proud of her strength, but just as she felt relieved at finding a place for herself, she would catch someone's eyes and quickly turn away, certain of having been discovered. She would work furiously until the warmth in her muscles made her brave again, until she was giddy with the thrill of her secret, the mystery of it enticing her to try a few manly gestures. She wiped her brow and hiked up her pants. She spit in the corner by the elevator but Mickey didn't flinch. Nore shook her head, amazed, stuffed her handkerchief in her back pocket and bent for another box. In the month she had been there, no one had had a conversation with her—talking was impossible over the din of the presses and she slipped out of the shop and trotted home before others could join her.

Nore couldn't figure it out, turning back towards the elevator. She knew how to act around men—she learned on the farm—but everyone there knew she was a woman, even after she had hacked off her hair. In the city, people were supposed to be sophisticated. How could they not know she was a woman: couldn't they see it in her face, her eyes, couldn't they smell it on her? Everything had been upside down since she boarded the train. First wearing a goddamn dress and some stupid little hat, then meeting city women who didn't mind the pants at all. It had been a horror trying to find a job, and now she didn't have to hide her pants but hide her breasts instead. She ate dinner with men who acted like women and wished for skirts, sitting beside beautiful women who slept with women as if they were men. No wonder Aunt Mildred had worried about her, Nore thought, as she heaved another box on the pile.

Nore practiced a wide-legged spread when she sat. That came easy, made her happy. She studied the stiff, arrogant walk. That made her unhappy. She slapped her bandana into her hand when she stood idle, squinted her eyes with menace when she surveyed the press room over a cup of water. She learned to pull her pant legs up slightly before crouching and cross her arms over her chest, pushing out her hips. Either the workers were too busy to notice, or, as she suspected and Zelda has assured her, they were too secure in their belief that anyone wearing the tag is the merchandise.

Occasionally, straightening up after loading a pallet, Nore would be aware of a movement inside her, a heat running through her belly and lungs that made her feel more like a woman than ever, more aware of the boundaries of her skin, and the difference between herself and the man she was expected to be. She had lived with this division in herself all her life but had never felt it as keenly as now. On the farm it had felt like a way to belong; now it seemed a cruel deception, a deception not of the public, but of her. For the first time, Nore felt as if the cloud she lived in was not a product of her own confusion but something forced on her, something held around her while she struggled to see clearly.

At these times she would act her most manly, scowl deepest and move with the most abrasive gestures she could summon, filled with fear that the self-awareness would show, that the men in the plant would see parts of her that she could only feel.

In the middle of an afternoon, while wheeling the pallet to the presses, Nore crossed in front of a thin woman in a simple green shift-dress and no hat. She clutched a small cloth bag in her hands. She was the wife of one of the typesetters and she arrived every day at this time to deliver his lunch and scurry out again.

Nore usually only caught a glimpse of her as she darted from the door to her husband who worked behind the tall wooden cabinets of type. Today, Nore was inches from her as she dashed to her husband's side and offered her little bag of food. He looked up from his work, his face suddenly creased and twisted with anger. He immediately raised a hand to slap her face, holding back from the punch just inches from her skin. She winced and Nore's breath caught short in her chest. The woman pushed herself against the cabinets as her husband brought his face close to hers, speaking in a way that made her hang her head and nod. Though she couldn't hear their words, Nore was frozen in front of the aisle. The other men, working across from the woman's husband, turned their backs on the scene and tightened their shoulders. The man asked questions with anger and the woman turned frightened eyes to him, denying, pleading, explaining. The man grabbed her arm and shook her. Nore twisted the bandana in her hand and stepped forward.

Suddenly the foreman was at Nore's side, startling her. Nore hadn't seen him coming and she didn't like him this close to her. He pointed towards the elevator and shouted something she couldn't hear. Nore turned away from the woman with the cloth bag and went back to the elevator.

Nore leaned on the wooden gate, looking down the black shaft towards the light on the first floor. There was no paper to unload when she arrived. The elevator was on the bottom floor, and the sound of the truck drivers having lunch echoed up the chamber. Nore turned around and saw the woman's hair poking above the top of the cabinet, saw her inching closer and closer to the corner. Did this happen every day? Why hadn't she ever seen it? Why hadn't she bothered to look?

Nore paced in front of the elevator. She, herself, had jumped when the foreman appeared, leaping out of her skin the same way the woman had. That's not the way Norman would have reacted, she thought. Nore had cowered, immediately, as a reflex. A man . . . well, a man would have looked the foreman straight in the eye. No one touches a man, Nore thought, kicking the gate of the elevator. No one makes a man grimace and cower or forces him to explain. She looked into the pressroom, saw the woman scurry away. The husband came around the side of the typecabinet and took a few steps towards Nore. She straightened, took a wide, offensive stance. He wiped his hands on a rag, scowling at her, then threw the rag on the floor and went back to his station.

Zelda ran to work in the morning as if dashing off to a rendezvous, coming home with the sheepish grin of the unfaithful. Most days she did nothing more than fold camisoles, marveling at the colors and the ribbons. Yesterday, the manager had asked her to count panties.

This morning, however, the department was busy as soon as she came in. Stock numbers and sizings replaced thoughts of women's bodies, lace on skin. Zelda had several women in the dressing rooms when a mother and her two daughters came into the department, moving with a slow elegance as if they had no destination but great purpose. They wore furs and jewels and a piece of lace tossed casually over a shoulder, a brocade bag flung about as if it were nothing, leather gloves dropped on the counter and only gathered up as an afterthought. The patterns of their skirts and coats folded into one another as they leaned together to whisper. Zelda clutched a handful of camisoles.

When they reached the rack of petticoats, the daughters became very animated. The older woman, in a large feathered hat and an imperious air, turned to Zelda.

"Miss? It seems my daughters will try on your petticoats."

The manager, talking with a customer at the end of the counter, dropped the merchandise and scurried to the mother.

"Yes, indeed. Let me get you chairs for the fitting room. Zelda?" the manager directed nervously.

The five women went into a large, curtained dressing room and the younger women began stripping off their coats and hats, flinging them across the chairs. Their mother sat down slowly. The manager bowed to her.

"This is Zelda. She will, I'm sure, help you find your fancy today."

Zelda stood in the dressing room as if she were a child again, facing women on the tram with her dress covered with fish scales and blood, this time without the security of her mother's hand. Zelda felt as if every particle of dirt that had ever touched her was now visible to these women, as if they could see how many years she had worn her first dress and how many scraps had been substitutes for dinner.

"Peach, Zelda," one of the young women cried. "Bring us your peach petticoats."

Zelda brought crinolines with lace, petticoats and bustles and slips with hoops. The women stripped down to their bloomers and cavorted in the dressing room, calling to her to bring them more. The petticoats began to fill the room, litter the floor like meringue puffs and they were still no closer to deciding. Instead, the women danced and played in the merchandise, leaning on their mother's chair and waltzing away, then crumpling into a heap on her shoes and putting their heads in her lap.

"Now girls, you may each choose one," the mother said and the girls laughed. Zelda wondered how long it would take to narrow their choices. The mother began laughing with her daughters.

"Well, Zelda, it seems that we'll just have to take them all."

"*All* of them?" Zelda asked.

The women turned their smiling faces to Zelda, hiding their mouths with their hands but drinking in the expression on Zelda's face. They hugged each other, laughing at Zelda's surprise until she stiffened, looked around at the disheveled room. Hadn't she been roped into their game? Wasn't her surprise necessary for the thrill of their purchase? Zelda wondered in how many other stores they had looked for a fishmonger's daughter so they could buy a boxcar of stockings or chimney lamps, a coach full of gloves? Zelda's shame turned to anger as she gathered the first handful of petticoats and marched towards the register.

The manager was thrilled and the other clerks amazed as Zelda tied the last bundles of boxes together and handed them to the women. They thanked her and sailed on to another department, giggling behind their gloves.

"Zelda," the manager said, "you have another fitting." Zelda strode back to the dressing room, glad to be out of sight of the little bits of lace and silk. Inside, however, stood a woman whose plain cotton bloomers were mended and without lace. She struggled into a boned corset that Zelda, even from across the room, could see was far too small.

By the end of the day, Zelda was tired and filled with conflict. The woman with the corset had twisted and strained, insisted on Zelda pulling the straps and lacings until the bones of the corset cut into her body. Zelda nearly cried with the effort and the pain of watching her, while her heart smarted from the torment of the young women and their petticoat money.

Zelda was the last to leave the department and as she gathered her ribboned hat, the manager came to her, smiling broadly, and handed her an envelope.

"Your first commission, my dear. You did very well."

Zelda shook her hand, and when the supervisor had gone, counted the money inside. There was nearly an additional week's wages there and she held it to her chest, head bent, eyes closed. Just a little extra money. Zelda opened her eyes. On the floor near the counter, at her foot, Zelda saw a lime green chemise, lying crumpled and forgotten. She deftly bent, slipped it under her skirt and stuffed it in the leg of her bloomers. Zelda strode out of the store and towards the tram, feeling at the same time battered and blessed.

She went to her room, splayed the money across her bed, threw her clothes into a chair and slipped on the chemise. It was silk. And lace. She hugged it to her before daring to walk to her mirror. Someday she would wear silk every day, Zelda whispered to herself. And someday there would be somebody. Somebody else. She took off her stockings, slipped on a robe over the lingerie and walked to Nore's room.

Zelda walked in without knocking and stood with her back against the door, looking down at Nore who lay on the bed fully dressed, still in her hat. Zelda couldn't think of anything witty to say, anything seductive. She looked down at her bare feet. How could she finally be willing to risk it, now of all times, when all she wanted was to be held and comforted?

"Sometimes it's too hard," Zelda said softly, then covered

her face with her hands and started to cry.

Nore slowly got up from the bed and stood very close to Zelda. On the farm, when one of the girls cried, Eleanora and the boys would leave the house. For the first time, Nore thought, someone was asking her for comfort, demanding something of her heart, not her muscles. Without the veil, the fog, the impermeable cloud between herself and others, Nore saw the crisp lines of Zelda's hair against her face, saw objects come into focus and deepen in color. Nore hesitantly brought her hand to Zelda's head, stroked her hair.

Zelda unbuttoned the house dress and dropped it at her feet. The silk clung to Zelda's ribs, hung lightly over the round of her breasts. Creamy lace barely concealed her nipples. The chemise hung just below Zelda's thighs, with a border of lace melding silk into skin. she pressed herself against Nore's chest, then grasped Nore's forearm and wrapped it over her own shoulder, nestling into the farmgirl's awkward embrace.

"When I'm rich, I'm going to dress like this every day," Zelda said.

Ellen tapped softly on the door, then peeked her head inside, withdrew and closed the door, then opened it again. Nore stepped away but Zelda grinned at her friend with some of the sparkle back in her face.

"We need you two," Ellen said, smiling.

"Is it tonight?" Zelda asked, wiping her wet face.

"Yes. The committee thinks we need two couples to be walking on the train platform just before it goes off to divert suspicion."

"Two couples?"

"Norman and Zelda, Ellen and Henry."

Zelda smiled. "Oh, Ellen, my first real boyfriend!"

The foursome walked slowly across the train platform, pretending not to notice the women from Ellen's meeting who crossed their paths, dropped little bags of explosives into every trash bin, then caught trams out of town. The two couples were the last to leave the platform as it closed for the day, the ticket taker rushing off to his dinner while Norman And Zelda, Ellen and Henry, dapper and confident and mistaken by passersby, slowly ambled into town for their celebration. When they were half-way up the path to the main street, the train station exploded, a portion of the roof scattering in all directions, benches thrown out into the path, glass shattering onto the torn platform. People from the streets came running towards the rubble, bumping into the women as they stood in awe. Zelda and Ellen pretended to be frightened, eager to be whisked away by their suitors.

At the top of a small hill, the four looked back at the chaos. Zelda sighed. Tomorrow the women from Ellen's group would hang a huge banner across the torn front of the station. "Votes for Women. Now." The twisted planks of the building and the horrified looks on the faces of the townspeople were another kind of justice, though, Zelda thought. She knew that the rich women and their petticoats had not really been destroyed, that the debris showering down was not money to buy more silk. It was, though, a kind of relief, as if it reaffirmed her feelings that she could play it, she could live it and she could tear it apart.

Nore was wide-eyed and jittery, standing with her arm around Zelda. She felt as if she were watching fireworks for her own special arrival, as if she had been given, with one explosion, a place to belong, a life to live. Nore looked around at the debris and the people running into the mayhem, looked at herself in her manly costume, standing solid and warm and, most remarkably, loved. Perhaps soon even able to give affection. Nore could hardly remember the awkward girl in the saucer hat, could hardly think why she would run from the women in the hotel lobby.

Zelda looked up at Nore and saw the change in her eyes, wanted so much to grab her by the ears, pull Nore towards her with the gesture of an elder whose heart has been caught by the brightened spirit of a child. Zelda wanted to hold Nore's cheeks between her palms and bring her close to her, drawing out the brightness in her eyes as if to find what finally made them come into the present and focus. The smoke billowed behind them, people rushed past on either side but Zelda noticed only the change in Nore's eyes. It seemed to have been a long time coming.

293

Contributors' Notes

Paula Gunn Allen is a professor of Ethnic Studies/Native American Studies at U.C. Berkeley. Among her publications are: *The Woman Who Owned the Shadows; The Sacred Hoop: Recovering the Feminine in American Indian Traditions* and *Spider Woman's Granddaughters: Native American Women's Traditional and Short Stories.*

Margaret Atwood was born in Ottawa, Canada. She is an editor, poet, essayist, short story writer and novelist. Her novels include: *The Edible Woman; Surfacing; Lady Oracle; Life Before Man; Bodily Harm; The Handmaid's Tale* and *Cat's Eye.*

Sandy Boucher is the author of four books, the most recent of which is *Turning the Wheel: American Women Creating the New Buddhism.* She is presently studying religion at the Graduate Theological Union, Berkeley.

Toni Cade Bambara edited *The Black Woman: An Anthology,* in 1974. She has published two volumes of short stories, *Gorilla, My Love* and *The Sea Birds Are Still Alive,* as well as a novel, *The Salt Eaters.*

Maureen Brady is the author of the novels *Give Me Your Good Ear* and *Folly,* as well as the short story collection *The Question She Put to Herself.* She is currently working on her third novel.

Dionne Brand was born in the Caribbean and now lives in Toronto, Canada. She has published five volumes of poetry, is the co-author of the non-fiction work *Rivers Have Sources, Trees Have Roots — Speaking of Racism,* and *Sans Souci and Other Stories,* which has just been published in the United States.

Anne Cameron lives and writes in Canada. Her publications include: *Daughters of Copper Woman; Dzelarhons; The Journey; Stubby Amberchuck and the Holy Grail; Earth Witch* and *The Annie Poems.*

Zoë Fairbairns is an English feminist writer whose books include: *Benefits; Stand We at Last; Here Today* and *Closing.*

Judy Freespirit has published short stories and poetry in a variety of journals and anthologies, including *The Tribe of Dina: A Jewish Women's Anthology*. *Daddy's Girl: An Incest Survivor's Story* was published in 1982 and is now part of a longer work, a collection of ten short stories about incest and its effect on different generations of the same family.

Sally Miller Gearhart is the author of *The Wanderground: Stories of the Hill Women* and *A Feminist Tarot* (with Susan Rennie). She has appeared in the documentary films "Word Is Out" and "The Times of Harvey Milk" and teaches at San Francisco State University.

Binnie Kirshenbaum has had short fiction published in *Kalliope, The New England Review/Bread Loaf Quarterly* and other magazines. Her first novel, *Short Subject,* was published in 1989.

Beryl Markham was born in England in 1902 and raised in East Africa. She was a trainer and breeder of race horses and, in 1936, she became the first person to fly solo across the Atlantic from east to west — taking off in England and crash-landing in Nova Scotia. Beryl Markham died in 1986.

Valerie Miner is the author of: *All Good Women; Winter's Edge; Movement; Murder in the English Department; Blood Sisters* and *Trespassing and Other Stories*.

Bonnie Morris has had stories, poems and essays published in a variety of journals and anthologies, including *The Second WomanSleuth Anthology: Contemporary Mystery Stories by Women*.

Merril Mushroom walked steel in 1979. Her writing has appeared in a number of journals and anthologies, including *We Are Everywhere: Writings By and About Lesbian Parents* and *The Original Coming Out Stories*. She has written a fantasy novel called *Daughters of Khaton*.

Grace Paley is the author of three short story collections: *The Little Disturbances of Man; Enormous Changes at the Last Minute;* and *Later The Same Day*.

Terri de la Peña is a fifth-generation Californian whose writings reflect the urban Chicana experience. She is currently working on a novel, *Margins,* which focuses on familial and sexual issues faced by Chicanas.

Natalie L.M. Petesch has published eight books, including: *The Odyssey of Katinou Kalokovich; Soul Clap its Hands and Sing* and *Flowering Mimosa*.

Irina Ratushinskaya was born in Odessa, USSR, in 1954. In 1982 she was arrested by the Soviet government for dissident activities and sentenced to seven years' hard labor and five years' internal exile. She was released in 1986. *Grey Is the Color of Hope,* a description of her life as a political prisoner, was published in 1988.

Joyce Renwick teaches fiction writing at the Writer's Center in Bethesda, Maryland. Her short fiction has been published in a number of journals and anthologies, including *Best American Short Stories*.

Teresa Noelle Roberts lives near Ithaca, New York. Her poems have appeared in many journals, including *Sojourner, Deviance* and *Kalliope*. Her first novel is currently in search of a publisher.

Canyon Sam is a third generation Cantonese American. Her short stories and articles have appeared in numerous journals and anthologies, including *Unholy Alliances: New Fiction by Women*. She is involved with the Tibetan movement as a cultural and political activist, and is a fundraiser for Tibetan nuns in India and Nepal. She supports herself as a freelance electrical contractor in her hometown of San Francisco.

May Sarton is the prolific author of numerous volumes of poetry, fiction and autobiography. Her most recently published journal is *After The Stroke* and her most recent novel is *The Education of Harriet Hatfield*.

Martha Shelley was born in Brooklyn and now studies martial arts at Wu Tao Kuan in Berkeley, California. Her two anthologies, *Crossing the DMZ* and *Lovers and Mothers* can be obtained through Sefir Publishing, 729 55th Street, Oakland, CA 94609.

Joyce Sikakane was born in 1943 and brought up in the Orlando district of Soweto, South Africa. She worked as a journalist before being detained for 17 months under the Terrorism Act. She left South Africa in 1973. Her autobiographical book, *A Window on Soweto*, was published by the International Defense and Aid Fund for Southern Africa, an organization which provides legal defense for political prisoners and aid to their families (P.O. Box 17, Cambridge, MA 02138).

Kitty Tsui grew up in Hong Kong and the United Kingdom. She immigrated to America in 1968. She grew up a stranger in many strange lands and started drinking when she was a teenager. A recovering alcoholic, Tsui survived a slip and is back in recovery. Her poetry and prose has been widely anthologized and she is the author of *The Words of a Woman Who Breathes Fire*.

Jess Wells is the author of four volumes of short fiction and one of women's history. Her short story collections include *Two Willow Chairs* and *The Dress/The Sharda Stories*. She lives in San Francisco and is currently working on her first novel.

Shay Youngblood was born in Columbus, Georgia. Her short stories and poetry have appeared in *Essence, Catalyst* and *Conditions* as well as in the anthology *The Stories We Hold Secret*. A collection of her short fiction, *The Big Mama Stories,* was published in 1989 and was adapted for the theater in a full length play titled *Shakin' the Mess Outta Misery*. She is at work on a novel set in Paris.

Irene Zahava (editor) has been the owner of a feminist bookstore in upstate New York since 1981. She has edited seven short story anthologies, including: *Love, Struggle and Change; Through Other Eyes: Animal Stories by Women* and two volumes of contemporary mystery stories by women.